# The Right

The lands[...] [...]ge change and transformation in recent yea[...] [...]cation and mas[...]cation. However, persistent pa[...] under-representation continue to perplex policy-makers and practitioners, raising questions about current strategies, policies and approaches to widening participation.

Presenting a comprehensive review and critique of contemporary widening participation policy and practice, Penny Jane Burke interrogates the underpinning assumptions, values and perspectives shaping current concepts and understandings of widening participation. She draws on a range of perspectives within the field of the sociology of education – including feminist post-structuralism, critical pedagogy and policy sociology – to examine the ways in which wider societal inequalities and misrecognitions, which are related to difference and diversity, present particular challenges for the project to widen participation in higher education. In particular, the book:

- focuses on the themes of difference and diversity to shed light on the operations of inequalities and the politics of access and participation both in terms of national and institutional policy and at the level of student and practitioner experience;
- draws on the insights of the sociology of education to consider not only the patterns of under-representation in higher education but also the politics of misrepresentation, critiquing key discourses of widening participation;
- interrogates assumptions behind widening participation policy and practice, including assumptions about education being an unassailable good;
- provides an analysis of the accounts and perspectives of students, practitioners and policy-makers through in-depth interviews, observations and reflective journal entries;
- offers insights for future developments in the policy, practice and strategies for widening participation.

The book will be of great use to all those working in and researching higher education.

**Penny Jane Burke** is Professor of Education, Roehampton University, UK.

**Foundations and Futures of Education**
Series Editors: Peter Aggleton, Sally Power and Michael Reiss

**Being a University**
*Ron Barnett*

**Education – An 'Impossible Profession'?**
*Tamara Bibby*

**Radical Education and the Common School**
*Michael Fielding and Peter Moss*

**Re-Designing Learning Contexts: Technology-Rich, Learner-Centred Ecologies**
*Rosemary Luckin*

**Schools and Schooling in the Digital Age: A Critical Analysis**
*Neil Selwyn*

**The Irregular School**
*Roger Slee*

**Gender, Schooling and Global Social Justice**
*Elaine Unterhalter*

**Language, Learning, Context: Talking the Talk**
*Wolff-Michael Roth*

**School Trouble**
*Deborah Youdell*

**The Right to Higher Education: Beyond widening participation**
*Penny Jane Burke*

# The Right to Higher Education

Beyond widening participation

Penny Jane Burke

Routledge
Taylor & Francis Group

LONDON AND NEW YORK

First published 2012
by Routledge
2 Park Square, Milton Park, Abingdon, Oxon OX14 4RN

Simultaneously published in the USA and Canada
by Routledge
711 Third Avenue, New York, NY 10017

*Routledge is an imprint of the Taylor & Francis Group, an informa business*

*British Library Cataloguing in Publication Data*
A catalogue record for this book is available from the British Library

*Library of Congress Cataloging in Publication Data*
Burke, Penny Jane.
The right to higher education : beyond widening participation / Penny Jane Burke.
p. cm. -- (Foundations and futures of education)
1. Educational equalization--United States. 2. Education, Higher. 3. Education,
Higher--Aims and objectives. 4. College attendance. 5. Education and state.
6. Right to education. 7. Educational sociology. I. Title.
LC213.2.B85 2012
306.43'2--dc23
2011036761

ISBN: 978-0-415-56823-4 (hbk)
ISBN: 978-0-415-56824-1 (pbk)
ISBN: 978-0-203-12557-1 (ebk)

Typeset in Garamond
by Taylor & Francis Books

1006577181

Printed and bound in Great Britain by
TJ International Ltd, Padstow, Cornwall

# Contents

# Foreword

*Carlos Alberto Torres*[1]
UCLA

## The world we live in

> It is again necessary for me to upgrade my knowledge of the world which is ingenuous, spontaneous, alienated and alienating. So I accept the world as the object of my epistemological mind, of my critical research, my vigilant curiosity. 'Conscientization' is primarily an act of vigilance by which I enter, little by little, into the very essence of the facts in front of me as knowable objects so I can discover their quiddity.
>
> (Paulo Freire, in Torres, 2005: 159)

People all over the world continue to demand more and better education. Families, communities and individuals have bought into the promise of the welfare state, a promise that they will be satisfied in their demands for more and better education and a host of other welfare benefits. Moreover, the promise included an implicit clause that the state will be willing and able to finance such enterprise. Today's reality, however, is the opposite and these promises have been broken.

School reform agendas have been launched in the United States, and internationally, focusing on 'restructuring' rather than merely transforming the efficiency of existing systems. Restructuring attempts the transformation of purposes, assumptions and methods of schools systems (Darling-Hammond, 1993: xi). Not surprisingly, this reform agenda is being implemented at times of serious financial retrenchment in public education everywhere. Because much of the 'schools-are-failing' literature blames the teachers for the ills of education, the relationships between teachers and educational authorities are also being reconsidered. Even where there is less focus on blame, there is considerable attention to competency testing, certification, national standards; in short, diverse attempts to improve excellence in instruction and learning. Trying to reduce expenses of financially overburdened school districts and attempting to make the systems more cost-effective often involves layoffs and substitution of lower-paid instructional personnel for fully trained, more expensive teachers.

Not only we are facing a restructuring of the systems, but also the impact of neoliberal globalization (Torres, 2009a). The dominant neoliberal agenda for globalization in K-12 education includes a drive toward privatization and decentralization of public forms of education, a movement toward educational standards, a strong emphasis on testing and a focus on account-ability. Specific to higher education reform, neoliberal versions of globalization suggest reforms for universities in four primary areas: efficiency and account-ability, accreditation and universalization, international competitiveness, and privatization (Torres, 2009b).

Those reforms associated with international competitiveness could be described as 'competition-based reforms', characterized by efforts to create measurable performance standards through extensive standardized testing (the new standards and accountability movement), introduction of new teaching and learning methods purported to create better performance at lower cost (e.g. universalization of textbooks), and improvements in the selection and training of teachers. Competition-based reforms in higher education tend to adopt a vocational orientation and reflect the point of view that colleges and universities exist largely to serve the economic well-being of a society. With regard to accreditation and universalization, major efforts are under way throughout the world to reform academic programmes through accreditation processes and various strategies that produce increased homogeneity across national boundaries.[2] It is against this background that we should consider the question of access and participation in higher education, the central topic of this comprehensive book.

## The promises of higher education: access and participation

There has been a systematic retreat, given the fiscal crises in the seventies, and the enshrining of neoliberal ideology from the early eighties, from these pro-mises of the welfare state. Yet, people are still eager to access higher education even if the politics of access, particularly with the growing privatization of higher education, have not been successful.

Professor Penny Jane Burke studies the themes of difference and diversity to shed light on the operations of inequalities and the politics of access and participation. These policies are studied both in terms of national and insti-tutional policy and at the level of student and practitioner experience. The author stresses the need to identify the location and identity of the writer. It is important because the author is herself not only a noted feminist scholar, but one who attended university as an adult, having achieved extraordinary success but also having to struggle with difficult conditions of access and participation.

This book is, to some extent, a biographical book that underscores some of the great dilemmas of students who come to the university with great dreams and encounter complex secondary institutions, and find difficulties to under-stand rules and regulations, standards and laws, and a host of hurdles and barriers that need to be overcome for a successful academic engagement. Yet, this book documents also the experience of the author, as a researcher and academic in the British system but who is also very knowledgeable of the experiences of other countries, collecting and analyzing a vast empirical data set using solid methodologies.

Because of her analytical premises and rigorous methodologies, Penny Jane Burke doesn't buy into the fetishism of method, nor does she buy into the positivistic approach that numbers themselves will offer a crisp and complete understanding of a particular problem and, through an undisputed evidence-based research, the clear, self-evident and painless choices for public policy — Chapters Four and Five are particularly useful markers for this discussion. Moreover, the author includes a substantial discussion on the epistemological and ontological perspectives embedded in the research problem that she chose to study.

The empirical work informing this book draws from several research projects directed by the author, including an ESRC-funded project on men accessing higher education, a qualitative study of admissions practices to art and design undergraduate courses funded by the National Arts Learning Network (NALN) and a project on transitions to Masters-level study, funded by the Higher Education Academy. Prof. Burke also draws on small-scale new research, involving interviews and written reflections with a sample of widening participation managers and practitioners across England.

Take for example the key problem that Prof. Burke analyzes, the widening of participation and access to higher education, but also the persistent pattern of under-representation, which continues to challenge policy-makers and practitioners. The arguments in this book fall squarely in the domain of a critical sociology of education with a healthy dose of critical reflexivity.

The author offers a substantial premise of her analysis: 'Meanings are understood as discursively produced, tied to power and author/ity and as non-linear, subjective and tied to emotional and intuitive, as well as rational, forms of knowing and meaning-making.' Thus, in a nutshell, all of this comes back to the question of the formation of subjectivity through competing dis-courses. If one focuses on research, despite the claim of 'scientists' who will challenge what I am stating here, the selection of the research questions, research problems and methodologies for data collection and data analysis are all related to the question of the subjectivity and positionality of the researcher. While positivistic researchers tend to discount this subjectivity, focusing instead on premises such as objectivity and neutrality in value judgement, Prof. Burke, from a Critical Feminist perspective, criticizes this point at the beginning of her work, informing with her logic of analysis the contextualization and analysis of the book. Raising aspirations discourse is deconstructed as part of this critical analysis of the assumptions of hegemonic discourses.

The key questions that Prof. Burke tries to answer include: how do the political, economic and social contexts shift the meanings behind widening educational participation and create different spaces and opportunities for learning?; and in what ways is access to higher education, rather than other forms of learning, privileged in these discourses and with what effects on social inequalities and differences?

Yet these questions are framed exposing the centrality of subjective construction and identity formation in the project of moving beyond hegemonic discourses of widening participation. The author identifies the key elements involved: 'As widening participation is about redressing historical exclusions and inequalities, it must grapple with the politics of social relations including axes of difference across age, class, disability, ethnicity, gender, nationality, race, religion and sexuality.'

This discourse of raising aspirations, which resulted from the theory and practice of the welfare state, confronts head-on neoliberalism, and we learn a sombre lesson. Neoliberals have made sure that there is a clash of raising expectations in identity formation with the educational and labour futures. There are no jobs, and we have all forms of evidence worldwide, from the Arab spring, demanding both democracy and equality of occupational opportunity through job creation, to the *indignados* in Spain, with multiple sit-ins protesting against not only the high unemployment (estimated at over 20 percent in Spain), but also the fragmented and limited occupational futures. So one may, in a very cynical way, ask how could we argue in respect of fair access that, 'through "transparent" sets of criteria, procedures, rules and regulations, admissions tutors and personnel are able to make fair decisions about accepting some candidates onto a course over others'; but in the end occupational futures are very sombre.

This question begs another important consideration. What are actually the true criteria to select or reject a candidate in an academic higher education programme? From this sceptical perspective, one may argue that there are literally no firm standards for equality of educational opportunity that can be invoked with certainty. Academic selection is based on all sorts of experiences, from individual to ideological preferences, from scholastic specialty to available number of slots in a given programme. Most recently in the United States, for instance, with the presence of academic capitalism, and the need to enhance revenue, additional applicants from outside the state or the country are selected in larger quantities because they pay a premium over the cost of the tuition to a domestic in-state student.

What are then the merits of meritocracy as the foundation for the (transparent and undisputed) standards for access and participation? Though everybody pretends that meritocracy is the mantra of academia, there is a systematic operation of selectivity, as Prof. Burke refers following Williams, to selections 'which are embedded in specific cultural values and assumptions, and often serve in the interests of historically privileged groups. Wider social discourses that legitimate certain sets of cultural capital ensure that candidates are identified and identify themselves as deserving or undeserving and this significantly effects decisions and choices.' If this could be considered a statement about barriers, and if the removal of barriers could be considered a non-sequitur in the attempt to enhance access and participation, the author goes one step further and offers very critical insights in dealing with this question of barriers to access in higher education.

> In Chapter Eight I argue that the concept of barriers is also limiting in many important ways. This chapter subjects the concept of barriers to critique, considering the ways it is used in policy and practice, the different meanings that students, WP practitioners and policy-makers bring to the concept and the limitations of the concept for thinking through the complexities of operations of inequality and misrecognition in shifting cultural, political and economic frameworks. In particular, attention is paid to the problematic analogy of the 'barrier' in a context in which local, national and global conditions are under constant change and are unstable rather than fixed.

In the end, this book is not only about access and participation but deals also with the perennial question of the politics of identity. Who are the students who access higher education, why do they do so, what are their desires, goals, dreams and utopias? How flexible and appropriate, how engaging and welcoming, are the institutions they want to access, seeking to empower themselves, to develop further the variety of their talents and intelligences, dexterities, skills and abilities, and also trying, in many cases, in the fortunate phrase of Paulo Freire, 'to read the word, reading the world.'

The reader will profit from reading this book because the reader will be challenged, upset, surprised, pleased, infuriated or convinced, but this is not the book that one reads on a quiet Sunday afternoon to fill up empty space or kill some time. This is a book that provokes and invites at the same time the reader to think and understand, but also to act and transform the world of higher education. Because of this, Prof. Burke should be congratulated for her work and contributions, and we should simply read this book and engage in conversation with her and with the traditions that she so aptly represents.

After all, she says it early on in the book, and says it very well: 'My key argument is that there is no way to challenge deep-rooted inequalities without engaging with the theoretical literature on educational inequalities that offers sophisticated ways of understanding issues of access, participation and inequality in higher education.'

I have learned many lessons from Freire and one of them is that there are books that are an 'act of epistemological vigilance'. This book exemplifies Freire's apothegm.

## Notes

1 Carlos Alberto Torres is a political sociologist of education in the Graduate School of Education and Information Studies, UCLA and Director of the Paulo Freire Institute. He is the former Director of UCLA Latin American Center, past President of the Comparative International Education Society (CIES), past President of the Research Committee of

Sociology of Education, International Sociological Association, and author of more than 60 books. He has been elected a Fellow of the Royal Society of Canada.

2 I have discussed these processes in my book with Rob Rhoads (eds) (2006) *The University, State and Markets. The Political Economy of Globalization in the Americas*. Stanford, CA: Stanford University Press.

# References

Darling-Hammond, L. (1993) 'Introduction' to *Review of Research in Education*, Vol. 19. Washington: American Educational Research Association, xi.

Torres, C. A. (2005) *La Paxis Educativa y la Educación Cultural Liberadora de Paulo Freire*. Xátiva, Valencia: Institute Paulo Freire D'Espanya.

——(2009a) *Globalizations and Education. Collected Essays on Class, Race, Gender, and the State*. 'Introduction' by Michael W. Apple, 'Afterword' by Pedro Demo. New York and London: Teachers College Press, Columbia University.

——(2009b) *Education and Neoliberal Globalization*. 'Introduction' by Pedro Noguera. New York and London: Routledge.

# Acknowledgements

I am indebted to the students and WP professionals who took part in the research for this book; thank you very much for sharing your experiences and perspectives. Additionally, I want to extend my great appreciation to Dr Andrew Wilkins and Dr Yu Ching Kuo for their excellent work in assisting me with the research, including the literature and policy reviews. I would also like to thank Dr Andrew Wilkins for conducting most of the interviews with WP professionals. Thank you to Professor Carlos Alberto Torres, Professor Sally Power and Jacqueline McManus for reading drafts of the book and for their helpful insights, feedback and comments. I am also very grateful to my family and friends for their patience in sharing my time with this book project and for all their love and support, without which this book would not have been possible.

# Introduction

Widening access to and participation in higher education (HE) has become a central policy theme nationally and globally. In England, the government has made a significant commitment to diversification, expansion and widening participation (WP), in the attempt to address the under-representation of certain social groups in universities (DfES, 2003a, 2003b). The landscape of higher education has undergone change and transformation partly as a result of the diversification of higher education, with new student constituencies and professional identities emerging and posing specific challenges for universities, colleges and schools. However, persistent patterns of under-representation continue to perplex policy-makers and practitioners, raising questions about current strategies, policies and approaches to widening participation.

In this book, I interrogate the underpinning assumptions, values and perspectives shaping current concepts and understandings of widening participation. Drawing on a range of perspectives within the field of the sociology of education, including feminist post-structuralism, critical pedagogy and political sociology, I examine the ways in which wider societal inequalities and misrecognitions, which are related to difference and diversity, present particular challenges for the project to widen participation in higher education. I focus in particular on the themes of difference and diversity to shed light on the operations of inequalities and the politics of access and participation both in terms of national and institutional policy and at the level of student and practitioner experience. I draw on the insights of the sociology of education to consider not only the patterns of under-representation in higher education but also the politics of misrepresentation, critiquing key discourses of widening participation, such as 'raising aspirations' and 'fair access', which might operate to reinforce deficit discourses of the 'disadvantaged groups' targeted by WP policy.

It is important to critique the assumptions behind WP policy and discourse. This includes assumptions about education as an unassailable good, the purpose of HE and what is meant by widening participation. The book will interrogate these assumptions, drawing on the accounts and perspectives of students, practitioners and managers who are subject/ed to the discourses of widening participation. This will add an empirical layer to the book to bring to life the conceptual and theoretical issues under discussion as well as to emphasize the importance of bringing together theory and practice in critical praxis to move beyond neoliberal and utilitarian discourses and practices of widening participation.

In questioning the assumptions that currently shape the meanings we bring to widening participation, and who is seen as having the right to higher education, I aim for this book to provide a dialogic space for thinking in different ways, against the grain, and to imagine new future directions. I hope the book will feel interactive in style and form; I draw on concepts of critical reflexivity throughout the book and want to extend that notion to the reader. I will draw on my own and others' experiences and perspectives; I invite you, the reader, to do the same, in making sense of the different and contested discourses, concepts and perspectives at play in this book and in the wider field of 'widening participation'.

Throughout the book, I will attempt to draw on critical reflexivity to explore and examine the identities, experiences and relations I bring to the ideas I am presenting, critiquing and arguing. I will draw on Jane Miller's concept of the 'autobiography of the question' to consider the ways that my experiences have shaped the questions I want to ask in this book. These questions include for example: who can be a student?; what do we mean by 'participation'?; what forms of learning are we concerned with when we talk about 'widening participation'?; what are the politics of access and participation, and how are these shaped by differences and inequalities? This relates to my own experiences of accessing higher education, my shifting sense of subjectivity and my relational position within and outside higher education. I will also draw here on the accounts of those I have spoken with, through formal research, to try to understand and tease out the different perspectives, values and understandings at play. How do these shape educational practices and discourses and the im/possibilities of the formation of a self as 'university student'?

This book aims to present a comprehensive critique of the concepts and discourses underpinning the body of work on widening participation and the ways in which it has informed and shaped policy and practice of and in higher education. Drawing on this critique, the book will offer insights for future developments in the policy, practice and strategies for widening participation, including practices beyond entry to higher education, for example pedagogical and writing practices. The book will consider ways of reconceptualizing WP and aims to provide reflexive and dialogic spaces to explicitly connect theory and practice.

## Structure of the book

This book is organized in four main sections. You might want to read each section independently, rather than following the book from start to finish. The book is not conceived of as 'linear' in its approach, although it does attempt to provide a structure that is clear and accessible and makes sense to the person reading it. For example, the book begins with a comprehensive review of widening participation policy and research, provides a critique of this and finally provides some suggestions for alternative futures. However, it is possible to read different parts of the book, without having to trace through this structure from chapter to chapter. This is deliberate; it draws on the critiques of academic writing, seeks to disrupt the conventions that might exacerbate exclusions and non-participation in higher education and also takes a post-structural approach to meaning-making. Meanings are understood as discursively produced, tied to power and author/ity and as non-linear, subjective and connected to emotional and intuitive, as well as rational, forms of knowing and meaning-making.

Part One attempts to provide a context for the book in its examination of widening participation. It aims to uncover the histories behind contemporary debates and understandings. The section will provide a detailed analysis of contemporary discourses by examining the impact of histories of classed, gendered and racialized social relations and practices on the constructions of the university student. This will contribute to a deeper analysis of the ways in which certain individuals become recognizable subjects of widening partici-pation policy against the construction of the normalized student subject. This section will also provide a theoretical framework for the book, exploring the different perspectives shaping current discourses of WP, and a wider context for understanding the discursive production of 'widening participation' in relation to changing economies and social relations.

Chapter One aims to expose the hegemonic discourses of widening participation that underpin policy and practice. The discussion considers the historical profile of widening participation as a discursive field to shed light on why particular perspectives have gained a hegemonic position within national and international policy. It also examines the implications of particular discourses for strategic direction and possibility. This chapter interrogates and analyzes specific policy developments, which relate directly to the contemporary widening participation policy agenda. To provide some international context, policy developments from the USA and India also are examined. The chapter aims to map out consistencies and contradictions across time and space in order to provide a more precise analysis of the competing discourses of widen-ing participation and their implications for social justice in higher education. Questions raised by this chapter include what is understood by 'educational participation' and why arguments are made to widen educational participation at different historical moments. How do the political, economic and social contexts shift the meanings behind widening educational participation and create different spaces and opportunities for learning? In what ways is access to higher education, rather than other forms of learning, privileged in these discourses and with what effects on social inequalities and differences?

Further developing on this discussion, Chapter Two considers the ways in which widening participation might be reconceptualized in relation to competing epistemological and ontological perspectives. The range of theoretical lenses and the different sets of values brought to the problem bear on the meanings given to the concept, and this chapter attempts to show some of the different ways that widening participation is conceptualized. A key argument of this chapter is that certain theoretical frameworks, such as post-structural feminism, critical pedagogy and political sociology, are particularly fruitful in developing a concept of widening participation that is able to address the complexities of inequalities, misrecognitions and exclusions that play out in educational fields such as colleges and universities.

Chapter Three exposes the centrality of subjective construction and identity formation in the project of moving beyond hegemonic discourses of widening participation. As widening participation is about redressing historical exclusions and inequalities, it must grapple with the politics of social relations including axes of difference across age, class, disability, ethnicity, gender, nationality, race, religion and sexuality. These differences continue to make a difference in higher education fields. Subjectivity is formed through the different discourses at play, and WP policy constructs recognizable subjects of its discourse: for example those seen as 'disadvantaged', 'non-traditional' and 'having potential'. This chapter draws on theories of identity and subjectivity to examine the implications of the construction of 'new student constituencies' within higher education, in terms of who can be recognized as a university student. Particular attention is drawn to the ways in which access to *higher education* is prioritized in widening participation policy debates, effecting the formation of learner and student subjectivities. This will include attention to the implications of this for marginalized and misrecognized learning and student subjectivities.

Part Two discusses the methodological implications of researching and developing practice for widening participation. A key argument is made that methodological considerations are often underdeveloped in both research and practice of widening participation, despite the central importance of methodological frameworks for combating educational inequalities and exclusions. The section also pays attention more specifically to the methodological issues involved in producing the research and writing for the book, including issues of re/presentation, which relate to the overarching conceptual theme of mis/recognition.

Widening participation has become a significant theme of educational research over past years, contributing to the growing field of higher education studies. However, this body of work has been critiqued as 'atheoretical' (Archer and Leathwood, 2003; Burke and Jackson, 2007) and lacking sophisticated levels of attention to methodological issues (Tight, 2003). Chapter Four argues that methodological issues are key to the contribution of knowledge about widening participation, and constructions of the 'right' to higher education, because different methodological frameworks profoundly shape the kinds of research questions formulated by researchers and the ways in which research is conducted. In this chapter, the importance of epistemological frameworks, which determine the ways that knowledge is produced, is emphasized. The chapter also argues for the importance of attention to onto-logical questions, such as the identity and positionality of the researcher and how this affects their interpretations and approaches. Methodologies shape the ways in which researchers collect and analyse data, the formulation of questions or problems, the ways ethical issues are handled and made sense of as well as the ways that knowledge is constructed and represented. This chapter aims to provide a set of tools for researchers to use in their work on widening par-ticipation, in order to contribute to deeper-level understandings of the key issues that impact on the project of widening participation. It also provides a set of tools for students and practitioners to critique some of the problematic assumptions that have shaped the body of work on WP and might limit our understandings and therefore the kinds of strategies and solutions formulated.

Chapter Five outlines the methodological framework for the book, discussing the approaches taken to collect and analyze data, the ethical dimensions, the epistemological underpinnings and the writing practices adopted. The book will draw on my current research projects, including an ESRC-funded project on men accessing higher education, a qualitative study of admissions practices to art and design undergraduate courses funded by the National Arts Learning Network (NALN) and a project on transitions to Masters-level study, funded by the Higher Education Academy. I will also draw on small-scale new research, involving interviews and written reflections with a sample of widening participation managers and practitioners across England (funded by a Higher Education Academy National Teaching Fellowship Award). The dif-ferent sets of data will provide insight into both student experiences and the perspectives and difficulties faced by an emerging professional body created by a national policy commitment to widening participation. The data will be used both to illuminate the conceptual and theoretical themes framing the book but will also be used to stimulate reflection and to create a more inter-active format to the text. The chapter will pick up on the themes outlined in the previous chapter in relation to the methodological and ethical implications of researching widening participation in the context of 'real research' conducted for this book. This will offer concrete examples of some of the issues and dilemmas that researchers face when attempting to shed light on a complex social and cultural set of issues, which circulate around a specific policy agenda.

Part Three focuses more specifically on the key strategies and discourses emerging in, and shaping, the English policy context, making connections to wider global concerns and socio-political contexts. The aim of the section is to provide a comprehensive critique of the values and perspectives shaping policy and practice and demanding major national investment, leading to the key policy discourses of raising aspirations, fair access and lifting barriers. The section considers both the opportunities presented by these discourses as well as the problematic assumptions behind them and the ways in which each of these might at times exacerbate rather than challenge complex educational exclusions. The chapters include the accounts of students, practitioners and policy-makers through data from previous and new research involving interviews with students and practitioners, as well as an analysis of policy texts. All four chapters keep in the frame an examination of the implications of changing economic, political and social contexts on policies and practices of widening participation in relation to challenging discourses of difference.

A central theme of contemporary WP policy is 'raising aspirations', leading to a focus on developing activities designed to target those lacking aspiration but with potential to benefit from higher education. The 'raising aspirations' discourse constructs the main problem for widening educational participation as those individuals and communities who fail to recognize the value of participating in higher education. Chapter Six deconstructs 'raising aspirations' to expose the underlying and problematic assumptions of this hegemonic discourse as well as the opportunities it produces for WP. The chapter argues that 'raising aspirations' does not pay ample attention to the complex processes of identity formation, which are situated and produced within the discursive fields and practices of schools, colleges and universities. It examines the interconnections between a subject's aspirations and their social positioning, drawing on data from qualitative interviews with students. It explores the cultural, economic and political contexts in which certain subjects are constructed, and construct themselves, as having/not having potential or ability or indeed not choosing to participate in higher education for a range of valid reasons (Archer and Leathwood, 2003).

Chapter Seven interrogates another hegemonic discourse at play in current WP policy: 'fair access'. The chapter argues that this discourse is premised on the assumption that, through 'transparent' sets of criteria, procedures, rules and regulations, admissions tutors and personnel are able to make fair decisions about accepting some candidates onto a course over others. It is problematic that such decisions are seen as being outside wider social relations and contexts assuming that candidates apply to higher education on a level playing field. The assumption that candidates can be selected on 'merit alone' is problematic, as the sociology of education has exposed the flaws of mainstream concepts of 'merit' and meritocracy, as well as the assumptions often made about ability and potential. This chapter seeks to expose the ways in which inequalities are hidden within the discourse of 'fair access', drawing in particular on data from the NALN-funded study of admissions practices in the context of art and design undergraduate degrees. I argue that the discourse of 'fair access' ignores the operations of selectivity (Williams, 1997), which are embedded in specific cultural values and assumptions, and often serve in the interests of historically privileged groups. Wider social discourses that legitimate certain sets of cultural capital ensure that candidates are identified and identify themselves as deserving or undeserving and this significantly affects decisions and choices (Webb, 1997; Williams, 1997; Reay *et al.*, 2001; Reay *et al.*, 2005). Those entering higher education from 'different' backgrounds are often seen as potentially contaminating of university standards and as a result a key policy strategy is to protect the quality of higher education by creating new and different spaces for those new and different students (Morley, 2003).

'Barriers' is a prominent concept in both WP policy texts and in literature on WP (e.g. Thomas, 2005; Gorard *et al.*, 2007). The concept is helpful in exposing some of the difficulties and challenges that students from traditionally under-represented groups might face in terms of broader national and institutional structures and policies (such as funding and financial support) and other practical issues relating to infrastructure and mechanisms of support (such as the accessibility issues of higher education institutions or need for childcare provision). However, in Chapter Eight I argue that the concept of barriers is also limiting in many important ways. This chapter subjects the concept of barriers to critique, considering the ways in which it is used in policy and practice, the different meanings that students, WP practitioners and policy-makers bring to the concept, and the limitations of the concept for thinking through the complexities of operations of inequality and misrecognition in shifting cultural, political and economic frameworks. In particular, attention is paid to the problematic analogy of the 'barrier' in a context in which local, national and global conditions are under constant change and are unstable rather than fixed.

Chapter Nine focuses on the processes of subjective construction in relation to those who have specific responsibility for WP in higher educational institutions. This chapter draws on data from interviews with WP practitioners, as well as their written reflections. Little attention has been paid to the production of new professional identities in higher education as part of the expanding WP market (Burke, 2008). Jones and Thomas argue that WP practitioners tend to work on the periphery of universities, in separate centres and outside academic faculties and departments (Jones and Thomas, 2005). This chapter considers the ways that these workers themselves might be constructed as 'non-traditional' and even marginal in academic spaces. Complex power relations are at play within universities, which are intensely hierarchical institutions, although of course this plays out in different ways across a highly differentiated higher education system. WP professionals have primary responsibility for developing and sustaining WP strategies within their institutions and in this way WP has its own special space, outside the main work of academic staff. The ways in which the new WP professional workforce is constructed matters and impacts on decision-making processes. Questions of identity matter as well in terms of power relations within institutions and the constructions of (lack of) authority that might facilitate or impede processes of change and transformation. This chapter explores these important issues in depth.

Despite significant investment in widening participation in terms of funding, resources and personnel, patterns of under-representation continue to persist amongst certain socio-economic groups. Even where students from 'non-traditional' backgrounds have been recruited successfully to higher education, there are patterns of non-completion and research, both in England and other international contexts, highlights that often such students experience a sense of not belonging and exclusion. Drawing on the insights of critical and feminist theory and pedagogy, Part Four sketches out the possibilities of inclusive higher educational spaces whilst acknowledging that contradictions, struggles and tensions will always exist. However, this part of the book will offer students, practitioners, policy-makers, educational leaders and academics possibilities for carving out more inclusive and dialogic educational spaces.

In Chapter Ten, I explore the potential of critical, feminist and post-structural theoretical perspectives for examining the complex ways in which social inequalities play out in higher education. Such theoretical perspectives place concepts of power and social justice at the centre of analysis, whilst mainstream perspectives of WP tend to ignore such issues. The book will have developed a strong argument that, despite substantial levels of financial and human investment in the project of WP, persistent patterns of under-representation amongst certain socio-economic groups raises crucial questions about the effectiveness of current frames of understanding. This chapter attempts to suggest more radical perspectives, which, when in dialogue with policy and practice, might work more effectively to dislodge and destabilize enduring relations of inequality, which continue to be reflected in universities.

Much of the work centering on WP emphasizes issues prior to access to higher education, most prominently 'raising aspirations' and raising levels of educational attainment. Although aspirations and attainment are certainly important, the book will have shown that mainstream approaches to aspirations and attainment do not have the capacity to address deep-seated and long-standing historical injustices within education. Furthermore, although it is significant to address the complexities of under-representation in higher education prior to entry, Chapter Eleven argues that it is equally important to tackle issues of inequality in terms of participation in higher education beyond entry. Indeed, issues of pedagogy, curriculum and assessment remain central areas of exclusion and it is therefore of great importance to explore possibilities for developing structures and frameworks that support inclusive practices, not just in terms of individual excellence but as a national and institutional commitment to widening participation.

# Part 1

# Contextualizing and theorizing widening participation

This part will put widening participation in context by uncovering the histories behind contemporary debates and understandings. It will also make connections internationally by exploring policy of widening access to, and participation in, higher education in the USA and India: two countries committed to widening participation but in quite different and contrasting ways. This will provide some context in which to make sense of the ways in which contemporary discourses of widening participation have emerged and have in turn shaped the discourses over who has the right to higher education, and who does not. In the English context, this is largely framed in terms of aspiration and potential and increasingly of being able to manage and accept the inevitability of large amounts of debt after graduation. Thus, a particular disposition is privileged in discourses about rights and higher education access and participation.

The urgency of making connections between widening participation and the complex ways that inequalities and misrecognitions play out in higher education is emphasized in Part One. This raises the necessity of drawing on the extensive body of theoretical work and research within the critical sociology of education that addresses the workings of educational inequalities and misrecognitions in sophisticated ways, providing conceptual tools to think through ways to disrupt inequalities. Chapter 2 thus considers the different theoretical perspectives available that might help those committed to widening participation to tackle these issues, moving away from narrow frameworks informed by the wider agendas of global neoliberalism to transformative, reflexive praxis which might destabilize long-standing and enduring inequalities. In this chapter, I explore the generative potential of Bourdieu's theory for understanding the ways in which inequalities in education are reproduced, so that common sense connections between 'right' and 'potential' are seen as about innate natural inequalities rather than social ones. I argue that Foucault's concepts of discourse and power are also of great value in understanding the ways that certain subjects are recognized or not as having the right to participate in higher education and how power is complex and unpredictable, so that utilitarian perspectives of widening participation miss the deeper and more subtle ways that power inequalities play out in the discursive fields of higher education.

In the final chapter of Part One, the impact of complex histories of classed, gendered and racialized social relations and practices on the constructions of the university student is examined through concepts of identity formation. This will contribute to a deeper analysis of the ways in which certain persons become recognizable subjects of widening participation policy against the construction of the normalized student subject. The key importance of identity in understanding issues of access to, and participation in, higher education will be emphasized.

# 1  Deconstructing the discourses of widening participation

## Introduction: widening inequalities

Despite the political commitment expressed through numerous international and national policies to widen educational access and participation, we are living in a time of increased, and widening, social and economic inequalities. Although we have largely moved from an elite to a mass higher education system in England and in many other countries, those benefitting the most from policies to expand HE are those with relative social, economic and cultural advantages, i.e. in the English context this would be those categorized in middle-class and/or professional groups.

The Government Equalities Office found that the large growth in inequality of the period of the late 1970s to the early 1990s has not been reversed (Hills *et al.*, 2010: 1). Although women are more likely now than men to participate in higher education (but this is highly gendered across different subject areas), women are paid 21 per cent less in terms of median hourly pay for all employees and 13 per cent less than men for those working full-time (Hills *et al.*, 2010: 11). In terms of ethnicity, 'nearly all minority ethnic groups are less likely to be in paid employment than White British men and women' (Hills *et al.*, 2010: 16). Indeed, 'social background really matters', for example, 'young people with GCSE results above the national median who have been on Free School Meals are less likely to go on to higher education than others with the same results' (Hills *et al.*, 2010: 25). Further, although only seven per cent of the population in Britain attend independent schools, 75 per cent of judges, 70 per cent of finance directors, 45 per cent of top civil servants and 35 per cent of MPs were educated in independent schools (Milburn, 2009: 12). The report, *Fair Access to the Professions* (Milburn, 2009: 15), points out that, increasingly, entry to the professions depends on having a good honours degree (and this is related also to the status of the university attended). The increase in vocational qualifications and provision has not necessarily enabled wider access to the professions. For example, only 0.2 per cent of apprenticeship learners progressed on to further or higher education, and few directly into the professions (Milburn, 2009: 15). Further, 'almost three times as many young people with parents from professional backgrounds attend university compared with young people whose parents have routine occupations' (Milburn, 2009: 39). Yet at the time of writing, the Coalition Government in England has just introduced the severest cuts to public spending since the Second World War, with funding to teaching in higher education cut by up to 97 per cent for some institutions. The cost of HE teaching is now expected to be almost entirely covered by students and their families, especially those studying subjects within the disciplines of arts, humanities and social sciences.

This chapter maps out consistencies and contradictions across time and space in order to provide an analysis of the competing discourses and perspectives of widening participation and their implications for access to higher education. I interrogate and analyze policy, which relates directly to the WP policy agenda in England. However, to provide some sense of international context and comparison, and to consider different policy approaches, a brief outline of relevant policy developments from the USA and India will also be presented. The USA and India have been selected as countries that have expressed explicit commitment to issues of access but in quite different and contrasting ways. Finally, I will deconstruct the policy discourses at play to consider the implications for strategic direction and the central aim of the book to move beyond the current hegemonic discourses of widening participation.

## A historical overview of English educational access and participation

Widening access and participation is largely concerned with redressing the under-representation of certain social groups in higher education. However, the concept of widening participation is highly contested and there is no one agreed definition. There have of course been particular policy interventions, for example by the Higher Education Funding Council for England (HEFCE, 2005), which has attempted to provide a concrete definition of WP and more specifically to offer guidelines to institutions, organizations and individuals who are involved in enacting WP policy. In the English context, during the period of New Labour Government (1997–2010), widening participation, often shorthanded as 'WP', gained discursive momentum and hegemony. I will argue throughout this book that the policy of widening participation (WP) has been framed by particular perspectives and assumptions, most powerfully that of neoliberal globalization. However, in order to understand the 'history of the present', I will trace the different histories through which particular policy discourses of educational access and participation come to be at play, and are contested with other discourses. In this section, therefore, I will present a historical overview of key policy moments in relation to widening educational access and participation from the late nineteenth century and up to the early twenty-first century. The aim is to provide historical background and insight in the specific English context and in terms of continuities and discontinuities, particularly around social and cultural inequalities of age, class, ethnicity and gender. This will serve as a context later in the chapter when I deconstruct the multiple and competing discourses of widening participation.

## Twentieth-century policy developments in HE access and participation

The language of expansion, massification and access have dominated the discourses concerned with issues of the right to higher education, often masking the intricate relations of inequality, which work at the complex intersections of class, gender and race, as well as other formations of sociocultural difference and inequality (such as age, migration, religion and nationality). The discourse of 'expansion' became increasingly significant over the twentieth century in Britain. The Education Act of 1944, for example, promised to increase the number of students qualified for university participation, with concerns to expand the supply of university-trained professions. The discourse of expansion became more prominent in the 1963 Robbins report on higher education (Robbins, 1963). A key aim was to raise the percentage of the age group receiving full-time higher education from about eight per cent to about 17 per cent by 1980. Expansion was supported by the human capital arguments put forward by economists and fully argued in the Robbins report, which legitimized the expansion that was already happening and made explicit the policy that all qualified applicants should find a place somewhere within a highly differentiated system (Kogan and Hanney, 2000: 72). This included the creation of 30 polytechnics from local authority colleges in 1970 (David *et al.*, 2009). The Government agreed to fund an expansion of up to 22,000 places in universities by 1971–72, but the University Grants Committee (UGC) told universities that their 'figures were not being laid down as precise targets or directives' (Shattock, 1994: 14).

The increasing tensions between aspirations for expansion and concerns to contain public funding came into full play in the 1970s. At the time, the Department of Education and Science was exercising much firmer control in order to achieve a balance between the university and the public sector of higher education. The Government cut back UGC's planning figure of 320,000 students by 1976–77 to 306,000 students by reducing the number of postgraduate places so as to preserve the more politically sensitive undergraduate places. This is a recurring theme in debates about widening access to HE, with undergraduate education prioritized in WP policy. Expansion was connected with concerns for containment. Thus, in 1978, the Department of Education and Science produced a Brown Paper on higher education, opening a public debate on ways of containing or planning the demographically driven expansion that might occur in the next few years (Kogan and Hanney, 2000: 72). The UGC negotiated with the Department of Education and Science to issue what amounted to an instruction (later withdrawn) that universities should restrict their student intake in 1980 to 94 per cent of the figure for 1979. In 1981–88, the UGC fined those universities that had exceeded their UGC targets (Shattock, 1994: 15). The concern about containment resulted in cuts, and in the early 1980s the UGC imposed a cut of around 15 per cent in total across the university sector (Trowler, 1998).

Funding presented an ongoing tension in relation to concerns about widening access and participation and, in 1984, the UGC developed a further strategy of selective research funding. Concerns were raised that failure to increase participation would lead to long-term shortages in many specialist skills. It was therefore proposed that more explicit guidelines should be drawn up to encourage a greater degree of self-funding, or joint funding and other forms of financial support (Kogan and Hanney, 2000).

Discourses of managerialism and enterprise crept into higher education policy developments. Charged with review and making recommendations about university management, the 1985 Jarratt Report recommended a raft of measures designed to make universities more effective and efficient through clearer management structures and styles (Trowler, 1998) and, in 1986, the research assessment exercise (RAE) began (David, *et al.*, 2009), which has had further implications for WP (see Chapter Four). The announcement of the 'Enterprise in Higher Education' initiative was made in 1987. This aimed to increase the supply of university graduates 'with enterprise'. A series of five-year schemes ran in universities and polytechnics with considerable amounts of pump-priming money attached to them. The idea was to vocationalize higher education, integrating 'enterprise' into degree schemes more generally (Trowler, 1998). Entrepreneurial discourses concerned with enterprise and efficiency, underpinned by neoliberalism and managerialism, thus increasingly shaped debates about widening access and HE expansion. Simultaneously, diversification of higher education was set in place, with research excellence central to processes of stratification.

The 1988 Education Act established the Universities Funding Council and Polytechnics and College Funding Council. The Act asserted that higher education should serve the economy more efficiently and have closer links with industry and commerce and promote enterprise (Trowler, 1998). The 1988 White Paper, *Employment for the 1990s* (Department of Employment, 1988), set out the nature and functions of the new Training and Enterprise Council, charged to meet the needs of local communities and government objectives with regard to vocational education and training. The 1990 Education Act (Student Loans) stressed the need for widening access to higher education in the context of a competitive international economic environment.

Meanwhile, racial tensions in Britain led to concerns during the 1980s with the need for more black and minority ethnic groups to enter professions such as social work and teaching. There was also acknowledgement that continuing expansion relied on recruiting mature 'second-chance' participants to higher education, as well as young 'non-traditional' students. There also emerged a more politicized educational movement, which aimed to redress social inequalities by transforming further and higher education to challenge the status quo and elitism. All of these different interests and concerns led to the development of locally based Access to Higher Education courses. The needs of students and local communities were placed as central in the design of Access courses, pedagogy and curriculum (Diamond 1999: 186). However, the practices across and within different Access courses ranged widely. There were mixed pedagogies; in some ways Access courses were radical in approach, with an explicit articulation of a political stance in terms of critiquing the educational system, paying attention to inequalities and exclusions. Yet, simultaneously, the pedagogical approaches were often embedded in traditional, didactic relations, underpinned by the aim to prepare Access students for hegemonic practices in universities (Burke, 2002). During the 1990s there were significant cultural and managerial changes to Access courses, resulting from its formalization and national recognition. As decision-making shifted from Access practitioners to national policy-makers, underpinning perspectives and values also shifted, from creating locally relevant courses to developing regulative systems of administration and organization (Burke, 2002).

The 1991 White Paper, *Higher Education: A New Framework* (DfE, 1991), proposed the end of a binary higher education system and established new funding councils, leading to polytechnics gaining university status in 1992. A framework around quality was introduced, with quality assessment to inform funding allocation. Continuing expansion was anticipated, with one in three 18–19-year-olds expected to enter higher education. All universities and colleges were brought within a single funding mechanism, and funding council grants and student grants were announced (Trowler, 1998). Expansion came back fully on the agenda in the 1994 White Paper which proposed to spend £300 million in 1997–98 on accelerated modern apprenticeships for 18–19-year-olds, leading to qualifications at NVQ Level 3. Later, the 1996 Education Act allowed students to borrow from banks on the same terms as from the Student Loans Company.

This brief history highlights the hegemony of a discourse of expansion, which is always in tension with policy concerns about the funding of higher education. This provides a context for the contemporary situation, which has moved increasingly towards the substitution of public funds with private individual fees (Carpentier, 2010). The landscape of higher education, as it has moved towards the aims of massification, has been increasingly diversified, but this has been tied in with processes of increasing stratification, differentiation and selection connected to the discourses of excellence, quality and standards. Higher education policy has been driven by an economic agenda, strongly underpinned by neoliberal discourses. Such discourses have had a major impact on the processes by which some individuals from traditionally under-represented groups have found new opportunities to access higher education, whilst others have been excluded from such opportunities. Gender has been one key aspect of such struggles over inclusion and exclusion, although it has always intersected with other social inequalities, such as social class and race, in the formation of who is seen, and who is not, as having the right to participate in (certain forms of) higher education.

*Examining the intersections of inequality in access to higher education*

Women have often been seen as a 'danger to the men' in higher education (Mirza, 2009: 116), and struggles over access often recast the gaze on women as threatening to the status quo. Yet women's recent success in accessing higher education (in certain parts of the world) is over-represented by women from privileged class and ethnic backgrounds. In understanding the history of inequalities in higher education, and struggles for the right to access and participate in HE, it is imperative to examine the complex intersections of gender with class and race.

It is easy to forget perhaps just how recently it was that women as a group were excluded from higher education. It remains that it is mainly women from middle-class white backgrounds who have benefitted from the 'massification' policies described above. Over the nineteenth and twentieth centuries, women from middle- and upper-class backgrounds struggled hard for their right to higher education. Initially, though, this was largely posed in terms that complemented rather than challenged the hegemonic understanding of 'being a woman' in late nineteenth-century Britain, emphasizing women's role in the domestic sphere. For example, Newnham College for women developed a female-oriented curriculum, drawing on constructions of the natural differences between men and women and also allowing women part-time programmes and longer periods for examination preparation. However, Girton College, set up by Emily Davies, insisted that women should have access to the same curriculum as men, to ensure the validity of their achievements on an equal standing. Such approaches were fiercely contested on the basis that such educational participation posed a serious threat to the family. It was often argued that women's participation in the intellectual pursuits traditionally preserved for men was detrimental to their health and well-being, with scientific arguments being made that the rigours of mental labour could cause 'menstrual disability' (Jones, 2010).

Despite these arguments, women continued to struggle for their right to higher education. Research was conducted by some of the women's colleges to interrogate the claims that intellectual work was dangerous to women's health. Such research found instead that educated women tended to be healthier than women who did not have access to higher education. Arguments against women's access to higher education were further undermined by the impressive achievements of some women. For example, Philippa Fawcet of Newnham College achieved far better exam results than the highest achieving male student in mathematics in 1890. Despite these achievements and struggles, women did not gain full access to higher education until the early twentieth century; women were finally awarded degrees at Oxford in 1920 and at Cambridge in 1921 (although they were not awarded full membership at Cambridge until 1948) (Jones, 2010). It is also important to take careful note of the ways in which women's access to higher education have often been constructed in relation to white, middle-class perspectives. Heidi Mirza describes the 'erasure of black women's genealogy in British academia' and explores the Indian suffragette movement in late nineteenth-century Britain to expose a 'counter-memory' that 'tells a different truth' (Mirza, 2009: 117). The erasure of black women in higher education represents a 'collective amnesia' and what Spivak (1988) names 'epistemic violence' (Mirza, 2009: 117). To counter this, Mirza describes the life of an Indian woman, Cornelia Sorabji, who went to Somerville Hall Oxford in 1889 and was given special dispensation to sit her law exams (Mirza, 2009: 119). Although Cornelia was not a feminist and was pro-British rule, Mirza considers her position as 'a special case' and the particular burdens connected with 'living a non-white existence in a consuming white world' (Mirza, 2009: 119).

Although there were some achievements with some women gaining access to higher education, as described above, there was a decline in the proportion of women in the university student population in the 1930s, with a long period of stagnation up until the 1960s. Carol Dyhouse establishes three main categories to explain this period of stagnation: (1) discrimination in access and provision; (2) limited employment opportunities for women graduates; and (3) demographic trends towards early marriage (Dyhouse, 2005). A key instance of discrimination in access and provision was the establishment of quotas by Oxford and Cambridge, restricting the numbers of women in their student populations; these remained in force until 1957 (Oxford) and 1960 (Cambridge). Giving an example of the explicit sexist discrimination expressed in higher education during the time, Dyhouse quotes Sir Raymond Priestley, Vice-Chancellor of the University of Birmingham, who stated in his 1945 report to Council that:

> The proportions of men to women have changed less than would have been the case had the University not adopted a self-denying policy. We are convinced that the pre-war proportion was about right and that any considerable increase in the proportion of women would so change the character of the University as to act to the detriment of both men and women students.
>
> (quoted in Dyhouse, 2005)

Here the right to higher education is seen in highly patriarchal terms, with women's access to higher education causing damage not only to women and men students but also to the 'character' of the university.

In the early years of the twentieth century, employment opportunities for women graduates were very limited: the majority went into school teaching. Many girls were discouraged from staying on at school and making long-term educational and career plans because of a social emphasis on the desirability of marrying young. Dyhouse (2005) argues that historians have underestimated the significance of the trend of early marriages after the war for women's participation in higher education. This is of course highly classed; women from working-class backgrounds have held an uneasy position in relation to marriage and domesticity, as they could never be 'the angels in the house', a social imaginary constructed in relation to the bourgeois white wife and mother. Working-class women had to saddle two impossible worlds of unpaid domestic labour and paid work and were often constructed as potentially patho-logical and polluting. Stanley explains the particular plight of working-class women in relation to education, arguing that the 'eroding phrase "working-class thicko" no longer even needs to be spoken, so well is it internalised' (Stanley, 1995: 171). Language signifies and reinforces class oppression, and educational institutions are places of 'systematic shaming and undermining', which help to keep working-class women out of higher education and in low and unchallenging social positions (Stanley, 1995: 171).

Importantly for contextualizing the recent debates about women's increasing access to higher education, often presented in relation to the perception of men's 'disadvantage' (see for example HEPI, 2009), Dyhouse examines the patterns of women's increasing participation in higher education beyond the 1970s. She identifies four main explanations for women's increasing participation: (1) demographic changes (the 'sexual revolution' and the woman student); (2) the attractiveness of the new universities of the 1960s to women; (3) feminism and equal opportunities legislation; and (4) changing employment opportunities (Dyhouse, 2005). She argues that it was the 'sexual revolution' that had the greatest impact on the lives of women students. Women's increased control over their bodies and fertility through legalized abortion and the contraceptive pill played a key role in women's aspirations and longer-term goals. Additionally, the new universities of the 1960s offered women broader curricula and broke down gender segregation and discrimination against women students. Equal opportunities legislation challenged sexual discrimination more broadly but also had a direct impact on women's access to and participation in higher education from the 1970s onwards. Although women were concentrated in teacher training, employment patterns in the 1970s began to change and, combined with second-wave feminism and equality legislation, employers' interest in women recruits to the labour market began to rise. However, Dyhouse notes that gaps in pay between men and women have continued, with the gap widening further in the five years following graduation. She states:

> Over the course of a working life a woman graduate can expect to earn some 12 per cent less than her male counterpart. The value of a university education, seen purely as a monetary investment, is still considerably less for women than for men.
>
> (Dyhouse, 2005)

High-profile debates about women's right to higher education continue to rage in the twenty-first century but increasingly in terms of a 'crisis of mas-culinity'. In a speech made on 1 April 2011, David Willetts MP, the UK Minister of State for Universities and Science, argued that feminism was prob-ably the 'single biggest factor' responsible for the lack of (working-class men's) social mobility in Britain, as (middle-class) women took up university places and well-paid work that might have gone to 'ambitious working-class men' (Mulholland, 2011). Willetts asserted that: 'The feminist revolution in its first round effects was probably the key factor. Feminism trumped egalitarianism. It is not that I am against feminism, it's just that it's probably the single biggest factor' (Willetts quoted in Mulholland, 2011).

Willetts reiterates an ongoing debate that poses the success of (white middle-class) women as the explanation for the low rates of (white working-class) men's participation in higher education. In a single sweep, 'the blame' of exclusion and under-representation is laid at the feet of women, without paying attention to the 'patriarchal dividend' (Connell, 2000) and its relation to sustained classed and racialized inequalities. Over the past decade, feminist scholars have extensively critiqued such explanations, which pose men and women as in competition and opposition through the narrative of a 'crisis of masculinity' and brush aside the intricacies of relations of gender, class and ethnicity in educational access, participation and attainment. The recent attention to men's 'under-representation' in HE dangerously recasts a battle of the sexes. This not only undermines the importance of girls' and women's achievements in recent years, which should be celebrated, but implies that women's success must be read as a direct threat to men's social position and status. This ignores the important, rigorous and sophisticated analyses contributed by feminist scholars to deconstructing gender discourses, subjectivities and relations and to developing a rich and nuanced understanding of the discursive constitution of masculinities and femininities within educational sites and the effect of this on boys' schooling, as well as the important ways that complex intersections of class, gender and race work to produce formations of inequality and exclusion. Questions raised by feminist scholars draw attention to the interconnections between gender and other formations of identity and subjectivity, which profoundly shape dispositions to learning.

## New Labour and widening participation policy

In 1997 the New Labour Government came to power, with Tony Blair as prime minister putting 'education, education, education' on the national agenda. The Dearing Report was published the same year, placing again the expansion of higher education as a central goal of policy, but also arguing that students should share part of the cost of funding higher education. The New Labour Government announced the introduction of tuition fees of £1,000 per year for students, to be introduced from 1998. These were to be means tested and repaid once the graduate was in employment (Trowler, 1998: 35). Further key themes, many of which resonated with earlier discourses, featured in the Dearing Report included: greater selectivity in research funding, more collaboration between institutions, an emphasis on lifelong learning, emphasis on improving teaching in higher education and the importance of information and communication technologies and making more transparent the objectives and outcomes for students, employers and other key stakeholders (Dearing, 1997).

Lifelong learning featured strongly in New Labour policy, and this was echoed internationally, connected with neoliberal concerns about global economic competitiveness, the need for flexibility in a continually changing labour market and the impact of 'the knowledge society'. In relation to such concerns, the Green Paper, *The Learning Age* (DfEE, 1998), was published in 1998, which set out the Government's vision of a learning society in which everyone, from whatever background, routinely expects to learn and upgrade their skills throughout life. Access to lifelong learning and expansion was a central theme of the Green Paper, with the aim of 500,000 additional students in further and higher education by 2002 and more young people to continue to study beyond age 16 with government aid. Other key proposals were to double the provision of financial support for basic literacy and numeracy skills amongst adults, with half a million people to be involved by 2002; inspection in further and adult education to be instituted; targets for the nation's skills and qualifications to be published; business, employees and trade unions to be involved in developing and supporting workplace skills; and simplification of the post-compulsory qualification system, with the aim being to give equal value to both academic and vocational learning, while addressing the needs of industry and employers.

The discourse of 'raising aspirations' took central stage as the Aimhigher: Excellence Challenge initiative was introduced in September 2001. This initiative set out the Government's aim to increase the number of young people from disadvantaged backgrounds who had the qualifications and potential necessary to enter higher education (Morris and Golden, 2005) but might have 'lacked aspiration'. The Secretary of State for Education and Employment announced that an extra £150 million was to be spent over the next three years to improve access to higher education for 'bright young students' from poorer backgrounds, whilst maintaining entry standards. At the same time, the Aimhigher: Partnerships for Progression scheme was set up to build on the extensive regional and local partnerships that already existed between HE and further education (FE), operating in nine regions covering the whole of England. This encompassed three broad strands of activity: (1) supporting and extending partnerships between HE and FE, with dedicated staff to work with schools and FE and training providers; (2) regionally co-ordinated activities including summer schools, mentoring and shadowing for successive age groups of school and FE students, across different progression routes; and (3) a national programme of research, evaluation and dissemination.

The White Paper, *The Future of Higher Education* (DfES, 2003a), set out the Government's plans for radical reform and investment in universities and colleges. The two Aimhigher initiatives were brought together into one single programme, in the government's aim to create greater coherence for its WP strategy. The main focus of Aimhigher was on the development of outreach activities such as visits to university campuses, residential summer schools, master-classes and open days and mentoring schemes. *The Future of Higher Education* signalled the introduction of an 'Access Regulator' to approve access agreements before any institution could charge higher variable fees. The Department published 'Widening Participation in Higher Education' (DfES, 2003b) on 8 April 2003, which included its proposals for the Office for Fair Access (OFFA) and its vision for widening participation, in the context of higher fees. The document outlined the Government's strategies to promote WP, focusing on attainment, aspiration, application and admissions. The Higher Education Act 2004 provided a framework for the work of the new Office for Fair Access, which was given two main responsibilities: (1) to make sure that the introduction of higher tuition fees in 2006–7 did not deter people from entering higher education for financial reasons; and (2) to ensure that universities and colleges were explicitly committed to increasing participation in higher education among under-represented groups. Outlining a number of financial support measures, the Government aimed to improve the current student support systems. These included concessions for students from lower-income groups with a new higher education grant of up to £1,000 introduced in October 2004, amongst a range of other financial support measures. In 2006, top-up fees were established, with a maximum fee of £3,000 for home students.

In June 2004 a further initiative to support the Government's widening participation agenda was introduced in the form of lifelong learning networks (LLNs). The focus of these networks was to develop a joint strategy to advance vocational and workplace progression into and through higher education, through the collaboration of several key bodies. A sum of £100 million was invested in the LLNs to support their aim to give vocational learners the same equality of educational opportunity as those students taking traditional academic routes into higher education. The task of each LLN was to develop specialist advice and personalized learner support systems to engage, and track, learner progress. This aimed to complement the work of the Aimhigher partnerships, which sought to raise aspirations and attainment to widen access and participation in HE more generally. HEFCE identified the main role of LLN as being to (1) develop curricula to make progression easier by removing barriers, promoting bridging provision and involving employers; (2) offer learners lifelong learning information, advice and guidance and track their progress; and (3) produce progression agreements that define for learners what they can reasonably expect from their universities and colleges and which these institutions have to commit to.

In November 2009, the former chief executive of BP, Lord Browne, was appointed to run a comprehensive review of the top-up fee system, examining the impact of tuition charges on who goes to university and the growing policy concern about the cost of universities to the public purse as student numbers expanded. The Browne review of HE funding and student finance was published in March 2010, setting out the following key claims: (1) top-up fees have not made the higher education system any less reliant on public funds, with every pound of fee income being matched by about a pound in additional cost to taxpayers; (2) the introduction of variable fees has not reduced participation in higher education, but there is a consensus that potential students need better advice and guidance to support their decisions; (3) there is clear evidence that bursaries are not understood by students early enough to have a substantial impact on their choices; (4) there is a consensus that potential students need better information, advice and guidance; and (5) although there has been some progress over the past five years in widening participation to higher education, this has been less marked at the most selective universities (Attwood, 2010).

## *Making tough decisions: the end of widening participation in England?*

At the time of writing this book, the UK has made the transition from a New Labour to a Coalition (Tory led with Liberal Democrat) Government. Suffering from a recession and financial crisis, the Coalition Government came in with the promise to make 'tough decisions', referring to significant funding cuts to the public sector. This has had serious implications for the widening participation policy agenda, arguably even bringing an end to WP, with universities becoming increasingly selective as student places have been severely decreased. In August 2010, approximately 190,000 students were still searching for a university place through the clearing system after being denied the place they applied to (Williams and Shepherd, 2010: 1). Yet, only 47,000 students found a university place through clearing in 2009 (Vasagar, 2010: 1). In 2010, the Government funded a total of 365,000 places at English universities. However, universities face a penalty of £3,700 if they exceed the government cap on university places. The University and College Union stated that '2010 would be remembered as the year when record numbers of qualified students were turned away from university' (Vasagar and Williams, 2010: 1).

As the English policy and funding framework has seen such dramatic changes, seriously undermining the last decade's commitment to widening participation in higher education, many students have devised alternative strategies for their futures. Jeevan Vasagar reports in the *Guardian* on 14 August 2010 that: 'high-achieving school leavers are skipping university and increasingly applying directly to companies once thought of only as graduate employers, as fears of student debt and unemployment deter teenagers from higher education' (Vasagar, 2010: 1).

This trend perhaps challenges discourses that higher education is the golden trajectory for young people, as well as opening up alternative forms of learning, including renewed interest in apprenticeships. For example, Network Rail noted an increase in 'academically capable' candidates opting for apprenticeships rather than university (Vasagar, 2010: 1). Pricewaterhouse-Coopers also observed the increasing number of applications for its A-level entrance scheme, which it suggests is motivated by concerns about rising levels of student debt and an increasingly competitive graduate employment market (Vasagar, 2010: 1).

The possible 'domino-effect' of the competition for university places was noted by the University and College Union (Williams and Shepherd, 2010: 1):

> Pupils who do less well in their GCSEs face being squeezed out of further education opportunities as colleges snap up higher performing students who have failed to get into university, the lecturers' union warns today as GCSE results are published.

This could negatively affect those students who have traditionally undertaken vocational courses in further education colleges, possibly further increasing the number of young people not in education, employment or training. Despite these patterns which raise serious concerns about educational inclusion, equity and widening participation, a spokesman of the newly formed Coalition Government Department for Education claimed that 'This government is working to give all young people, regardless of background, the best opportunities to progress' (Williams and Shepherd, 2010: 1), maintaining a discourse of neoliberal fairness and meritocracy.

However, whilst the Government argues that it remains committed to WP, those institutions that have been most successful in widening participation are likely to suffer the most from the recent cuts to funding. Overall, there will be a 12.6 per cent reduction, with a total of £940 million being cut across teaching, research and buildings for the academic year 2011–12. However, research-intensive universities are predicted to suffer the least from these cuts, whilst 'newer universities focused on teaching will be worst affected' (Vasagar and Carrell, 2011: 14). Science, Technology, Engineering and Mathematics subjects will have some protection, while Arts, Humanities and Social Science subjects will face the full onslaught of the cuts. The costs of teaching in higher education are expected to be met largely through a graduate contribution, in the form of tuition fees of £6,000–£9,000 per year. Although students will receive loans to cover the costs of these fees, they will leave university with considerable levels of debt, arguably deterring those from poorer backgrounds and cultural traditions of avoiding debt. OFFA has announced that those institutions who choose to charge the highest fees of £9,000 will be responsible for ensuring that a proportion of this will be used towards widening participation. However, the University and Colleges Union, in a report that analyses the likely impact of these cuts on different institutions, shows that it is those universities that recruit the highest numbers of students from working-class backgrounds who are at highest risk of financial instability in this new funding framework (UCU, 2010). The policy decisions currently being made about HE funding therefore seem to have the worst implications for institutions and students associated with widening participation, and there is growing anxiety that this marks the end of widening participation in England.

# International discourses of widening higher educational access and participation

Although this book focuses on the policy discourses and historical developments of widening higher educational access and participation in the English context, I do not want to suggest that these discourses, or the related issues raised in this book, are unique to England. Indeed, concerns with widening access to higher education have been expressed internationally, and this has become an increasing focus of policy as neoliberal globalization has taken hold. Thus, policy attention to widen access to higher education has been driven largely by concerns with globalization, economic stability and growth, development and prosperity, national competitiveness and notions of a knowledge society. However, discourses of 'widening participation' in higher education are not monolithic or homogenous; and it is the aim of this section to examine the different discourses at play across and within different national contexts. I focus on two national contexts, India and the USA, both of which express strong commitment to issues of widening access and participation, but in interestingly different ways.

## *A brief outline of the Indian context*

In the Indian context, discourses of equality and egalitarianism are hegemonic in shaping policy approaches to widening participation in higher education. The current gross enrolment ratios in Indian HE are extremely low. Only seven per cent of the population in the age group 17 to 24 attend higher educational institutions in India, as against 92 per cent of the eligible age group population attending higher educational institutions in the USA and 52 per cent in the UK. The majority of students, nearly two-thirds, are enrolled on arts and sciences courses, with only about 18 per cent enrolled on commerce and management courses. It is also important to note that the gender composition of student enrolment tends to vary considerably according to region. For example, women constitute about 40 per cent of all student enrolments, varying from as low as 20 per cent in Orissa to as high as 58.8 per cent in Kerala (Kapur and Mehta, 2007). Domestic labour of girls in their families often prevents their parents from encouraging them to access education at all levels. Thornton explains that:

> educating daughters is a double burden for rural families because they cost rather than attract a dowry, and any future economic contribution will benefit their husbands' family rather than their family of origin. Boys are still valued more than girls especially in poor, rural families, and dowry continues, despite its illegality.
>
> (Thornton, 2006: 25)

Although educational participation rates are variable across different regions, poverty characterizes the rural areas in India, and state schools are perceived as not meeting the needs of poorer children in multiple ways. This perception is linked to teaching standards as well as the ways that pupils from lower castes are treated. Furthermore, the cost of the equipment required to attend school often discourages poor families in addition to the fact that the labour of children in the family is often relied upon.

Despite this highly challenging context, WP policy in India is deeply influenced by principles of egalitarianism. Mary Thornton argues that there are programmes in India that offer important insights into widening participation for other national contexts. To illustrate this, she draws on a case study of Rural Development Society educational programmes in West Bengal, and the aims of these programmes to 'empower' poor communities and provide 'integrated support' (Thornton, 2006: 26). She identifies four key features of the programmes that are particularly valuable for other national contexts, which are:

1. *a non-alienating environment*, where disadvantaged and non-traditional students actually 'fit in' and whose life experiences and motivations are understood and valued by their teachers;
2. *teachers and facilitators who come from the community*, who can relate to their students and their students' goals;
3. *valuing and extending skills and abilities that the targeted community already have*, thus empowering rather than disempowering its students; and
4. *the validation and valuing of diverse identities and experiences*, which raises the status of disadvantaged and non-traditional students and their chances of achieving success within.

(Thornton, 2006: 29)

However, despite these important insights and the commitment of government to equality in higher education, HE is a low priority in public expenditure in India. This might be connected to the increase in private sector participation in Indian HE (Kapur and Mehta, 2007: 4). In contrast to the English context, the Indian middle classes have little stake in their national HE system. This is largely due to a growing tendency among these 'elites ... [to] send their children abroad even for undergraduate education' (Kapur and Mehta, 2007: 9). One of the reasons for this, according to Kapur and Mehta, relates to the inadequate 'signalling effect' performed by many HE institutions. The signalling effect highlights the function of higher education to 'act as signalling device to potential employers and labour markets' (Kapur and Mehta, 2007: 21).

Kapur and Mehta argue that the focus of policy on egalitarianism has not supported the development of the higher education system in India. They argue that an 'overemphasis' on equality has translated into increased government regulation, bureaucracy and a centralization of power that undermines freedom of private enterprise. Banerjee *et al.* (2002) make a similar claim when they criticize the 'excessive egalitarianism and politicisation' shaping education policy in India, in particular HE policy, where the formal principle of equality is most vigorously asserted.

During the late 1990s the Department of Economic Affairs released a discussion paper entitled *Government Subsidies in India* (Government of India, 1997), which argued for a reduction of subsidies in HE. The concern was that such subsidies were likely to be accrued primarily by the middle classes, therefore undermining the principle of egalitarianism driving HE policy development. Instead, private rates of return and more private sector participation in public sector management in HE was emphasized as a lever for widening access to HE for the disadvantaged, namely the Scheduled Tribes, the Scheduled Castes and the Other Backward Castes, sometimes referred to as tribes or tribals (see Sundaram, 2006 and Desai, 2008 for details on the Indian caste system and its ambivalent relation to Indian HE).

Compensatory or positive discrimination policies in favour of allocating certain HE resources to people from the lowest caste is therefore key to Indian HE policy, with improved enforcement and increased funding into these programmes since the 1990s (Gupta, 2005). Additionally, quotas were set up, informed by a concern about the continued absence of dalits and adivasis (known as the 'untouchables', people who form groups contained in the lowest position in the caste hierarchy) from certain sectors of the labour market, namely the civil service. Additional schemes include the provision of scholarships and fellowships at all levels, midday meals, uniforms, stationery and books. However, there has been an increased backlash against this policy and a growing sense of resentment among some members of Indian society:

> This action followed the report of the Mandal Commission and led to widespread riots in 1990. The resentment flared up again as the government sought to introduce quotas for other backward castes in highly competitive engineering and management schools in 2006. This dissent has unified higher caste Hindus against affirmative action and led to increased sabotage at the local level, where these policies are to be implemented. Upper caste Hindus express their resentment by arguing that while compensatory discrimination seeks to redress the inequities suffered by dalits and adivasis, the individuals taking advantage of these benefits belonged to a rich 'creamy layer' and were never subject to the severe discrimination faced by their poorer brethren.
>
> (Desai and Kulkarni, 2008: 6–7)

In contrast again to the English policy context, redistributive measures in Indian HE tend to cluster around divisions concerned with religion and caste rather than income and class, region or gender. The Indian Constitution (Articles 29, 30) for example, outlines special protection to linguistic and religious minorities, which enable these individuals and groups the right to preserve their culture and traditions in HE institutions. The mobilization of specific kinds of identity politics in Indian HE policy therefore tends to preserve and allocate preference to divisions based on caste and religion as the main axes of difference and stratification.

The Indian policy approach has been to emphasize concerns with equality and egalitarianism, with entrepreneurialism and concerns with quality being marginalized. Although this is criticized by writers such as Kapur and Mehta as contributing to a large number of mediocre higher education institutions in their view, this also highlights that global discourses of widening participation are contested and heterogeneous. The construction of such differences however is problematic; it reinforces binary oppositions across a political spectrum and in this way might constrain our educational and pedagogical imaginations; how might we reconceptualize widening participation in a way that disrupts such binaries and creates a framework for reconstructing the discourses at play?

## A brief outline of the US context

The US approach to access to higher education is framed by a market-oriented approach, in which the federal and state governments play a limited role. Although US higher education (HE) borrows its structure from European HE, in particular British and German HE, much of US HE policy and practice is informed by particular American values of limiting government control and seeking to 'protect' HE institutions from government interference and centralized planning. Some US HE institutions are even asking for less money in exchange for more autonomy in order to free themselves from structures and accountability requirements that supposedly impede their capacity to be effective and efficient. Therefore, similar to some HE institutions in Europe, US HE promotes the rationality of the market and competition as necessary devices for achieving diversity and excellence in HE. There is also in evidence a commitment to ideals of social justice and inclusion and widening access to and participation in HE for non-traditional entrants. In US policy, non-traditional entrants refer to people who possess one or more of the following characteristics: they are aged 25 or older, have delayed entry into HE after completing high school, did not earn a traditional high school diploma, are married, attend college or university part-time, work full-time or have children (US Department of Education, 2002). Because such entrants typically juggle work or family responsibilities with college or university attendance, it is extremely common for these students to formally transfer from one institution to another, sometimes attending two institutions simultaneously. This is possible because of the 'credit' system set up in US HE institutions in which course credits accrued by students at one institution may be transferred to another institution, assuming the receiving institution accepts the value of these credits as roughly equivalent to its own. This ensures that some students benefit from a level of mobility that allows them to suspend enrolment for some period before enrolling at another institution and to minimize the individual cost of HE participation as much as possible.

In 2001 the US Department of Education counted 6,500 post-secondary institutions that participated in its student financial aid programme, including 4,200 colleges and universities that award degrees and 2,300 institutions that award vocational certificates. US HE institutions that grant degrees are typically divided into four major groups and a considerable amount of diversity exists between them:

- public two-year institutions or community colleges award vocational degrees and tend to recruit the largest share of students (6 million students counted in 2001);
- public four-year colleges and universities concentrate on undergraduate teaching and gradate preparation in professional fields such as teaching and business, while research-intensive universities offer undergraduate, graduate and professional degree programmes (6.2 million students counted in 2001);
- private not-for-profit institutions are extremely diverse. They consist of faith-based institutions, women's colleges, historically black colleges and institutions, liberal arts colleges, research universities and specialized institutions (3.2 million students counted in 2001);
- for-profit institutions that offer vocational programmes that result in certificates rather than degrees (750,000 students counted in 2001).

In terms of governance, US public colleges and HE institutions tend to be governed at the local level, where some colleges and universities enjoy more autonomy than others. This means that funding levels, admission standards, accountability measures and policy settings are often negotiated by a locally elected board of trustees. Accredited organizations monitor quality assurance and member associations represent institutions to the federal and state governments. The federal government relies on these organizations to determine whether colleges and universities demonstrate fiscal soundness and managerial competence, fair admission and recruiting practices, and evidence of student achievement in order that they be included in the federal student financial aid programmes. Since there is no mention of education as a federal responsibility in the Constitution, the federal government plays a limited role in governing education. It was only during the Second World War that federal funding for scientific research at colleges and universities was first established, but its main aim was to build on and extend US military capacity.

In terms of funding, US colleges and universities generate their revenue through student fees, which have risen at twice the rate of inflation since the 1980s; appropriations, grants and contracts from federal, state and local governments; private donations from individuals or corporations; endowment and other investment earnings; and sales from auxiliary enterprises and services, such as managing real estate and running conference centres. Traditionally, state appropriations have made up the bulk of institutional revenue at public institutions, but they are diminishing both as a share of state expenditures and as a percentage of institutional revenue. In response, state governments and public institutions have raised student fees, shifting the responsibility from taxpayers to students.

Admission requirements and selection procedures differ dramatically from institution to institution. Admission selection, however, is often determined by a fixed set of academic criteria, including high school coursework, grade point average and class rank, and admission examination, as well as a more flexible account of non-academic characteristics such as demonstrated leadership ability, creativity and community service. 'Tensions between meritocracy and democracy remain at the centre of academic selection processes in the United States' (Lamont and Moraes da Silva, 2009: 4).

Certain polices have been taken up in order to increase diversity: affirmative or positive discrimination. Such policies have very often been disputed and held to be counter-intuitive to the goals of excellence or meritocracy in education. Guinier and Sturm (2001) highlight the way in which critics of affirmative action regularly pit meritocracy against diversity with the intention of setting them up as mutually exclusive goals that undermine each other. Indeed, the goal to increase the enrolment rates of low-income students is often represented as conflicting with other central tenets of US HE, such as the importance of market competition and resistance to excessive government control.

## Deconstructing contemporary discourses of widening participation

I have shown through this overview of WP policies that struggles over access to higher education have a long history, with different, competing and contradictory concerns emerging in policy over the past century and in different national and international contexts. There have been clear themes suggesting some continuity across time and space, for example, struggles over access for particular social and cultural groups, notions of meritocracy and liberalism, concerns with fairness and social justice and attention to patterns of social exclusion and mobility. It is also possible to trace some discontinuities and contradictions over time and in different national locations, including for example, tensions between egalitarian ideals and entrepreneurialism, expansion of student numbers and public funding, concerns with social justice against economic competiveness, the increasing interest in quality and standards versus concerns about equality and fairness, to include a shift in focus from social groups to individuals and from education to training. Over the past century there has been a shift from concerns for women's access to higher education, to a concern with men's (particularly in high-income countries), from publicly governed and funded education to quasi-markets and entrepreneurialism, and from concerns with the development of disciplinary, subject-based knowledge to concerns with skills-development, employability and the commodification of knowledge. Naidoo explains that economic concerns underpin policies to widen participation internationally:

> Governments across the world are making concerted efforts to boost participation rates in higher education. Government policies have portrayed

intellectual capital in the era of knowledge capitalism as one of the most important determiners of economic success.

(Naidoo, 2003: 250)

A growing body of international literature has interrogated the dominance of neoliberal perspectives of widening participation, which fail to take account of deeply embedded and complex histories of exclusion, inequality and misrecognition. Naidoo considers the impact of 'the global template of neo-liberalism' on higher education, in which the 'industry of HE' has overshadowed 'social and cultural objectives of higher education generally encompassed in the conception of higher education as a "public good"' (Naidoo, 2010: 71). Connected to this, new managerialist and marketized frameworks are 'likely to erode the potential of higher education to contribute to equity' (Naidoo, 2010: 74) and also have implications for quality (Naidoo, 2010: 75). She demonstrates that the interests of dominant countries and powerful international organizations hinder governments '[from] devising policies that are appropriate to the local socio-political and economic context' and the development goals of low-income countries Naidoo, 2010: 83).

Within different national contexts, the neoliberal emphasis on links between higher educational participation and the economy compels individuals to be responsible for their 'employability' by ensuring that their skills are up to date to meet the needs of increasingly unstable, turbulent and highly competitive employment markets. In this way, WP policy can be seen as part of the broader neoliberal technologies of self-regulation (Walkerdine, 2003: 239), which operate to shift responsibility from the state to the individual. The neoliberal project of self-improvement through higher education is presented as available to all who have the potential to benefit, regardless of social positioning and volatile economic conditions.

Research by Jones and Thomas (2005) identifies 'utilitarianism' as the dominant approach to WP across different English higher education institutions. The focus is on changing individual attitudes and compensating for their lack of academic skills and qualifications. They characterize this approach as the 'double deficit model' and one that strongly emphasizes the relationship between higher education and the economy (Jones and Thomas, 2005: 618). The purpose of HE in the utilitarian framework is reduced to enhancing employability, entrepreneurialism, economic competitiveness and flexibility (Morley, 1999; Thompson, 2000; Burke, 2002; Archer, Hutchings *et al.*, 2003; Bowl, 2003). Contemporary education policy concerned with widening access and participation is strongly framed by the 'common sense' of neoliberal globalization (Torres, 2010), although there are of course competing discourses at play, as I have shown through this chapter.

Widening participation must be understood in the context of an increasingly highly differentiated and hierarchical HE system. Jean Barr asserts that 'one of the most pernicious effects of the (New Labour) government's widening participation strategy could be to solidify existing hierarchies (of institutions and knowledge) within higher education' (Barr, 2008: 36). Research-intensive, elite institutions continue to recruit students largely from affluent socio-economic backgrounds, whilst newer post-1992 institutions are associated most strongly with recruiting students from traditionally under-represented and 'diverse' backgrounds. The institutional identities of universities within this differentiated system are strongly tied up with student identities and this profoundly shapes individual aspirations and choices in relation to HE participation (Reay *et al.*, 2005; Reay *et al.*, 2001) as well as student experience (Crozier and Reay, 2008). Such hierarchies are re/produced through neoliberal frameworks, which deploy market mechanisms such as league tables to 'exert pressure on universities to comply with consumer demand' (Naidoo 2003: 250).

## Final reflections

This chapter has examined different and competing discourses at play in relation to widening educational access and participation across time and space. I have argued that there have been both continuities and discontinuities in the issues, debates and concerns framing policies of widening educational access and participation over the past century and in different national contexts. These have emphasized different political, economic and social concerns and perspectives, including questions about who has the right to higher education, and in what forms, notions of meritocracy versus a commitment to social justice and egalitarianism, concerns with economic development and market competitiveness, attempts to redress cultural differences and inequalities, the rise and hegemony of neoliberalism and discourses of entrepreneurialism, shifts from a focus on state responsibility to individualism, and debates about curricular issues as well as binary constructions, such as academic and vocational education, knowledge and skills, and university and other (less esteemed and less culturally valued) forms of learning.

I have shown through examining the different contexts and discourses of widening participation that the aim to widen access to higher education has been an ongoing concern, although with a particular focus on certain social groups at different times and in different places. In the English context, women's access to higher education was a particular concern in the early twentieth century, and continued to be a concern until more recently, when the concern with gendered access to higher education has shifted to boys and men. Throughout the twentieth and into the twenty-first centuries, social class has remained a key focus in struggles for the right to higher education in Britain, although I have argued that gender and class must be conceptualized as intersecting social differences with other forms of social inequality. In the Indian context, the concern with widening participation has been more recent and has paid specific attention to issues of caste, rather than class. Redressing racialized inequalities has been a central theme in US policy initiatives to widen participation. In recent global policy debates, concerns to widen educational access have been largely connected with economic issues, including global economic development and market competiveness, with the economically driven aim to ensure that there is a highly skilled labour force and the notion of the necessity to build a 'knowledge society'.

However, different forms of higher education have been identified as appropriate for different groups and, in the contemporary English context, widening participation in higher education has been linked to the formation of new kinds of courses and provision (including the provision of HE in further education colleges). Diversity has become increasingly connected to the diversification of higher education and the development of different kinds of institutions and forms of provision. There has been an overarching expression of anxiety linked to widening participation policy debates, with fears about 'lowering standards' and 'safeguarding' traditional academic courses (DfES, 2003a). A central argument of this book will be that the privileging of access to, and participation in, higher education, as the 'best' form of learning, has particular implications for the reproduction of wider social inequalities. The development of new forms of higher education for new student constituencies, although it might be a positive, valuable and creative way to redress the under-representation of certain social groups in higher education, also contributes to the re-privileging of certain institutions, courses, academics and students. I will explore these issues in greater depth in further chapters. In the next chapter, I will turn my attention to the different theoretical and conceptual tools available for reconceptualizing widening participation, with a particular emphasis on disrupting social inequalities, exclusions and misrecognitions.

# 2 Re/conceptualizing widening participation

> My ethical duty, as one of the subjects, one of the agents, of a practice that can never be neutral – the educational – is to express my respect for differences in ideas and positions. I must respect even positions opposed to my own, positions that I combat earnestly and with passion.
>
> (Freire, 2009: 66)

## Introduction

Further developing the discussion presented in Chapter One, I consider the ways that widening participation in higher education might be re/conceptualized, drawing particularly on critical and post-structural theoretical perspectives. The range of theoretical lenses and the different sets of values brought to the problem shape and re/fashion the competing meanings given to the concept. This chapter will attempt to show some of the different ways in which widening participation might be re/conceptualized. A key argument of this chapter will be that critical theoretical frameworks are particularly fruitful in developing a conceptual framework of widening participation that is able to address the complexities of inequalities, misrecognitions and exclusions that play out in educational fields such as colleges and universities. In particular, I draw on concepts of power and subjectivity to move beyond current hegemonic discourses of widening participation.

In Chapter One, I have presented some of the key policy discourses shaping understandings of issues of access to, and participation in, higher education, for those groups historically under-represented in higher education. This discussion and review has shown that there are both similarities and differences across different historical, national and regional contexts, shaped by hegemonic frameworks and perspectives, including neoliberalism, meritocracy, rationalism, instrumentalism, utilitarianism and globalization. I have also shown the continuities and discontinuities in debates about access to, and participation in, higher education across the twentieth century and shaping understandings into the early twenty-first century. Continuities have included struggles over access for particular social and cultural groups, notions of meritocracy and liberalism, concerns with fairness and social justice and attention to patterns of social exclusion and mobility. Discontinuities include a shift in focus from social groups to individuals, from education to training, from concerns for women's access to higher education to a concern with men's, from publicly-governed and funded education to quasi-markets, private forms of funding and entrepreneurialism, and from concerns with the development of disciplinary, subject-based knowledge to concerns with skills-development, employability and the commodification of knowledge.

In this chapter, I want to move from deconstructing policy discourses to a concern with re/conceptualizing higher education access and participation and to begin to move beyond the hegemonic discourses of widening participation. I focus on access to, and participation in, *higher education*, as this has been a key focus, and has profoundly constructed policy discourses and strategies of widening participation in England as well as in many other national and transnational contexts. However, this is not to suggest that higher education is the most superior form of learning. I do not agree that it should be assumed that all young people deemed to have potential to benefit from higher education should go straight on from school to university. My own position is that there are other forms of learning, some non-formal, which are as important and profound, sometimes more so, as higher education. However, I strongly argue that, because higher education remains a social institution where life chances and privileges are reproduced, and certain groups continue to be significantly under-represented and are excluded from such opportunities and social privileges, then we must pay close attention to the ways that inequalities in higher educational participation play out. This includes, however, attention to the ways in which higher education carries social esteem to the detriment of other forms of learning experience. Life chances and social privileges should not depend on the chance to participate in (certain forms of high-status) higher education or not; and therefore part of a conceptual framework for reconceptualizing widening participation must interrogate assumptions that higher education is the gold standard for those with 'high levels of potential and ability'.

During its time in government in the UK, New Labour set a goal of increasing participation to 50 per cent of 18–30-year-olds by 2010, a goal that has not come to fruition. However, the point I want to make in relation to this target is that, in constructing this as an ideal, there are increasingly significant implications for non-participation in higher education. Such targets tend to exacerbate exclusion and inequalities for those who do not have access to the most esteemed forms of learning and educational institutions. Such targets also exacerbate the constructions of certain forms of education as being 'better' than others. Binaries and divisions, for example between academic and vocational, knowledge and skill, higher and further, become more significant as access to higher education (particularly high-status forms) becomes more important to the life chances of the individual. All of this is further exacerbated by the current economic crisis, when valuable commodities, such as gaining a university degree, become scarcer and more expensive and competitive. It is important therefore to have the critical conceptual tools to reveal the underlying assumptions behind access to, and participation in, higher education and the ways that inequalities might be sustained, reformulated and reproduced through such assumptions within material and structural contexts of social inequities.

A key argument and premise of this book is that a project of widening participation is necessarily a project of social justice. The emphasis on *widening*, rather than simply *increasing*, access to, and participation in, higher education places focus on those groups who have been traditionally excluded or under-(mis)represented in higher education. This must then pay attention to the patterns of social inequality in higher education. However, my position is that it is not enough to identify patterns of under-representation or to develop 'quick-fix' solutions to 'lift barriers'. As well as identifying patterns of under-representation, it is important to develop sophisticated, theorized and critical approaches, which depend on long-term strategies embedded in deep-level understandings of the subtle and insidious operations of classed, gendered and racialized inequalities in higher education (and education and learning more generally). Attention also must be placed on the different and contradictory ways that inequalities play out in different local, institutional, disciplinary, subject-based, regional, national and global contexts. Ultimately, praxis of widening participation is needed to develop deep understandings, which draw together critical theories of inequalities in higher education, practice-based perspectives and lived and embodied educational and pedagogic experiences.

This chapter draws on critical and post-structural theoretical perspectives to consider the different conceptual tools offered for the project of reimagining widening participation. I will argue that such theoretical frameworks offer valuable insights that help to disrupt problematic assumptions and reconceptualize widening participation, with close attention to the insidious workings of power and inequality across educational contexts. I will also draw on the work of feminist scholars and will look at the ways that other critical theories have been used to draw attention to the reproductive discourses of widening participation, which might help to expose the complex ways that inequalities in higher education, and in other stages of formal education, have been sustained, reconstituted and exacerbated.

## Theorizing power in educational access and participation

As critical and feminist theorists of education have pointed out, education is never neutral but is always a site of struggle over meaning-making and knowledge (e.g. Lather, 1991; Torres, 1998). Education is a potential space for transformation but it also is an institution of regulation, control and marginalization. Struggles over access to higher education illuminate explicit processes of exclusion and marginalization – the persistent under-representation of certain groups and communities from a key site of the re/production of privilege and life chances. Universities are significant institutional sites of the legitimization of certain forms of knowledge and identity. Exclusion from higher education has huge implications not only for individuals but also for the wider differential positioning of social groups in society, not least in the participation of knowledge production and the processes by which different forms of knowledge are legitimated. In order to study the processes of exclusion and inequality in higher education, it is of great importance to have a conceptual framework that enables close attention to the complex and detailed operations of power at multiple levels. This requires a sophisticated conceptual framework that pays detailed attention not just to explicit moments of oppression and discrimination but also to the subtle, micro-level, relational, embodied and insidious workings of power and inequality, across, between and within educational fields.

Power and difference are two key concepts underpinning the analyses of widening educational participation offered in this book. Educational spaces are always sites of struggle, in which shifting, complex and discursively produced power relations are at play in the formation of identities and subjectivities and in the privileging of particular epistemological and ontological perspectives and frameworks. For example, recent policy developments of widening participation have largely been shaped by neoliberal perspectives, which tend to prioritize and emphasize the importance of higher educational participation in relation to economic imperatives, orientations and concerns. Furthermore, meritocratic discourses have largely shaped policy discourses of widening higher educational access and participation, emphasizing issues of 'fair access' and the notion of an openness of the university to all who have the potential and ability to participate. Concerns with power and difference within such theoretical perspectives are largely absent, with a discourse of social inclusion framing the focus. Social inclusion within economically centred and meritocratic views of access to higher education ignores issues of 'difference' and celebrates 'diversity' as a key aspect of widening participation. An engagement with issues of power is missing from such approaches; diversity is constructed as unproblematic, whilst difference is to be controlled through standardization and monitoring processes (such as quality assurance). Inclusion, from this perspective, requires the transformation of those individuals deemed to be 'different' from the 'standard' student through processes of self-improvement. Louise Archer explains that the hegemonic view of inclusion expressed in widening participation policy aims to:

> include those who are excluded into the dominant framework/state of being, rather than challenging existing inequalities within the mainstream system, or encouraging alternative ways of being.
>
> (Archer, 2003: 23)

A critical theoretical perspective of hegemonic discourses of inclusion and diversity points to the centrality of power relations and the ways in which inequalities and power underpin social diversity. A critical perspective asserts the significance of theorizing inclusion and diversity in relation to concepts of power and difference. For example, in what ways does the discourse of 'inclusion' regulate and misrecognize those seen as outside the boundaries of what counts as being 'included'? Inclusion implies exclusion, and is tied in with what Jenny Williams (1997) calls 'polarising discourses': being 'included' implies the opposite, being 'excluded'. Being constructed as 'excluded' has implications for the formation of identity, for the ways that the person or group of people are seen and positioned by others and for institutional categorizations, which frame possibilities for participation in higher education or not. Furthermore, certain values are assumed to be 'good': if a person decides not to participate in higher education but has the standard qualifications and/or perceived potential and ability, that person is constructed as a 'problem', or as having 'low aspirations'. The value judgement that higher education is the 'best choice' for all those deemed to be potential HE students has important implications for assumptions about inclusion and exclusion, as well as the ways in which certain learning trajectories are recognized as superior to others. This is deeply tied in to the re/construction of the 'problem' of widening participation in classed, gendered and racialized ways. The 'problem' is re/located to the individual or communities, who are seen themselves as the 'problem', and this is often understood in deeply classist or racist ways and certainly in terms of the ways those individuals or groups are seen to be 'lacking' (e.g. the 'right' kinds of attitudes, values and/or aspirations).

Furthermore, the problem of who participates in higher education, and who does not, has largely been constructed through research that draws on statistics and benchmarks to measure patterns of HE participation of different social groups. Such large-scale work has made an invaluable contribution to tracing the patterns of under-representation in higher education, as well as other stages of educational provision. This has helped to expose historic exclusions and inequalities as well as to make arguments for change and strategic intervention. Producing data that highlight how some groups have persistently been excluded from a key social institution such as higher education is important not only to research, but also to policy formation and implementation as well as the shaping of educational and pedagogical practice. Thus, the contribution of such forms of research has been important in recognizing that there is a significant problem that requires serious attention, concern and strategy at the level of research but also of policy and practice.

Although such evidence is clearly important and needed to develop strategies to widen participation, post-structural perspectives have problematized some of the assumptions that have emerged from social science categorizations. In asking questions about who participates in higher education, institutionalized categorizations of difference are re/constructed: ways of dividing and classifying groups of people; marking out groups of people as 'included' or 'advantaged'; and marking out other groups as 'excluded' or 'disadvantaged'. A question shaped by post-structural perspectives might be raised: What are the implications of such technologies of classification? For example, in what ways do such classifications homogenize groups of people? Historically, women have struggled for access to higher education, but such struggles have been problematized by questions of power and difference. Black women have argued for example that the struggles of 'women' have privileged the perspectives of middle- and upper-class white women, thus silencing and ignoring the different experiences, positioning and perspectives of black and working-class women. In contemporary discourses, men's struggle to access higher education has been constructed as a key concern, with arguments being made that men are the new 'educationally disadvantaged' group (see e.g. HEPI, 2009). Feminist scholars have contested such discourses, as overlooking the differences between groups of men, as well as reconstructing a 'battle of the sexes', which undermines the achievements of (some groups of) women. Similar points of concern apply to other constructions of social groups: 'black and minority ethnic', 'working class', 'disabled', 'mature', 'part-time', 'lower socio-economic'. These classifications are useful in offering statisticians and policy-makers variables to produce data sets and then to analyse them, thus providing some of the tools in which to formulate policy; however, they are simultaneously problematic in the constructions that they produce and reproduce. These constructions frame and constrain the ways we are able to think about questions of educational access and participation. Importantly, such classifications are always enmeshed in power, reconstructing power relations and social differences that make a difference. We both need these categorizations and yet are constrained by them, so that large-scale quantitative research and in-depth critical, feminist and post-structural research are important in teasing out the complexities of the problem of widening participation in higher education. In this book, I focus on the significant contribution of critical, feminist and post-structural approaches to *reconceptualizing* widening participation, whilst acknowledging the important work of large-scale studies that have helped uncover patterns of under-representation and inspired those policy interventions that have aimed to tackle such inequalities.

A key concept for thinking beyond hegemonic approaches to widening participation is power. Post-structural concepts of power are particularly generative for reconceptualizing widening participation and have been influential in my own work on gender and access to higher education (see e.g. Burke, 2002, 2006, 2009, 2010). Drawing on Foucault (1982, 1984), power is not only always tied to knowledge but is produced through the discourses that shape the ways in which we know. Power is not something to be redistributed or given to those who don't have it; power is exercised, disciplinary, relational and tied to the formation of the person, or the subject. Power circulates everywhere, is unpredictable, shifting, generative and regulatory. This conceptualization of power destabilizes binary notions of the oppressor/oppressed, advantaged/disadvantaged, included/excluded, participant/non-participant, male/female, empowered/disempowered, agency/structure, which have profoundly shaped policy discourses of widening educational participation. Such theoretical frames arguably lock us into ways of thinking that are reproductive of, rather than challenging to, the status quo. Understanding power as relational, discursive, productive and simultaneously regulatory and constraining is useful for thinking through the complexities of inequalities in sites of education and struggles for access to meaning-making and becoming a subject. Importantly this also disrupts rationalist discourses premised on binary distinctions, unsettling essentialist assumptions about class, ethnicity, gender, race and sexuality.

However, critical theories, such as feminism and Marxism, remain important in addressing material and structural inequalities, such as poverty and the resources available to some groups and not to others. Nancy Fraser offers an important framework to conceptualize issues of social justice, presenting two key forms of injustice to analyse (Fraser, 1997). The first is socio-economic injustice, which requires a politics of redistribution, for example making sure that all students have equal access to educational resources, such as books and lecture materials, as well as clear advice, information and guidance, regardless of their background. This requires all individuals and social groups to be treated equally or the same. The second form is cultural or symbolic injustice, which draws attention to cultural differences and requires a politics of recognition, for example recognizing that literacy practices or ontological dispositions are differentially valued. Widening participation strategies have tended to either be concerned with socio-economic injustices, in the sense of identifying material barriers and attempting to eradicate these, or have in some ways exacerbated cultural injustices through the misrecognition of those constructed as excluded and/or lacking in aspirations, experience and knowledge. This raises challenges for rethinking widening participation and offers useful analytical tools to develop more nuanced and sophisticated strategies that address different forms of injustice in higher education. It is important to develop a theoretical framework that enables the destabilization of regimes of truth, which constitute subjects through symbolic and discursive mis/recognitions. Yet, simultaneously, it is important to recognize the impact of material inequalities, which deeply affect the lives of individuals and groups, as well as the persistence of particular social inequalities across intersections of class, gender and race.

## Power, cultural capital, field and habitus

The nature of power, and the ways it might be theorized, is important in thinking about the complex inequalities at play across and within educational contexts. For example, the ways some groups of students are constructed in critical research as 'privileged', and others as 'disadvantaged', reflects a particular theoretical perspective of power relations. The notions of 'privilege' and 'disadvantage' rely to some extent on structuralist perspectives, for example, how some groups have access to resources, funding and networks, which reproduce social and cultural privileges and disadvantages. Pierre Bourdieu's work has been particularly compelling and sophisticated in thinking through power in these ways, developing such foci to explore how material and cultural differences also become embodied dispositions, or habitus. Bourdieu has helped researchers concerned with inequality in a range of educational sites to analyse the processes of social and cultural reproduction. Drawing on structuralist concepts of 'power', Bourdieu argues that the dominant groups in society have the power to impose meanings and to render these as legitimate. 'The high value placed on dominant culture in society as a whole simply stems from the ability of the powerful to impose their definition of reality on others' (Paton, 2007). Bourdieu is concerned with the ways that different forms of capital – social, cultural, economic and symbolic – benefit the dominant groups in society and how educational institutions are central to the reproduction of (class) inequalities. Different forms of capital are 'capable of conferring strength, power and consequently profit on their holder' (Skeggs, 1997: 8). The concept of cultural capital, and its possible conversion into symbolic capital, is highly generative for understanding struggles over access to higher education. Bourdieu defines cultural capital as 'a form of knowledge, an internalized code or a cognitive acquisition which equips the social agent with empathy towards, appreciation for or competence in deciphering cultural relations and cultural artefacts' (Bourdieu, 1993: 7).

Bourdieu's work is helpful in thinking in critical ways about processes of exclusion and relations of power and difference in higher education fields. He talks about this in terms of the social function of elimination and, in particular, the 'elimination of members of the working class from higher levels of education', accomplished in two key ways: through formal examinations and through processes of self-exclusion (Paton, 2007). Lack of the legitimated forms of cultural capital makes it less likely that working-class groups will succeed in school examinations, which are the main form of entry to HE. However, and significantly for arguments made in much of the WP literature on the importance of educational attainment at school, the decision not to participate in higher education, or a process of self-exclusion, 'accounts for a higher proportion of elimination' (Paton, 2007). Thus, non-participation in higher education, from a Bourdieudian perspective, is explained by the (legitimate) attitudes of working-class groups, formed through internalized 'objective conditions' (Paton, 2007).

Importantly, Bourdieu moves away from the binaries of structure and agency through his concept of habitus, providing a powerful lens by which to theorize, not only the under-representation of working-class groups in HE, but also the classed experiences of HE participation. Habitus is a set of socialized dispositions, which unconsciously incline people (agents) to 'act or react' (Bourdieu, 1993: 5) in certain ways in particular social spaces (fields). Habitus is 'the result of a long process of inculcation which becomes a "second sense" or "second nature"' (Bourdieu, 1993: 5). One of the important insights of Bourdieu's theoretical contributions is that the accumulation of cultural capital and the development of embodied habitus takes time 'and is not readily available to everyone on the same basis' (Mills and Gale, 2010: 44). His work emphasizes the importance of context, but not in a flat way, considering context as simply the 'backdrops' in which people live their lives and form their habitus. His concept of field shifts the way in which context is conceptualized to consider 'the external constraints bearing on interactions and representations' (Bourdieu and Waquant, 1992: 10–11 in Mills and Gale, 2010: 30). A field has its 'own laws of functioning and its own relations of force,' (Bourdieu, 1993: 6). A field is a particular social setting or context, both actual and abstract (Silva, 2004, cited in Reay *et al.*, 2005), and gives habitus its dynamic quality (Burke and McManus, 2009). Habitus becomes practice (Reay *et al.*, 2005) and generates behaviour, feelings and practices depending on the field (Burke and McManus, 2009). Each field is comparable to a game with its own set of rules; those with a 'feel for the game' (Bourdieu, 1993: 5) and the 'right' habitus are free to play the game:

> To enter a field one must possess the habitus which pre-disposes you to enter that field and not another, that game, not another. One must possess at least the minimum amount of knowledge, or skill or 'talent' to be accepted as a legitimate player.
> (Bourdieu, 1993: 8 cited in Burke and McManus, 2009: 20)

If habitus confronts an unfamiliar field, although the experience can be transformative, it more often produces feelings of 'discomfort, ambivalence and uncertainty' (Reay *et al.*, 2005: 28). In addition to generating certain feelings, emotions and practices, habitus produces various forms of resources, or 'capital' (Burke and McManus, 2009: 20).

Bourdieu has been extensively critiqued for producing a theoretical framework that focuses only on education as reproductive and thus being overly deterministic. For example, Brooks (2005) is concerned that a theory of sociocultural reproduction is unable to account for the examples of mobility within higher education and why some individuals from working-class backgrounds do successfully access higher education. Furthermore, such a theoretical perspective is unable to explain 'the changes to the social class profile of specific universities over time' (Paton, 2007: 13). However, Mills and Gale (2010) argue that such critiques significantly misunderstand Bourdieu's work, which offers possibilities for educational transformation. His concepts 'transcend the subjectivist/objectivist dichotomy, providing new ways of relating subjective human dispositions and actions and the objective social world within which they are framed' (Mills and Gale, 2010: 20).

> There is a great deal of striving, resistance and action aimed at changing current circumstances as many of the poor and dispossessed, interviewed by Bourdieu and his colleagues, search around for ways of changing and transforming their lives.
> (Reay, 2004: 437 in Mills and Gale, 2010: 17)

At the heart of Bourdieu's work, then, is attention to *struggle* rather than reproduction. His concept of 'symbolic violence', which is 'the imposition of systems of meaning that legitimize and thus solidify structures of inequality', illuminates 'the social conditions under which these hierarchies can be challenged, transformed, nay overturned' (Waquant, 1998: 217 in Mills and Gale, 2010: 17–18).

## Researching WP from a Bourdieuian perspective

Research on widening participation has drawn extensively on Bourdieu's theoretical perspectives to understand the reproduction of sociocultural inequalities in education and possibilities for transformation. For example, Diane Reay (2001), drawing on an ESRC-funded study on student choice (Reay *et al.*, 2001, 2005), has explored the contradictions that working-class students experience in terms of their sense of self and their aspirations to participate in higher education. Her analysis suggests that this causes confusions and ambiguities about 'the sort of self they are seeking', and the research participants' accounts of accessing higher education 'hint at a delicate balance between realizing potential and maintaining a sense of authentic self'. She draws on the notion of 'pretention' to highlight the ambiguity connected to being aspirational, arguing that 'almost by definition, aspirant working classness is pretentious – a hankering after "the Other" rather than an acceptance of the self'. Reay explains that Bourdieu defines pretention as 'the recognition of distinction that is affirmed in the effort to possess it' (Bourdieu, 1986: 251). Building on this insight, she argues that there is a threat of 'losing oneself' in the search to find a university where one has a sense of belonging. Although the university sector 'epitomizes middle-classness' (Bourdieu and Passeron, 1977), there appears to be 'an attempt to match the habitus of the home to the habitus of the university' (Reay, 2001: 338).

Similarly, Archer and Leathwood (2003) discuss the implications of 'identity change' in relation to working-class participation in higher education. They highlight how higher educational participation of working-class groups is often framed in WP policy as being partly about achieving changes such as 'becoming more educated, skilled, affluent, socially mobile, "civilized" and (implicitly) middle-class' (Archer and Leathwood, 2003: 176). They found in their research that there was widespread resistance to the possibilities of identity change, although some working-class students embraced 'becoming middle-class' in terms of taste and accent. Students resistant to identity change 'drew clear boundaries between themselves and the middle-class institution, positioning themselves as able to benefit from participation while not belonging to, or feeling ownership of, the institution' (Archer and Leathwood, 2003: 177). Research has also shown though that students seek to find a place to study where they might feel a sense of belonging or 'fitting in' (Burke, 2002). Reay *et al.*, (2001, 2005) theorize students' choice of higher education institution by drawing on Bourdieu's notion of 'objective limits' and how choices become 'transformed into a practical anticipation of objective limits', which lead to processes of self-exclusion (Reay *et al.*, 2001: 11). They argue that 'choices are governed by what it is "reasonable to expect"'

(Bourdieu and Passeron, 1977: 226) and that students tend to have a strong sense of their 'proper place in the world' (Bourdieu, 1984: 474). They draw on Bourdieu's work to demonstrate that habitus operates not only at the level of the individual but also the institutional.

Crozier and Reay (2008) build on the concept of institutional habitus (Reay *et al.*, 2005). They argue that the institutional habituses of universities and colleges are connected to organizational culture and ethos, as well as wider socio-economic and educational cultures (Crozier and Reay, 2008). In their analysis of students' experiences in four higher education institutions, with a focus on social class and students' identities, they found that there are 'greater differences between student experiences at different universities than between the experiences of students from different backgrounds in each university' (Crozier and Reay, 2008; Crozier *et al.*, 2008).

Connolly and Neill (2001) also draw on concepts of habitus to explore the educational aspirations of working-class children in relation to gender and locality. They use Bourdieu's concept of 'symbolic violence' to illuminate how the undermining, marginalization and exclusion of working-class groups, perceived as normal, natural and legitimate, is a form of 'symbolic violence'. They explain that:

> the way that the children's habitus has encouraged them to develop specific attitudes towards education and future aspirations tends to limit powerfully their life chances – it is this act of restriction that forms the basis of the symbolic violence.
>
> (Connolly and Neill, 2001: 115)

Similarly, Raphael Reed, Croudace, Harrison, Baxter and Last argue that forms of misrecognition present 'unequal access to cultural capital as something natural when it is in fact a social construction underpinned by differential access to economic capital' (Raphael Reed *et al.*, 2007: 23). They further argue that experiences of traumatic and highly negative formal education, including bullying and violence, and humiliation and shame, often contribute to the formation of particular habitus, for example what they call 'disengaged learning identities', which represent in part self-protection strategies (Raphael Reed *et al.*, 2007: 29). Similar to Crozier and Reay (2008), they argue for the 'establishment of *respectful* and *relational practices* as the basis for improving educational engagement' (Raphael Reed *et al.*, 2007: 33).

In my own recent research with Jackie McManus, we deconstruct the perspectives and practices of admissions tutors in processes of selection of students for art and design courses across five higher education institutions in England (Burke and McManus, 2009). We draw on Bourdieu's *The Love of Art* (1991), in which he argues that middle-class habitus and cultural capital makes the middle classes more likely, and more comfortable, to visit galleries and museums compared to the working classes. This is important because in selection interviews of candidates for art and design courses, of which we observed 70 in our research, questions are posed to interviewees about their habits of visiting galleries and museums, as well as their familiarity with different artists and works of art. Bourdieu argues that 'art is implicated in the reproduction of inequalities, and that the relationship between culture and power is such that taste creates social differences' (Bourdieu, 1984). Certain kinds of art can only be decoded, and appreciated, by those who have been taught *how* to decode them (Burke and McManus, 2009). Recent work by Bennett *et al.* (2009), drawing explicitly on Bourdieu's earlier research and examining its relevance in the UK context, argues that:

> Visual art remains a strong field of classification of social position. Engagement with visual art, as part of a broad visual culture, is widespread, the availability of art substantial and access increasingly available. Yet core participation by better off groups remains resilient, even though fissures and cleavages occur across group boundaries. The grip of legitimate culture remains firm. This is partly a matter of being able to afford to own works of art, the more prestigious of which are comparatively expensive. Acquiring objective cultural capital in this field, through possession, is for a minority. It is also evident in the tendency for the more highly educated middle classes, and especially the elite, to be far more likely to visit art galleries and have views about the quality of art. They, and their children, are disproportionately likely to develop a knowledge and appreciation that serves to increase institutional [legitimate] capital.... Art remains a relatively exclusive field.
>
> (Bennett *et al.*, 2009, cited in Burke and McManus, 2009: 21)

In our observations of selection interviews, we found that there was a distinct preference for a particular kind of privileged cultural capital, acquired through familial and academic background, which privileges white racialized and middle-classed habitus. For example, we found that the majority of applicants had portfolios that were deemed average – that is neither exceptional nor unexceptional. This enabled some applicants, predominantly those who were middle class, to talk their way onto the course by demonstrating the possession of symbolic cultural capital, capital which is valued and can be traded in the field/market of art and design higher education for a place on a course. It was standard practice to construct the interview around a series of canonical questions and acceptable answers that reflect middle-classed habitus and cultural capital (McManus 2006). Examples of such questions include:

- Who is your favourite artist/designer? Who are your design heroes? Who or what influences your work?
- What galleries do you visit? What is your favourite gallery? What exhibitions have you been to lately? If you could exhibit your work in a gallery, where would that be?

- What is your favourite film? What films have you seen recently? What is your favourite advert? Who is your favourite director?
- What books do you read? What are you reading at the moment?
- What is your favourite shop? Where do you like to shop?

(Burke and McManus, 2009: 39)

Bourdieu's framework enables the researcher to disrupt the problematic focus on individual attitudes, which tends to construct those targeted by widening participation policy as deficient and needing remedial help through the intervention of the (middle-class) professional. Rather, Bourdieudian theoretical approaches highlight and emphasize the strengths of working-class students, for example, their great resilience and commitment to their studies, which is often in the face of adverse structural discrimination and oppression (Crozier and Reay, 2008). The problem of widening participation is thus reconceptualized as a need to understand the ways that sociocultural inequalities are reproduced within educational fields, as well as to identify possibilities for transformation.

## Power as discursive and relational

Foucauldian post-structural perspectives offer an alternative and compelling perspective of power, understanding it as productive, dynamic, discursive, intimately bound to, and inseparable from, knowledge and potentially transformative. In the next section, I will outline post-structural concepts of power, drawing in particular on the work of Foucault:

> Power produces knowledge. Power and knowledge directly imply one another. There is no power relation without the correlative constitution of a field of knowledge, nor any knowledge that does not presuppose and constitute at the same time power relations.
>
> (Foucault, 1980: 93)

Foucault offers a framework for conceptualizing power at both the level of the person (subject) and at the social level, which is important for reconceptualizing higher educational access and widening participation. Power is exercised within institutional spaces through technologies of regulation, discipline and control. Power and knowledge are always connected through discourse: the way in which meaning is given to the social world and to the self. Discourse is 'a structuring of meaning-making whose major characteristic is its disciplinary and hence regulatory power' (Edwards, 2008: 22). Discourse defines what can be included and is constitutive of knowledge, rather than a reflection of a pre-existing 'truth'. Discourse (power/knowledge) produces 'regimes of truth', which profoundly shapes the meanings and understandings we give to concepts such as 'widening participation', 'inclusion' and 'exclusion'. Indeed, these discourses themselves have exclusionary practices as part of their effects

(Nicoll and Fejes, 2008: 5). Regimes of truth regulate subjects and their actions, which are then reproductive of those same regimes of truth. 'All knowledge, once co-implicated with action, has real effects, and in that sense becomes true, or more accurately counts as true' (Edwards, 2008: 23). As Sue Jackson and I have argued,

> It is the constitution of knowledge claims as 'truth' that is linked to systems of power: those who have the power – institutionally as well as individually – to determine and legitimize 'truth' also have the power to determine dominant discourses. This exercising of power happens so thoroughly, so powerfully, and so ideologically, that the political nature of discourses becomes hidden.
>
> (Burke and Jackson, 2007: 6)

Through what Foucault names 'dividing practices', binary divisions are produced, constructing subjectivities and normalizing discourses that create exclusionary practices. The concept of dividing practices is useful in understanding the ways in which different candidates and students in higher education are constructed through the familiar discursive binaries, which impose normalizing judgements, such as standard/non-standard, traditional/non-traditional, worthy/unworthy, academically able/academically weak. Jenny Williams (1997) explains that such 'polarising discourses' frame admissions practices in higher education, because reference to the standard, worthy student implies the opposite: the non-standard and unworthy candidate, who is constructed as a threat to the quality of higher education.

Although such discourses and regimes of truth are disciplinary and regulatory of who and what the subject can be, the subject is dualistically implicated in these processes. S/he is both subjected to and active subject of the discourses that regulate her/him.

> It is through mobilization into discursive regimes that people become active subjects inscribed with certain capacities to act. Here the beginning of human agency does not entail an escape from power, but consists rather of a specific exercise of power – one is empowered in particular ways through becoming the subject of, and subjected to, power. Capacities are brought forth and evaluated through the disciplinary technologies of observation, normalization, judgement and examination, the extent, criteria and methods for which are provided by the discourses at play.
>
> (Edwards, 2008: 24)

Importantly, Foucault is concerned with the ways that power is positive and productive, rather than repressive and negative. He argues that

> we must cease once and for all to describe the effects of power in negative terms: it 'excludes,' it 'represses,' it 'censors,' it 'abstracts,' it 'masks,' it

'conceals.' In fact, power produces; it produces reality; it produces domains of objects and rituals of truth. The individual and the knowledge that may be gained of him belong to this production.

(Foucault in Rabinow, 1984: 205)

Thus, power produces subjects of and in (and outside of) higher education contexts. Foucault's concept of disciplinary power is the 'inversion of visibility' and 'compulsory objectification' in which the subject of disciplinary power is made constantly visible through the normalizing gaze, by which the subject is differentiated, classified, judged and objectified. The regime of disciplinary power differentiates individuals in relation to an average, measures the subject in quantitative terms and places the subject in a hierarchy of levels and values. Disciplinary power compares, differentiates, hierarchizes, homogenizes, excludes and normalizes (Foucault in Rabinow, 1984: 195).

Foucault's work offers the possibility for approaches to widening participation that put at the centre concerns for critical change and transformation. A key focus of Foucault's work is understanding how the subject might be re/constituted in transformatory ways. This involves questions such as 'how the self comes into being, what the costs of the self might be, and how the self might be made *again differently*' (Youdell, 2006). As noted in Chapter One, Foucauldian approaches are concerned to develop methods, strategies and practices to interrogate the 'nature of the present' and to expose the relationship between the subject, truth and the constitution of experience. However, such approaches are not only concerned with questions about how the present is made, but also how it might be *unmade*. Foucaudian approaches argue that no particular manifestation of power is inevitable but that 'freedom' concerns the will to exercise power differently.

Using the notion of the 'experience-book', Foucault wants not only to understand processes of subjectification but also processes of de-subjectification, in which the self is written or made differently. He perceived his own books as 'direct experiences which aim to tear me away from myself, to prevent me from being myself', or a process of 'de-subjectivation' (Foucault in O'Leary, 2002). He similarly aims for his writing to transform the subjectivity of the reader. Such aims of de-subjectification offer potential tools for transformatory approaches to widening participation, which do not focus on creating 'docile bodies' through the disciplinary technologies of higher education, but on creating new ways of being and doing within higher education, which place ethics and equity at the centre of the project to widen participation.

However, Foucault also emphasizes the power of processes of subjectification, which take place within institutional contexts. He says:

If I tell the truth about myself, as I am doing now, it is in part that I am constituted as a subject across a number of power relations which are exerted over me and which I exert over others.

(Foucault, 1988)

Foucault illuminates the complex processes in which the subject is both sub-jected to, and subject of, the relations of power. He highlights that a range of insidious technologies of subjectification are at play within institutions, in which the subject is individualized, categorized, classified, hierarchized, nor-malized, surveilled and provoked to self-surveillance. The metaphor of the panopticon provides a powerful illustration of this process. Foucault draws on Bentham's architectural device, the panopticon, to shed light on the complex operations of power within institutions that are no longer tied to an individual authority figure but rather 'a certain concerted distribution of bodies, surfaces, lights, gazes; in an arrangement whose internal mechanisms produce the relations in which individuals are caught up' (Foucault, 1977: 202). Foucault explains that, 'whenever one is dealing with a multiplicity of individuals on whom a task or a particular form of behaviour must be imposed, the panoptic schema may be used' (Foucault, 1977: 205).

The panopticon is a useful theoretical tool to shed light on the ways that subjects are caught up in complex relations of power both within and beyond institutional spaces. For example, I used this conceptual tool to analyse the processes of gendered subjectification of a group of working-class white women in my study of widening participation (Burke, 2002). I found that the women in my study identified education as a potential space for the transformation of gendered subjectivity. Yet, as they searched for new ways of being, their subjectivities as wives and mothers were increasingly policed in the home. In this context, the home seemed to serve as a space of permanent visibility in which the women's subjectivities were regulated and controlled.

> Home seems to operate as a 'panopticon', Bentham's architectural device, which for Foucault represents the triumph of disciplinary technology (Foucault, 1991: 195–228). In such conditions of permanent visibility, women seem to be always watched, to the smallest detail of their activities. Home is therefore turned to a locale where even if there are discontinuities and dispersion in the gaze of the other, women's integral surveillance is being carried on.
>
> (Tamboukou, 1999: 132)

The women's accounts suggested that, in the struggle for a space of their own outside the home, the space within it became increasingly regulated and controlled. One of the women in my study, 'Vicky', undertaking an Access to Higher Education course in the late 1990s in an English further education college, explains: 'How can I put it … in a way … now I'm doing what I want to do, I feel as though certain people are watching me and it's suffocating me … the suffocation frightens me' (Vicky quoted in Burke, 2004).

Foucault's work is valuable for reconceptualizing widening participation as it helps to understand both the complex, subtle, invisible and insidious working of power on the self and on the body. However, his work also helps us to imagine possibilities beyond this, ways of being and doing that not only go beyond but also destabilize hegemonic discourses, including the discourses of widening participation. These might focus on transformatory practices and relations that aim to alter subjectivities and knowledges. In the final section of the book, I will explore such possibilities in detail, thinking about the kinds of transformatory practices that are available to imagine new forms of being and knowing in higher education, beyond widening participation. Formations of identity are key sites of potential transformation and feminist post-structuralism offers the conceptual tools to both interrogate processes of subjective construction but also to imagine transformatory possibilities.

## Feminist concepts of identity, subjectivity and difference in widening participation

Identity and subjectivity is a central concept for developing a deeper under-standing of the operations of inequality and exclusion within educational contexts, such as schools, colleges and universities. How we understand who is a learner, who is a student, who is a teacher, and so on, is crucial to understanding who has access to privileged forms of learning and who does not. Furthermore, it is important to explore beyond issues of access to consider relations of and practices of educational participation. This might include, for example, con-sideration of the ways that pedagogical relations and practices work to legitimize certain selves, whilst excluding others.

Identity is something that tends to be taken for granted in everyday talk. Certain notions about identity tend to predominate, for example the idea of the inner self, which is a core identity separate from the social forces at play. The idea of individual autonomy is also important, as it rests on notions of individual agency and freedom, including freedom of choice. Within such perspectives, individuals are seen to make free 'choices' about whether or not to participate in higher education, and if they are seen to make the 'wrong' choice, there are assumptions about attitudinal problems, such as having 'low aspirations'. The theoretical perspectives outlined above, help to problematize such assumptions and to question some of the taken-for-granted ideas about selfhood and the individual.

Feminist theories reveal the significance of identity formation and subjective construction for understanding the politics of higher educational access and participation (Archer and Leathwood, 2003; Burke and Jackson, 2007). A transformatory approach to widening educational participation requires that the taken-for-granted meanings and discourses at play in policy and practice are interrogated by drawing on the conceptual tools and perspectives developed by critical theorists to develop deeper-level understandings of inequality and misrecognition at play in schools, colleges and universities and in the formation of pedagogical identities. Such perspectives aim to reveal the multiple layers of injustices that operate around processes of identity formation and subjective construction in relation to embodied intersections of age, class, ethnicity, gender and race (Mirza, 2009). Post-structuralism sheds light on the multiple, contradictory and shifting sense of self that unsettles hegemonic versions of the individual as a coherent, rational, knowable and stable self.

The fluidity of processes of identity formation means that the naming of a subject as 'student' does not in itself guarantee the subject will be read off as 'student' because 'every identity is constituted in relation to who may not occupy the subject position as much as who may occupy it' (Winstead, 2009: 132–33). It is through complex processes of 'doing' as well as 'being' and the embodiment of particular identities that an individual may or may not be recognized as a 'student', and this is shifting across space and time and according to social, political and cultural context. It is not only the process of naming or being named that constitutes the identity position as 'student'; it is through the taking up of particular practices and ways of doing and being within particular cultural contexts that the subject may be recognized as a student. Furthermore, these processes are not purely rational; they are entangled in emotional as well as structural, cultural and discursive relations and practices. This includes not only how I might feel about 'me' but also how I might feel about 'you' and what 'you' mean to 'me'. The complex web of discourses, relations, practices and emotions that constitute subjectivities and identity positions profoundly shapes educational decisions, aspirations, desires, choices and experiences, and thus access to, and participation in, higher education.

These ideas have usefully been put to work in research on widening participation in higher education, focusing on the ways that identities profoundly shape educational decision-making processes. This has included attention to the complex ways that forms of gendered, class and racialized identities, as well as other sets of identification (such as religion and sexuality, for example) profoundly shape the processes of becoming a student in higher education. This is interconnected with social practices, power relations and the emotional dimensions of subjectivity. For example, Archer *et al.* (2001) explore the impact of formations of masculinity and religious identifications and practices on decisions not to participate in higher education. They show how some young Muslim males position HE participation as ideologically incompatible with some forms of Muslim masculinity, since university is often seen to involve drugs and drinking, which are in tension with the kinds of familial and cultural dispositions signified, valued and practised through the Muslim religion. Similarly, Archer *et al.* (2001) argue, drawing on their research data, that some young men from minority ethnic backgrounds view HE participation as incompatible with a 'cool' identity since it often involves impoverished lifestyle and financial hardship, and therefore lacks the kind of immediate material and monetary rewards made available by going to work (also see Archer and Leathwood, 2003). In this way, participating in HE appears to interfere with practices of maintaining residual or emerging versions of masculinity for some men, since it locates them 'within an arena where middle-class men exercise greater power/competency' (Archer *et al.*, 2001: 441), leaving them struggling with feelings of dispossession and exclusion. However, in my research on masculinities and aspirations to participate in higher education, most of the men, including those from Muslim and minority ethnic backgrounds, saw higher education as a potential space of transformation and social mobility (Burke, 2006, 2010).

Archer and Leathwood (2003) also observed among some young women a tendency to frame HE participation as a threat to hegemonic forms of hetero-sexual working-class femininity. At the same time, the main motivation shaping working-class women's participation in HE was the desire to improve the self through cultural and academic learning. Therefore, working-class women were far more likely than working-class men to frame HE participation in positive terms as a way of improving and reshaping the self to fit with those images of the self often presented as more desirable in hegemonic discourses of 'success', including being educated, middle class and aspirational (Archer and Leathwood, 2003). On the other hand, Archer and Leathwood (2003) point to the way in which women students are often more likely than men students to talk about 'feeling alienated by the academic culture within the university' (p. 190), especially aspects of academic practices, conventions and language, highlighting the contradictory experiences of HE participation in relation to identity formations. My research on working-class women supports this; women in my study often found formal educational institutions intimidating places where they did not have a sense of 'fitting in' (Burke, 2002).

For Archer and Leathwood, certain young people from poorer socio-economic backgrounds often resist and challenge the 'middle-class transformative ideal' (2003: 178) that shapes the culture and ethos of many HE institutions, choosing instead to sustain and reconstruct themselves as working class. Indeed, Reay *et al.* (2001) highlight the process of disidentification among some working-class and minority ethnic students with certain HE institutions and the forms of middle-class belonging and attachment made available through those institutions. Drawing on qualitative interviews with HE applicants conducted as part of an ESRC project on access to higher education, Reay underlines the way in which working-class HE applicants engage in complicated practices of 'trying to negotiate a difficult balance between investing in a new improved identity and holding onto a cohesive self' (2001: 337). Reay is interested in the different kinds of emotional investments shaping working-class students' transition from further to higher education, and those dimensions of experience that inform class feeling – the place of memory, feelings of ambivalence, inferiority and superiority and the distinctions and markings of taste. According to Reay (2001) a central problem facing working-class students as they enter HE institutions (HEIs), especially the pre-1992 'elite' HEIs, is the 'problematic of reconciling academic success with working-class identity' (Reay, 2001: 339). This is because being aspirational and working class often demands having to negotiate competing sets of pressures and seductions based on distinct forms of class identification – being aspirational might involve a risky process of 'losing oneself' (Reay, 2001). Reay argues that formal educational institutions and practices are structured in relation to a middle-class imaginary, where middle-class values are treated as the norm, while working-class students are constructed through a deficit model which positions them as lacking aspirations, information or academic preparation. Thus a concern has been raised in feminist research of the ways that higher education operates to pathologize working-class experiences and identities, since it facilitates forms of recognition that afford little pride and respect to gendered, working-class positions, identities, relations and practices. Indeed, the explicit denial or rejection of working-class history and identity is central in such processes of exclusion and misrecognition. It is those elements of middle-class subjectivity that are positioned as the norm, as something to aspire to, and this directly contributes to the inferior construction of many young working-class people, feelings that often cut a deep wound in the psyche (Skeggs, 1997; Reay, 2001; Burke, 2002). Importantly, feminist theory uncovers the intricate relations and operations of class with gender, ethnicity and other social differences, identities and inequalities.

## Final reflections

This chapter draws on different theoretical and conceptual tools to theorize and develop reconceptualizations of widening participation. Drawing on critical theory provides the resources to problematize and interrogate some of the assumptions underpinning contemporary practices, strategies and understandings of 'widening educational participation'. It also provides the tools to shed theoretical light on the more insidious and subtle forms of inequality in higher education that profoundly affect access and participation but largely remain invisible. Such tools provide us with analytical frameworks to uncover the hidden forms of exclusion, discrimination and mis/recognition at play and to develop methodological frameworks that go beyond collecting information about inequality and diversity. Importantly, such tools allow us also to re-imagine widening participation in transformatory ways, getting to the heart of the workings of inequality to enable us to find new ways of 'doing' WP. In Part Three of the book, I will draw on empirical data to illuminate the value of such critical tools for understanding complex inequalities in higher education. In the next chapter, I will develop my discussion of the importance of concepts of identity and subjectivity for reconceptualizing widening educational participation as a social project of transformation.

# 3 Subjects of widening participation: Identity and subjectivity

In this chapter, I argue for the importance of a conceptual framework that includes subjective construction and identity formation in the project of reimagining widening participation beyond hegemonic discourses shaped by neoliberalism. As widening participation is about redressing historical exclusions and inequalities, it must grapple with the politics of social relations, including the intersections of difference, inequality and identity across age, class, dis/ability, ethnicity, gender, nationality, race, religion and sexuality. I will argue that these differences continue to make a difference in higher education access and participation, and in the re/production of educational inequalities. Subjectivity is formed through the different discourses at play and WP policy constructs recognizable subjects of its discourse, for example, those seen as 'disadvantaged', 'non-traditional' and 'having potential'. This chapter draws on theories of identity and subjectivity to examine the implications of the construction of 'new student constituencies' within higher education, in terms of who can be recognized as a university student. Particular attention will be drawn to constructions of aspiration, potential and choice in the processes of accessing higher education and the ways that access to *higher education* is prioritized in widening participation policy debates, affecting the formation of learner and student subjectivities. This will include attention to the implications of this for marginalized and misrecognized learning and student subjectivities. In returning to my earlier argument about the importance of connecting the personal with the theoretical, and with recognizing the autobiography of the question, the chapter will end with an analysis of my autobiographical account of accessing higher education and the ways that concepts of identity, subjectivity and recognition are valuable in theorizing WP.

## Relational identities: disrupting individualist discourses

Although identity is often a taken-for-granted concept in everyday discourse, a critical, post-structuralist theorization of identity raises key challenges to common sense understandings of what it means to be an 'individual' in Western societies. Much of the everyday understanding of identity draws on individualist perspectives and rests on notions of a coherent, fixed, core self – the 'notion of a "true" or "deep" self, which is seen as somehow outside the social' (Lawler, 2008: 5). This informs taken-for-granted notions of potential, which, through the intervention of professional and pedagogical agents, can be 'unlocked'. Individual potential is thus seen as something essential and core to who the person is, rather than as socially constructed and contextualized and intimately tied in with subjective processes, including those of learning and being a student. The interconnection between identity and potential is deeply tied in to historical inequalities and the social and institutional markers of differentiation, as well as the politics of identity formation.

As Stuart Hall has insightfully theorized (1992, 1997, 2000), identity rests on notions of difference, as well as 'sameness', and processes of disidentification are as important as identification in forming a sense of self. I understand myself as a 'woman' *in relation* to seeing myself as different from 'being a man'. Identity formation is thus a relational process – I understand 'who I am' in relation to others – who I see myself as different from and who I identify with through narratives of 'sameness'. This has been at the heart of much debate in critical and feminist theories. For example, in early second-wave feminism, there tended to be a strong emphasis on women's shared experiences. However, this was later critiqued by black and working-class women who pointed out that women's experiences differed significantly across 'race' and class (e.g. Hooks, 1982; Lorde, 1984; Bryan *et al.*, 1985; Carby, 1987). Furthermore, post-structural theorists importantly highlight that what it means to 'be a woman' is contested, socially constructed and discursively produced, as well as differently experienced. Indeed, identity is always constructed through difference:

> Precisely because identities are constructed within, not outside, discourse, we need to understand them as produced in specific historical and institutional sites within specific discursive formations and practices, by specific enunciative strategies. Moreover, they emerge within the play of specific modulations of power, and thus are more the product of the marking of difference and exclusion. Above all ... identities are constructed through, not outside, difference.
>
> (Hall, 2000: 17)

We form our identities through the multiple, contradictory, social positionings that we take up in and through time, place and space, including for example the teacher, mother, son, worker, student, professional. However, these different identity positions are not simply additive, so that being 'black' or 'middle class' or a 'woman', simply build on one another. Rather, these different positionings intersect and are mutually constitutive, yet also might contradict and be in tension. Furthermore, some aspects of our identity might be more visible or influential at a certain moment in space and time and this is tied to complex relational processes of subjective construction. Importantly though, the idea that our identities are multiple and that identities might be in tension challenges assumptions of a coherent unified 'self'. These theoretical insights are significant in understanding the complex experiences of students and the ways they negotiate the competing expectations, practices and discourses of different identity positions in and outside higher education fields. For example, in my research on mature, white, working-class women students, I found that the women's negotiations of their identities as wives, mothers and students were not necessarily smooth and supportive positionings to organize, manage and negotiate; rather, they caused pain, fragmentation, contradiction and the tight regulation of the women's (hetero)sexualized identities in the home (Burke, 2002, 2006).

Such insights are important in understanding the complex processes by which different subjects in higher education get fashioned and refashioned through contradictory policies, practices, and discourses. Identity formation is a fluid process, linked to shifting contexts, micropolitics and wider struggles over meaning, being, doing and knowing. Identity is a continual process of becoming through identifications, a discursive project that is, however, always linked to particular social and personal histories and experiences that are connected with deeply embedded social and material inequalities and differences (Hall, 2000).

## Narrative identities

This book draws on narratives throughout to understand issues of educational access, participation and experiences and the formations of identity that shape these. In Chapter Four, I will explore narrative as a methodological approach that helps to deepen understanding of social identities, experiences and practices. Here I want to think about the ways that narratives are used in the everyday lives of people as a tool to interpret and reinterpret their memories and experiences and to give meaning to their identities and lives. This conceptual tool helps to think through how narratives shape personal and social sensibilities about entitlement and the 'right' to higher education.

Through the telling of stories about ourselves, we actively produce our identities through an assemblage of the memories and experiences we reconstruct in the telling process. Identity is constituted through these narratives, in which we remember certain episodes or events that give meaning to our narrative and sense of self. Lawler argues that narratives, or stories, are central to Western culture, and indeed perhaps all cultures, although what counts as a narrative will differ in different historical and cultural contexts (Lawler, 2008: 12). The important point to make here is that we participate continuously in telling stories about our past, present and future and through this process we engage in re/interpretation about who we are and might become. Our stories always involve others, and so a narrative perspective of identity emphasizes the social and relational in identity formations. Lawler (2008: 13) explains that narratives are not simply reflections of a set of autobiographical facts, but rather 'identities are produced through the autobiographical work in which all of us engage every day'. The importance of this perspective is the emphasis that it places on interpretation and reinterpretation in the ways in which we create self-meaning:

> [T]he self does not know itself immediately but only indirectly by the detour of the cultural signs of all sorts which are articulated on the symbolic mediations which always already articulate action and, among them, the narratives of everyday life. Narrative mediation underlines this remarkable characteristic of self-knowledge – that it is self-interpretation.
>
> (Ricoeur, 1991: 198 quoted in Lawler, 2008: 17)

The sense of continuity that we give to our identities is tied to the process of telling and retelling stories 'which produce it as something continuing through time' (Lawler, 2008: 17). In this process, we draw on our memories, which themselves are interpretations and reconstructive of the events that appear in our narratives as significant for explaining who we are. Yet we interpret our memories based on what we know about our present and in relation to the wider social circumstances of our lives. In this way, there is the suggestion of movement through time, from past to present and present to future and this makes 'later events seem the natural and inevitable culmination of earlier ones' (Lawler, 2008: 19). This is important for understanding how people make sense of their lives in relation to educational experience and 'being a student', the processes of aspiration-forming, as well as the ways that their narratives are read off by others, contributing to judgements about 'potential' and 'ability' and shaping judgements about access, choice and selection. Narratives thus contribute to the processes of recognition that create possibilities for participation in higher education, based on particular assumptions and values, such as what counts as 'potential'.

## Subjectivity and mis/recognition

Recognition is central to processes of identity formation, including the formation of student identity. Identity formation is tied in with processes of subjective construction or, in post-structural terms, 'subjectivity'. Constituted through discourse and what Butler calls 'performativity', subjectivity disrupts notions of identity as fixed and stable. Miriam David and colleagues explains that performativity is 'the idea that identity does not prefigure action but is made through action, discourses or the words we speak or behave' (David *et al.*, 2006).

> Discursive performativity appears to produce that which it names, to enact its own referent, to name and to do, to name and to make. ... [g]enerally speaking, a performative functions to produce that which it declares.
>
> (Butler, 1993: 107)

Butler's work on the constitution of the subject through processes of exclusion and differentiation highlights the ways that the subject creates an illusion of autonomy, which disavows dependency on others and the need for inclusion. The illusion of autonomy is: 'accomplished through subjection to dominant discourses and a simultaneous relationality with others that opens up new dependencies and potentially new subversive forms of recognition' (Claiborne *et al.*, 2009: 47).

A central concept of subjectivity is recognition, which is achieved through the dual processes of submission and mastery. That is, the subject both practices agency and intent whilst also being subjected to the discourses that name and position her.

> Central to the dual process of submission and mastery in the formation of the subject are the mutual acts of recognition through which subjects accord each other the status of viable subjecthood.
>
> (Davies, 2006: 427)

Subjectivity highlights the relational, discursive and embodied processes of identity formations and focuses on the ways people 'are both "made subject" by/within the social order and how they are agents/subjects within/against it' (Jones, 1993: 158). Subjects move across and between fluid and contradictory positions, and are subjected to, as well as resistors of, the competing discourses at play (Davies, 1997: 275). The discursive constitution of subjectivities is located within debates and policies that generate particular understandings of 'widening participation', 'access', 'higher education' and 'university student'. Hegemonic discourses of WP, for example, constrain and make possible competing understandings of what it means to be a university student as well as to profoundly shape educational policies and practices (Burke and Jackson, 2007: 112).

WP policy and practice is implicated in the dual processes of submission and mastery in the formation and recognition of the WP subject. Those recognized as 'WP students', as 'having potential' and as 'disadvantaged' (see e.g. HEFCE, 2006) are subjected to the 'disciplinary gaze' (Foucault, 1984) of WP policy discourses. To be recognizable as a subject of this policy, the person must be subjected to the discourses of disadvantage, re/positioning the WP subject as the different and 'Other' (Said, 1977) of educational policy, yet actively engaged in a project of self-improvement through educational participation, 'mastering' the skills needed to succeed (e.g. DfEE, 1999). The subject of WP policy is positioned through difference and the 'polarizing discourses' that are entangled with the imaginary ideal-student subject: the traditional, standard, 18-year-old student (Williams, 1997: 26). The subject of WP, struggling for recognition as a viable student-subject, attempts to avoid the subject positioning of 'Other', the identifiable 'non-standard' subject of the often derogatory discourses of WP, which are embedded in classed and racialized assumptions about lack and deficit (Williams, 1997: 25). The ideal (imaginary) student-subject of policy discourse is constructed in relation to middle-class and white racialized norms and values 'where autonomous individual motivation is prized and where dependency on others is considered a sign of vulnerability and weakness' (Raphael Reed *et al.*, 2007: 22).

## Naming (and shaming) the WP subject

Forms of symbolic, emotional and physical violence regulate and police the production of identity in educational sites. Lynn Raphael Reed and her colleagues found that the young people they interviewed about their participation in HE talked powerfully about experiences of violence at school. Experiences of violence operated through peer group bullying and 'outcasting', undermining academic effort and aspiration, 'to normalize attempts to be different and to exert a form of "collective agency" in pursuit of socially valorized goals' (Raphael Reed *et al.*, 2007: 18). My own research on men, masculinities and access to higher education found similar accounts of bullying and violence shaping the men's memories of schooling and their identities as students (Burke, 2006). Bourdieu's concept of 'symbolic violence' helps uncover the more subtle forms of violence at play in educational institutions: the ways that feelings of being an outsider or 'thick' in educational contexts are made to appear natural through the legitimization of particular forms of cultural capital and habitus. Raphael Reed and her colleagues (2007) argue that 'shame' is a social emotion that is internalized as a feeling of lack of self-worth or sense of failure.

> [Shame] exists with reference to how we anticipate others may see and reject us' – but it is experienced as internalized disappointment with self i.e. it exists with reference to how we judge our own shortcomings, feelings of failure or inadequacy.
>
> (Raphael Reed *et al.*, 2007: 19)

Foucault's concept of 'dividing practices' helps to develop such themes of difference and otherness in the constitution of a student-subject positioning. Dividing practices 'objectify individuals *and* provide them with the means to construct a sense of self' (Atencio and Wright, 2009: 33). Foucault explains that 'the subject is either divided inside himself or divided from others. [ ... ] Examples are the mad and the sane, the sick and the healthy, the criminals and the "good boys"' (Foucault, 1977: 326).

Dividing practices are a 'form of objectification' in which subjects are 'made objects that can be known' (Fejes, 2008: 90). Dividing practices contribute to 'a subjectification wherein the normal and abnormal are created and divided. Such a practice, related to the political ambition to govern, was made possible by pedagogy, education, sociology, psychology and statistics' (Fejes, 2008: 90).

These disciplines contribute to the institutional frameworks in which a subject is named and recognized as a (particular form of) university student. A dilemma for research on widening participation in higher education that aims to problematize identity as fixed and fully knowable is that, in discussing social inequalities, it is important to use descriptors such as 'women', 'mature' and 'working class'. This risks essentializing identities as fixed and reproducing pathologizing discourses that reposition and re/class/ify certain individuals and groups in derogatory ways.

Yet, feminist and critical theory insists on the importance of analysing particular social groups and identities to understand the workings of power and inequalities. Feminism aims to understand the ways in which women and men are gendered subjects, negotiating formations of femininities and masculinities across complex power relations and intersections of difference, and to theorize the ways in which experiences and knowledge are also gendered. Yet, post-structuralism aims to destabilize the subject, deconstructing hegemonic understandings of identity as stable and reconceptualizing identities as always constituted through discourse. In these ways, as I have considered in previous work (Burke, 2002), feminism and post-structuralism are discordant theoretical perspectives. However, the conceptual tools of post-structuralism are powerful in deconstructing processes of gendered subjectivity, in understanding the subject as formed through doing as well as being, and as theorizing the subject of gendered discourse as always in process and thus open to transformative ways of being.

Feminist post-structural theory, in disrupting essentialist and coherent notions of identity, illuminates the significance of processes of recognition in the ongoing formation of the gendered and classed subject. Yet, the naming of a subject position in itself does not constitute a definite identity position. Winstead, in discussing the dilemma she faces in drawing on post-structuralism, which disrupts identity as fixed and knowable, whilst also naming the participants in her research in relation to particular social identities, explains that:

> The naming of a subject position does not assure its meaning or its relation to other subject positions, because the grounds of differentiation are constantly shifting. Indeed, the incitement of a unitary identity is necessarily a culturally specific political act, in that every identity is constituted in relation to who may not occupy the subject position as much as who may occupy it. In other words, notions of unitary identities rest on myths of allegiance. The incitement of a given unitary identity often hints at a struggle for power in the distribution of various forms of social, cultural, and economic capital, but it rarely reveals the fictional 'sameness' for the people who are subjected similarly. Therefore, the reader should view my use of identity categories as more than a post-structuralist tension (which it remains); such identities should also serve as indicators of where I position myself, and am positioned, in relation to the participants in the telling of the stories.
>
> (Winstead, 2009: 132–33)

Winstead points to the significance of considerations of who may not occupy a particular subject position, for example of the 'non-traditional' student.

Furthermore, she highlights that categories construct fictions of 'sameness', and so constructions of sameness in relation to the 'traditional' student-subject is as much a fiction as the 'non-traditional' student-subject. Further, the researcher produces certain narratives or stories through the research from the particular identity positions that she occupies in the research in relation to the research participants. This is tied to the processes of recognition and subjective construction, as well as notions of 'sameness' and difference, which are embodied as well as discursive.

## Embodied identities

Foucault's work on processes of subjectfication and the constitution of the subject emphasizes the ways that discourses regulate, govern, classify and exclude bodies within institutional spaces, such as schools and universities. Identity is embodied and, through disciplinary practices and discourses, bodies are controlled and rendered 'docile'. However, Foucault also theorized the ways that embodied subjects engage in 'practices of the self', both being 'acted upon' but also actively engaged in the constitution of the self. Subjects participate in 'practices of the self' by 'idealising, contesting and investing in discourse, power relations, and social practices in ways that are indicative of a more "ethical" relationship to their self and to others' (Atencio and Wright, 2009: 34). Subjectivities are constituted through embodied practices, discourses and the particular ways that bodily behaviour is regulated and moulded. In their study of two 'black' young women participating in dance classes in an inner-city American high school, Atencio and Wright (2009: 45) suggest, based on their analysis, that 'schools and teachers must critically reflect upon how they (re)produce hegemonic practices and power relations that only serve to support particular types of bodies and subjects whilst devaluing those constituted as "Other"'.

Bourdieu's concept of habitus also provides a compelling theoretical framework for understanding identities as embodied. At the heart of the concept of habitus is practice, which implies that 'oppression is deeply rooted in psychological and physical dispositions' (McNay, 2008: 181). Habitus is the incorporation of 'the regularities and tendencies of the world into the body' (McNay, 2008: 181). Identity emerges through practice, which is the 'product of power relations that have been internalized into the body and also of an active engagement with social structures' (McNay, 2008: 182). Embodied subjects are situated within a 'given set of relations that comprise distinct spheres of social action', or 'fields' (McNay, 2008: 182). In the context of widening participation in higher education, habitus illuminates the ways that unequal relations of power become internalized and naturalized so that decisions and aspirations to participate in higher education (or not) are seen as freely made individual choices. The ways that students are differentiated and live out those differentiations through practice is embodied and perceived as about differences in (innate) potential and ability rather than as the interplay of embodied dispositions, the intersubjective relations of the field and social structures (McNay, 2008: 187).

In drawing on habitus and notions of embodied identities, Beverley Skeggs argues that class is made through different processes and in relation to other classifications. She explains that 'We need to think how bodies are being inscribed simultaneously by different symbolic systems; how inscription attributes difference and how we learn to interpret bodies through the different perspectives to which we have access.'

The concept of embodied identities emphasizes the working of power and difference and the ways that these are marked and inscribed on the body, as well as resisted or subverted through 'practices of the self'. This is powerful for thinking through difference and transformation in the context of policies and practices of widening participation and the ways that different bodies are positioned, mobilized and regulated in relation to complex inequalities across space. Embodied identity helps to think through the ways different bodies take up and use the different higher education spaces available, and the ways that higher education spaces are constructed and re/shaped in relation to the different bodies that move through and are positioned within them.

## Theorizing difference and diversity in the formation of student identities

As noted above, identities are formed as much through difference as they are through 'sameness'. Difference and differentiation, linked to discourses of 'diversity' are central in understanding the formation of student identity in higher education and in relation to struggles over access and participation. Beverley Skeggs points out that in contemporary societies recognition of difference is more difficult to maintain with the proliferation of difference through a range of sources, including markets, advertising and popular media (2004: 97). Drawing on Homi Bhabha, she points out that the problem of differentiation in contemporary social contexts is not distance but *proximity*. 'The problem is of perceived similitude by those who feel too close' (Skeggs, 2004: 96). As higher education is becoming increasingly characterized by diversity, the anxiety about closeness of the 'Other' to those deemed to be worthy of higher education participation is expressed through narratives about contamination by the lowering of standards and the 'dumbing down' of university curricula and pedagogical practices (Morley, 2003).

Thus the marking out of difference is central to subjective construction and the processes of becoming a (certain kind of) student in (a highly differentiated) higher education. Processes of the marking out of difference, and the connected technologies of exclusion, misrecongition and inequality, tend to be hidden through the citation of 'diversity', with its contemporary positive connotations in HE policy discourses. However, diversity is underpinned by difference and the ways that identities are formed, embodied, performed, invoked and constructed through social and cultural inequalities. 'Diversity' is generally presented as a positive phenomenon in higher education, without reference to the ways that unequal and hierarchical relations of difference underpin diversity. Indeed, diversity in higher education has become one of its defining features (Maher and Tetreault, 2006: 5). However, although 'diversity' is now a central theme of higher education discourse, and often used by universities to promote their profile, being recognized as 'too different' requires self-correction and self-regulation.

In their study of the implications of increased diversity in higher education, Chris Hockings and her colleagues argue that diversity extends beyond the traditional structural divisions of class, gender and ethnicity, also encompassing diverse student entry routes and the different ways that students combine life, work and study (Hockings *et al.*, 2008). They avoid the terms 'traditional' and 'non-traditional' students since they mask the complexity of the student population (Hockings *et al.*, 2008), which reiterates the point made above about fictions of 'sameness' constructed through particular institutionalized classifications of difference. Instead, Hockings *et al.* (2008) are interested in the ways that 'individual students and teachers negotiate their identities by marking themselves out as similar to or different from their peers'. They examine the ways that difference is used as a source of diversity, enriching the lives of others, or as a mechanism of isolation and marginalization of those who are seen as not fitting in or as 'others' (Hockings *et al.*, 2008).

In the US context, in *Privilege and Diversity in the Academy*, Maher and Tetreault draw on the concept of diversity to 'analyse the challenges to institutional privilege brought about by the entrance of new groups into the academy' (2006: 5). They understand diversity to mean 'people and ideas that are different from the assumed norm of white, heterosexual, middle-class and college-educated men' (Maher and Tetreault, 2006). Brah explains that 'difference' might be conceptualized as 'experiential diversity', to explore the different ways that 'ideological and institutional practices mark our everyday life' (Brah, 1996: 89). Difference is a social relation 'constructed within systems of power underlying structures of class, racism, gender and sexuality' (Brah, 1996: 88). Brah argues that it is important to make a distinction between difference as the 'marker of collective histories' and difference as 'codified in an individual's biography' (Brah, 1996: 89). However, both forms of difference are significant in the understanding and making of the self and in social and personal identity formation. Such distinctions help emphasize the importance of understanding issues of access and participation in higher education, not in terms of raising individual aspirations but in relation to collective and personal histories of under- and misrepresentation, as well as the ways that some subjects (are made to) feel different and 'unworthy' of higher educational access and participation.

In order to illuminate these concepts of identity formation, I will now draw on and theorize my own autobiographical narrative.

## The auto/biography of the question: theorizing the self

One of the most compelling concepts I have encountered in my personal journey of accessing higher education is Jane Miller's autobiography of the question (Miller, 1995). This concept emphasizes the researcher's relationship to the questions she's exploring, requires careful consideration of the experiences, identities and perspectives she brings to the research process and asks her to make connections between herself, the research participants and other voices in the field. Miller's concept has helped me understand my relational position across multiple and contradictory subjectivities. In the final section of this chapter, I draw on my autobiography to explore processes of identity formation in relation to the complex processes of accessing and participating in higher education.

My journey through higher education became possible through the serendipitous discovery of an Access to Higher Education course, offered at my local further education college. At the time, I was newly married, and had the full-time responsibility of caring for my two sons, in our reconstituted family unit. It was the early 1990s; I was a survivor of domestic violence and had lived for a considerable period of time in a Women's Aid refuge. The experiences of violence, escaping and surviving altered my world perspectives and sense of self profoundly. My traumatic experiences politicized me and I wanted to seek answers and, like many others, I wanted to find a way to 'give back'. This sense of purpose and urgency was partly connected to the identity project of redefining a legitimate subjecthood, as I often described myself as 'rebuilding my life'.

As a young woman, I had been completely submerged and invested in becoming a ballerina, and this powerfully defined my sensibilities as a gendered subject. I constituted myself through the discourses and practices of femininity, drawing on particularly delicate and 'ladylike' subject positions, my sense of self strongly formed through the Hollywood glamour and the romanticized ballet world that I grew up in. My subject position as a recognized young lady revolved around being seen as demure and elegant. The loss of the ballerina subject position, which came with my escape, followed by the tremendous support offered by Women's Aid, reshaped my sensibilities.

The Women's Aid refuge was managed in a feminist way; it was my first explicit experience of feminism. This provided an empowering framework in which to make sense of painful and transforming life experiences. Domestic violence was often understood through terms such as 'battered wife syndrome', which distorted the issue, placing negative attention on the victim, often leading to the internalization of guilt, humility and shame.

Unlike many other forms of crime, domestic violence is still often perceived as private, a shameful secret, not to be spoken about in public spaces. Yet the scale of domestic violence indicates the depth of the social problem. Approximately half of all rapes are committed by a current or former partner. At least one in four women will experience domestic violence in their lifetime and about two women a week are killed at the hands of their partner or former partner (Women's Aid, 2009). While I lived in the refuge, I continually heard about shocking and horrendous stories of terror and violence, and I began to see certain patterns emerging, which helped me to move beyond my personal experience. I recognized that domestic violence is a serious social and gendered issue; and I saw that I had a valuable insight as a survivor. This made me feel strongly that I needed to speak out, refusing to be silenced by the regulatory discourses of shame often connected to domestic violence. All of this formed some of the most powerful learning I have experienced in my life; and through these lessons I was able to turn a traumatic set of events into a transformative and invaluable set of resources that deeply reshaped my ontological position and helped me to discover the positive forms of power and subjectivity available to me.

My initial aspirations were to become a primary school teacher. Becoming a teacher felt possible and realistic. I had my own children and I was already an experienced children's ballet teacher. Teaching primary school felt like a natural extension of my existing sense of self. Furthermore, there were real practicalities as well as emotional dimensions; the Access course accommodated my material needs as a mother – the nursery was on campus – but also my emotional need to be recognized as the talented subject with potential.

The move from 'budding ballerina' to college student had a sense of continuity; one supported the other in a seamless move from being disciplined through the strict demands of ballet class to being disciplined through the intellectual rigour of academic study. I identified as the 'non-traditional' Access student but I was also striving towards recognition as the (imaginary) ideal-student subject. The cultural practices of the Access course fit in well with those of the ballet world: it was all about listening, learning and reiterating the discursive and performative practices of the teacher. I immersed myself in the cultural practices and discourses of higher education, which powerfully reshaped my gendered subjectivity.

After completing my Access course, and giving birth to our third son just two days after my final exams, I decided to pursue my newly discovered love for Sociology. Like many Access students, I did not consciously select a university but simply applied to the local post-1992 university. However, the transition to university provoked uncertainties about my self-worth. The university was big, intimidating, and the academic and pedagogical practices were unfamiliar. Large lecture theatres were alienating places and, although I looked forward to the smaller seminar groups, I was often anxious about speaking out in case I got it wrong and exposed myself as unworthy and 'not belonging'.

Certain cultural practices though resonated with my previous experiences of ballet; although the focus was on intellectual rather than physical rigour, the disciplinary regimes of academic practices felt in some ways familiar. I was able to draw on some of the everyday practices of classical ballet training, which had become part of my embodied habitus. Simultaneously, I discovered a passionate focus for my intellectual development through exposure to feminist theories. I began making connections between the experiences of the other mature women students on my course and the theoretical insights of feminism. This gave me a strong sense of purpose in my studies; I wanted to find a theoretical language to make sense of gendered experiences of accessing higher education and the ways subjectivity was performed and constructed in and through university spaces.

Through such engagements, I began to develop a sense of myself as a university student. This was linked to my narrative of survival, my apparent ability to master academic practices and my passionate commitment to women's access to higher education. This was reinforced through the recognition of others with institutional authority and status and the excitement I felt at being encouraged to continue on to a Master's Degree. My point here is that I was able to draw on some valuable resources and experiences that allowed me to negotiate inclusion and recognition as a legitimate university student. My story is partly about individual determination to succeed and the personal transformation that higher education participation can offer. However, I want to emphasize that my story is also about the social and cultural contexts, capital, discourses, conditions and relations that supported me through what was at times experienced as intimidating, alienating and unsettling. My social and cultural location, more than my individual determination, enabled me to move through the university system.

## Final reflections

Much of the WP policy discourses have focused on implicit assumptions about identity, which draw on the notion of a core, inner self, that is formed mostly 'within' and separate from the social world (Lawler, 2008). Everyday discourses of identity, such as the notion of 'finding yourself' profoundly shape assumptions about issues of access to, and participation in, higher education. For example, in my research on working-class women accessing education through Access and Return to Study programmes (Burke, 2002, 2004) the women offer the idea of 'finding myself' as a key motivation for participating on their courses.

The idea of 'finding yourself' reinforces assumptions that there is a core self to be discovered and unlocked. This rests on notions of 'hidden' or 'untapped' potential as well as notions of innate ability and talent. The concepts of identity and subjectivity outlined in this chapter trouble such notions and challenge assumptions that talent and ability is something natural or innate that the individual 'has' and that can be objectively assessed, for example through fair and transparent admissions or assessment criteria. Rather, identity is understood as constituted through discourses and ways of 'doing' identity and taking up available social positions. Ability, talent and potential are similarly constructed through discourses, norms and values that focus on particular sets of attributes that are seen to signal or indicate a person who is 'talented', 'able' or 'has potential'.

Formations of identity and subjectivity rely on processes of recognition – the 'talented' person can only become this kind of person through being recognized by others as 'talented'. Processes of recognition take place within social contexts where power relations play out so that those recognitions must fit into socially sanctioned notions of 'talent' as well as be legitimated by those who occupy the social positions of power and authority to do so. Thus, being recognized as a 'potential student' in higher education is deeply inter-connected with not only institutional structures and practices but also discourses (the power/knowledge nexus).

Identity and subjectivity are central then in understanding the complex forms of exclusion and inequality that play out in educational contexts and the ways some people are not recognized as being worthy of or having the right to higher educational access and participation. Such concepts help to tease out the complexity of inequality in struggles over access to higher education, which include material and structural barriers but also more subtle processes of mis/recognition tied to complex formations and the (micro)politics of identity.

In the next section, I take up the theoretical perspectives outlined in Chapters Two and Three to consider the implications of different methodo-logical approaches for the development of strategies to widen educational participation. I will argue that widening participation strategies, practices and approaches are profoundly shaped by the methodological frameworks that make such strategies, practices and approaches possible. Struggles over access to and participation in higher education are not just material struggles, but also ontological and epistemological ones.

# Part 2

# Methodologies and approaches

This part discusses the methodological implications of researching and developing practice for widening participation. A key argument is made in Chapter Four that methodological considerations are often underdeveloped in both research and practice of widening participation, despite the central importance of methodological frameworks for combating educational inequalities and exclusions. Concepts of reflexivity and praxis are drawn on and critiqued to place power relations, ethics and re/presentation at the heart of research for social justice in higher education and to emphasize the importance of bringing together theory and practice. The significance of thinking about voice and author/ity are also explored. A key concern of the chapter is to make certain methodological debates and tools accessible to all those who are committed to widening participation and to research for transformation.

Chapter Five considers more specifically the methodological issues involved in producing the research and writing for the book, including issues of re/presentation, which relate to the overarching conceptual theme of mis/recognition. I provide an overview of four of my research projects on widening participation, which will be drawn on later in Part Three to explore key issues and bring to life some of the abstract theoretical and methodological points discussed in Parts One and Two of the book.

# 4    Methodological approaches

Widening participation has become a significant theme of educational research over past years, contributing to the growing field of higher education studies. However, this body of work has been critiqued as 'atheoretical' (Archer and Leathwood, 2003; Burke and Jackson, 2007) and lacking sophisticated levels of attention to methodological issues (Tight, 2003). This chapter argues that methodological issues are key to the contribution of knowledge about widening participation because different methodological frameworks profoundly shape the kinds of research questions formulated by researchers and the ways in which research is designed and conducted. In this chapter, the importance of epistemological frameworks, which determine the ways that knowledge is constructed and produced, is emphasized. The chapter also argues for the importance of attention to ontological questions, such as the identities, perspectives, values and positions of researchers and research participants in the field and how this affects their interpretations, relations and approaches. Methodologies shape how researchers collect and analyse data, the formulation of questions or problems, the ways ethical issues are handled and made sense of, as well as the ways that knowledge is constructed and re/presented. This chapter aims to provide a set of tools for researchers to use in their work on widening participation, in order to contribute to deeper-level understandings of the key issues that impact on the project of widening participation. It also provides a set of tools for students and practitioners to critique some of the problematic assumptions that have shaped the body of work on WP and might limit our understandings and therefore the kinds of strategies and solutions formulated.

## Power, truth and the politics of knowing (and being known)

A key argument of this book is that we need theoretical and methodological frameworks that enable us to move beyond instrumentalist discourses of widening participation that are underpinned by neoliberal perspectives, in order to develop educational policies and practices that engage a politics of both redistribution and recognition. Although a body of research has provided important insights into which socio-economic groups have been under-represented in higher education at different times and places, policy and practice has not been able to fully tackle deeply engrained historical inequalities and mis-recognitions at play in higher education. I argue in this chapter that this is partly due to an *overemphasis* on the collection of measurable, objective data and 'evidence' for widening participation, and an *underemphasis* on methodologies that engage the subjective, emotional and experiential dimensions of cultural and subjective experiences, identities, relations and inequalities in different educational and pedagogical contexts.

Critical, feminist and post-structural methodologies concerned with social justice in and through education challenge hegemonic perspectives that research must always aim for objectivity, generalizability and neutrality. Social research interested in examining educational inequalities and mis-recognitions must explicitly address complex relations of power and (micro) politics, thus challenging those re/presentations of the social world as decon-textualized and disembodied sets of evidence to be collected, measured and classified. Critical, feminist and post-structural methodologies expose that knowledge and power are inextricably connected and are not reducible to measurable facts or information. Contesting those epistemological perspectives that insist that research must be neutral, apolitical and value-free, critical and feminist methodologies argue that knowledge produced through social and educational research is necessarily partial, embodied, underpinned by particular values and ontological perspectives, highly contextualized and constructed through, and indeed structured by, classed, gendered, racialized and sexualized relations, epistemologies and discourses. Researchers committed to social justice in education raise the concern that lack of close attention to the socially and discursively constructed and contextualized nature of meaning-making tends to exacerbate cultural and material inequalities and misrecognitions, because these remain unproblematized and embedded in HE and WP policies and practices.

Carlos Alberto Torres develops a political sociology of education to contest the common sense and privileging of research frameworks rooted in positivist traditions and to work towards educational research for social transformation and justice. A political sociology of education explicitly interrogates positivist epistemologies, which insist on 'the dispassionate environment of technical reasoning through the manipulation of empirical data that, despite potential problems of reliability, generalization, and sample size, cannot be suspected to be social constructions' (Torres, 2009: 49). Such technocist epistemologies are seen as servicing 'truth', rationality and objectivity and demand that educational research is value-free and apolitical. A political sociology of education 'aims to study power and relations of authority in education, and the political under-pinnings and relations of educational policies' (Torres. 2009: 40). In this critical methodological framework, power is seen as central to educational research practices and to the production of knowledge.

Such methodologies, which critique the hegemony of positivism and technocism, are important for moving beyond widening participation because they require close attention to the complex and micro-level workings and relations of power and inequality in educational sites at multiple levels and across different contexts, identities and social locations. Such methodological approaches enable the researcher 'to deconstruct and critique the premises of the principle of common sense' (Torres, 2009: 37) and to place culture at the centre of analysis of the production of hegemonic discourses and perspectives at play in everyday contexts and practices. Critical methodologies disrupt the positioning of the social scientist as the dispassionate researcher describing the world as it is. Indeed, there is no one 'truth' to be discovered or claimed by the dispassionate researcher; rather, there are multiple 'truths', which are contested over and tied to complex relations of power and inequality. The critical researcher aims to pay particular attention to the truths of those who have been silenced, excluded and pathologized through the colonizing, regulating, normalizing and paternalistic gaze of some of the hegemonic forms of social science research and policy.

Critical and feminist researchers are committed to the development of methodologies 'which empower those involved in change' as well as in critically understanding the social world (Lather, 1991: 3). However, the concept of 'empowerment' itself is subject to critical deconstruction so that it 'opposes the reduction of the term as it is used in the current fashion of individual self-assertion, upward mobility and the psychological experience of feeling powerful' (Lather, 1991: 3). Rather, empowerment is a conceptual tool, which enables the analysis of ideas about powerlessness, systems of oppression and ways to effect change (Lather, 1991: 4). The focus of critical and feminist approaches to 'empowerment' is to draw on different methodological resources so that all involved in the research process participate in the analysis, critique and deconstruction of structures, subjectivities and discourses tied to complex and unequal relations of power. Within critical methodological frameworks, 'the politics of knowing and being known take on urgency in our discourse about what it means to do social inquiry' (Lather, 1991: 86).

Such methodological frameworks compel the researcher to engage in self-reflexivity in order to interrogate the values, perspectives, experiences, assumptions and meanings she or he brings to the research process. Concerns about doing research reflexively emerge from epistemological debates about the nature of knowledge and research, as outlined above. Such perspectives highlight the situated nature of knowledge, which is always understood to be contextualized, contested, discursive and socially constructed. Such debates are profoundly important in research concerned with challenging inequalities in higher education, as HE is a key site of knowledge production and of the legitimization (and marginalization) of certain forms of knowledge and ways of knowing and being known (and thus recognized as a valid subject of knowledge). Reflexivity has been conceptualized as a framework in which the researcher might 'become more sensitive to the power relations embedded in the research process' and move 'to interrogate their own social location and to disentangle how it shaped their definition of the situation' (Haney, 2004: 297).

Critical, feminist and post-structural perspectives illuminate the importance of reflexivity in research that takes seriously the complexity of inequalities, misrecognitions and exclusions in and beyond widening higher educational participation.

## Reflexivity as critical research practice

Reflexivity involves acknowledging the '"world-making", constructive quality of research' (Usher, 1997: 36).

> It is in a sense to *research* the research, to bend the research back on itself, to ask by what practices, strategies and devices is world-making achieved? By asking this question, the research act is made self-referential or *reflexive.*
>
> (Usher, 1997, original emphasis)

Reflexivity requires that we examine how our values insert themselves in the social processes of conducting research (Lather, 1991: 80). Reflexive researchers reject universalized claims to knowledge, challenging epistemological frameworks that forbid and reject knowledge emerging from the personal and emotional realm of human life (Ellsworth, 1992). Feminist post-structuralists (e.g. Flax, 1995; Kenway, 1995; Luke and Gore, 1992) have argued that knowledge construction and meaning-making is a gendered process that is ongoing and is always changing and fluid. Knowledge is eternally incomplete, because we are unable to fully access the unconscious, and to separate ourselves from our subjective views of the world (Ellsworth, 1997). Values, culture and social positioning are not dynamics that can be 'removed' or isolated when convenient to the researcher; rather, the researcher (and teachers and learners) are always entrenched in the historical, geographical, political, personal, emotional, economic, psychological and social dynamics of the moment, shaping their interpretations, perceptions and ways of seeing, hearing and knowing. These dynamics cannot be fully known, as they are never fully visible or audible to us.

'Hearing' and 'representing' are thus key concepts for the researcher to examine and interrogate, including how participants are 'heard', for example, in an interview situation, how this is transformed into a textual form of transcript, how bits of the transcript are then selected, included or discarded, and finally how research participants' stories and identities are re/presented in the written and spoken text. To exclude such examinations while claiming objectivity is to deny the existence of unequal power relations within the research process, while ignoring the central role of the researcher in shaping the research design, process and relations and in producing the final text. A researcher who practises reflexivity in the field, during their analysis of data and in writing the research will address these issues and the dilemmas that they raise for participants through reflexive practices, placing ethics at the heart of research process.

Furthermore, research that is largely descriptive and that fails to examine issues of power and representation is likely to reinforce dominant, problematic, exclusive and common sense assumptions about higher education and the subjects of WP policies (including students, staff and institutions). This is because of its lack of critical attention to the underpinning assumptions and truth claims being made. Descriptive, unreflexive research is thus limited in its contribution to methodological and theoretical debates about higher education inequalities, including what and how we can 'know' about HE, who can claim to know and who is the object and subject of knowing. A reflexive researcher pays close attention to their epistemological and ontological positioning(s) and perspectives and the complex and fluid power relations at play throughout the research process. The researcher considers how these positionings and perspectives shape the research design, data collection and analysis and the ways that knowledge is produced in and through the research. For example, detailed attention is given to the development of a theoretical framework that supports the researcher in moving from a descriptive interpretation of the data collected to a critical analysis that uncovers the problematic assumptions and discourses in narratives and accounts of higher education institutions and people's experiences and practices within it. Complex issues of ethics and power are brought to the centre of attention in the processes of meaning-making and knowledge claims. For example, issues of author/ity are foregrounded rather than hidden, through the explicit consideration of the values, experiences and knowledge that the researcher brings, rather than hiding the voice of the author through the use of the third person or passive voice, a dominant convention of social science research.

## Problematizing reflexivity in critical research practice

However, critical and feminist researchers have also brought to attention the problematic nature of reflexivity, which also needs careful consideration. This raises questions about the use of reflexivity to author/ize the self. Lisa Adkins argues that some versions of reflexivity ironically 'allow only certain subjects to speak' (Adkins, 2004: 332). Although reflexivity is often seen to make visible the relations between the researcher and participant, thus revealing 'normatively constituted speaking positions', Adkins argues that 'reflexivity privileges a particular relation between knower and known even as it ostensibly appears to challenge – indeed undo – such forms of privileging' (Adkins, 2004).

Beverley Skeggs makes an important distinction between different approaches to reflexivity, on the one hand drawing on reflexivity as a cultural resource to authorize the self, and on the other *doing* research reflexively (Skeggs, 2002). In the former, reflexivity becomes a 'property of the researcher's self *not* of the practice of the participants' (Skeggs, 2002: 359). Furthermore, those 'others' who are excluded from selfhood 'become the object (often objectified) by those who have access to the subject positions of researcher/writer which they use to constitute themselves as interlocutors' (Skeggs, 2002: 357). Skeggs argues that the 'ability to be reflexive via the experience of others is a privilege, a position of mobility and power, a mobilization of cultural resources' (Skeggs, 2002: 361). The latter, which focuses on reflexivity as practice, aims to be challenging and disruptive to existing power relations (Skeggs, 2002: 367). Reflexivity is a practice:

> that understands the relations of production, that is aware of the possibilities for appropriation, that knows about the constraints of disciplinary techniques and the power relations of location and position, and that does not reify and reproduce the categorizations that enable exploitation and symbolic violence.
>
> (Skeggs, 2002: 363)

Mauthner and Doucet (2003) argue that not enough attention has been paid to the actual methods of reflexivity, which would support researchers in developing ethical practices of reflexivity. They usefully suggest key questions that the researcher might ask of herself to guide the reflexive process. These include:

- Is the subject's voice one that can be rendered transparent or is it viewed as an interactive resource between different research subjects?
- Is the subject's account regarded as meaningful only in the particular research context in which it was produced?
- Is the subject viewed as data to be discovered or, alternatively, as constructed?

Such questions support the reflexive researcher in critical practices that aim to draw on the resources available to the researcher to expose the insidious ways that some subjects are misrecognized and pathologized through hegemonic, regulative and normalizing discourses. The reflexive researcher should utilize her access to the 'explanations and interpretations that do offer some epistemological authority, but this need not contradict the moral equality between researcher and participant' (Skeggs, 2002: 363). Skeggs suggests that rather than asking the question of whether those seen as marginalized can speak, researchers should be asking if they can hear (Skeggs, 2002: 369). She reminds researchers that 'telling has always been moral' and reflexivity requires accountability and responsibility in research, not self-formation and self-promotion (Skeggs, 2002: 369).

## Narrative research approaches

In Chapter Three, I highlighted narrative as an important conceptual framework for understanding the ways in which people produce accounts of and make sense of identity, subjectivity and notions of self. In this section, I want to build on that discussion to consider the value of narrative methodologies for researching higher educational access and participation, pushing researchers and practitioners beyond the hegemonic discourses of WP to collaborative methodologies and praxis for widening participation.

As outlined in Chapter Three, narrative serves as an 'interpretive device', which is drawn on by people in processes of self-representation (Lawler, 2002: 242). Narratives are not simply 'transparent carriers of experience' but are social products created within specific social, cultural and historical locations (Lawler, 2002). Importantly, narratives do not originate with the individual but are part of a wider set of cultural resources that individuals draw on to produce their own stories and to make sense of their experiences and social locations (Lawler, 2002). Furthermore, Lawler (2002) points out that the 'social world is itself storied'. The concerns raised by critical approaches to social research make narrative methodologies particularly compelling in recent years. These include increasing interest in the ways that texts, both written and spoken, produce what we count as social reality, and the need to then interrogate texts, as well as to critique the problematic notion of the individual, self-contained, coherent self. This has led to the critique in social research of conventional binaries such as structure and agency, individual and society, self and other (Stanley and Morgan, 1993 cited in Lawler, 2002: 245). In order to explain the processes of narrative construction and deconstruction, Lawler draws on the work of Paul Ricoeur, who understands narrative as a 'category by which people make an identity' (Lawler 2002: 245). Narrative includes the components of transformation, plot line and characters but these are brought together through a process of 'emplotment', or 'a synthesis of heterogeneous elements' (Ricoeur, 1991: 21 quoted in Lawler, 2002: 245). Ricoeur poses three forms of synthesis at play in processes of emplotment, which include the synthesis between: (1) many events and one story; (2) discordance and concordance; and (3) two different senses of time (Ricoeur, 1991 quoted in Lawler, 2002). The point is that emplotment turns disparate events into 'episodes' and 'even if the events seem unrelated they will be brought together through an overall coherence of the plot' (Ricoeur, 1991 quoted in Lawler, 2002: 245–46). This process makes the episodes that constitute the plot seem inevitable, so that a narrative must have a point. The significance of events is 'rooted in personal and social histories' and 'in what gets to count, socially, as significant' (Ricoeur, 1991 quoted in Lawler, 2002: 246).

Over the past decade and a half in the UK context, during the period of the New Labour Government, particular stories of widening participation have been in circulation, which have drawn from, but also contributed to the formation of WP policy and practice. This has created certain understandings of widening participation, which has also shaped the possibilities for the formation of higher education identities and subjectivities. The ways that certain selves are recognized, or not, as targets of WP policy is part of the social narrative of widening participation and, more broadly, higher education in the early twenty-first century. Although narratives of WP have produced particular meanings and subjectivities nationally, these are produced in relation to wider globalized narratives. The narratives of higher education, and who has the right to be a university student, are produced at multiple levels, which are interconnected: institutional, local, regional, national and international. A critical researcher drawing on narrative methodologies will focus on uncovering the processes by which particular narratives of WP are produced and the effect of this on WP policy, practice and identity formation across different contexts and fields.

Narrative approaches help the researcher to uncover the processes by which certain stories are privileged in policy and practice and the complex ways by which such stories become narratives of the self. In my own narrative of accessing higher education for example (see Chapter Three), I highlight key elements of social narratives of WP in the UK context, including the story of survival against the odds, individual tenacity and determination, ability to decode the practices of higher education through previous experience and knowledge and the importance of mentors and networks. The different episodes of my personal narrative: classical ballet training as a positive foundation, surviving domestic violence, discovering feminism, and benefitting from the mentorship of those more experienced than me – all of these episodes come together to provide the inevitable and significant plot of my story: becoming recognized as a university student. Narrative approaches help to highlight the ways that we create meaningful stories about ourselves, our relationships with others and the social world. Such approaches are connected to concerns about understanding the ways that knowledge is situated in personal experiences and social contexts and is tied to complex subjectivities. Concerns about the auto/biographical and subjective are thus central to such methodological approaches.

## Auto/biographical research: exploring the authorial voice

> Whenever I have tried to carry out a piece of theoretical work it has been on the basis of my own experience, always in relation to processes that I saw as taking place around me. It is because I thought I could recognize in the things I saw, in the institutions with which I dealt, in my relations with others, cracks, silent shocks, malfunctionings ... that I undertook a particular piece of work, a few fragments of autobiography.
>
> (Foucault, 1988: 156)

As Diane Reay argues, all research is either autobiographical or the avoidance of autobiography (Reay, 1998: 2). People usually do social or educational research because they are interested in exploring or examining an issue in more depth. It is rare that a researcher will have no sense of interest in the area that she or he is investigating or that the researcher does not believe that the research focus is of some greater importance, beyond their personal interest. Furthermore, researchers always bring to their research their experiences, values and perspectives, even if this is the value to do research in a 'neutral' or 'objective' way. Whether the researcher formulates a hypothesis or a set of research questions, the researcher's values, perspectives and understandings – about the research focus and about knowledge itself – shape this.

> It is my contention that researchers conduct research in order to resolve the tension between what we know, and what we don't know. Research therefore primarily reflects our 'self' – our questions and our need to explore phenomena and find answers – and only secondarily, research attempts to find answers to broader social questions, and the questions of others. The science of research, and particularly qualitative research, is therefore not an objective process. It is a personal process.
>
> (Bell, 2003: 172)

Such concerns about the nature of the researcher, and the experiences and identities she or he brings to the research, are accentuated when the focus is on issues of educational access and participation, which must in some way tackle questions of under and/or misrepresentation, exclusion and inequality, whether from a quantitative or a qualitative approach. Research that is about educational equalities must pay close attention to the workings of power through and in research at all stages of the process: the proposal and submission to a funding body, the processes of accessing the field and research subjects or participants, the ethical issues involved throughout the life of the research, the research design, the methods of data collection and analysis, and the production and dissemination of knowledge.

Jane Miller's concept of the 'autobiography of the question' emphasizes the researcher's relationship to the questions she's exploring, requires careful consideration of the experiences, identities and perspectives she brings to the research process and asks her to make connections between herself, the research participants and other voices in the field. The autobiography of the question helps the researcher examine the questions, knowledge and experience she brings to a particular research focus. As such, it supports practices of reflexivity, which are concerned to locate the researcher in wider social relations of power and inequality, and engage her in critical processes of interrogation, with a strong level of sensitivity to inequalities and misrecognitions. However, such processes are always constructed as both personal and social, moving beyond individualist concepts of 'reflection' and 'being critical' to making sense of how the 'personal is the political'. This helps the researcher to consider her sense of self as relational, to acknowledge and pay close attention to complex power relations and to consider identity formations across intersecting and embodied sets of difference. Miller (Miller, 1997: 4) explains that the autobiography of the question, will involve the researcher in:

> beginning with the story of [her] own interest in the question [she] is asking and planning to research into. From that initial story she may

move towards the mapping of her developing sense of the question's interest for [her] onto the history of more public kinds of attention to it. This becomes a way of historicising the questions [she is] addressing and of setting [her] life and educational history within contexts more capacious than [her] own. Theory becomes theories; historically contrived to address or explain particular questions; and we are all theorists.

(Miller, 1997 quoted in Burke, 2002: 5)

This concept highlights that research is not only autobiographical but also biographical in that the researcher is not just an individual asking questions that arise out of her own life experiences but is socially connected to wider social and cultural histories, questions, debates and discourses that will have in turn impacted on the ways she (and others) constructs her research interests and questions. Researchers must always map their questions in relation to those of others in the connected fields of study, relating their understanding and claims to other 'voices'. Furthermore, the representation of these questions and concerns will be open to the reinterpretation of the reader and in this way research is a deeply dialogic process.

However, these connections between the personal and methodological are not always made explicit in research. Indeed, hegemonic academic and research conventions often work to obscure the position of the researcher and the values and perspectives she brings to the arguments and the claims she makes for her research. Miller's concept invites educational researchers to critically reflect on their experiences, values and identities, to understand what brought them to ask certain research questions and then to do the work of critically connecting these to wider literatures, theories and debates. The notion of the objective, neutral and detached researcher is deeply challenged by this concept, requiring the researcher to develop a reflexive orientation to her work and to the research process. Ethical concerns are seen as ongoing issues and challenges, embedded in the research relationships and processes. Issues of author/ity are central, so that the author of the research must interrogate writing practices and methodologies as a key concern in developing her research and understanding and its relation to other connected fields.

## Writing methodologies: ontology and knowledge production

Writing is deeply enmeshed in wider power relations that subtly construct the 'author' in classed, gendered and racialized ways. Writing is relational; authorial subjects are constructed around notions of 'voice', which are located in wider politics of identity and knowledge. Writers are socially situated subjects and the meanings they produce through their writing are constituted through the contested and multiple discourses at play in different social fields. This raises important epistemological and ontological questions about the processes of writing research.

Often, writing is seen as a research activity, which takes place at the later stages of the research process, when the researcher 'writes up' the 'findings' in the final report. In this perspective of writing, the research findings are seen to be reflected in the writing, in a rather straightforward way. Language is seen as reflective of a truth or reality, rather than discursive, contextual and open to different and contested interpretations or meanings. Writing is seen primarily as a tool of communication, in which the researcher reports the main findings of a study in a highly formal, rational and objective format. By writing in the third person, the researcher is seen to present the research in an unbiased, neutral and apolitical way, taking out any remnants of her personal experiences, values, identities and opinions. Such a perspective reflects the conventions of positivist methodological frameworks, in which the researcher must take a distanced and objective position to the research and the final reporting process. As far as possible, the author is 'written out' of the text.

Critical sociologists, ethnographers, feminist scholars and qualitative researchers, amongst others, have extensively critiqued such perspectives of writing, language and research. Writing, rather than a technique of telling, is conceptualized as a social practice and tied to different methodological perspectives. The ontological perspectives of the writer in this view matter, whether or not the author writes in the first or third person. The author always brings to the writing process, whether explicitly or not, her or his experiences and values, which shape the decisions she makes about the ways she positions herself in the text. For example, the decision to write in the third person might be a strategy of textual positioning that brings a sense of authority and power to the writer's voice. By writing herself out of the text, the claims being made appear to be 'more objective' perhaps than if she used the first person.

Some feminist scholars have argued that hegemonic knowledge within academia is oriented towards those qualities associated with masculinity, and operates around traditional binaries that privilege the masculine over the feminine (e.g. Alcoff and Potter, 1993; Morley, 1999; Anderson and Williams, 2001; Currie, *et al.*, 2002). Knowledge that is legitimized by universities is often constructed as large-scale, attached to quantitative methods, objective and value-free (Morley, 1999; Quinn, 2003; Burke and Jackson, 2007). It is often characterized as detached from the personal and political, although feminist theorists have argued that knowledge is always situated and tied to wider power relations that are classed, gendered and racialized (e.g. Collins, 1990; Lather, 1991). The production of knowledge therefore operates in the interests of certain groups over others. In a feminist framework, who the knower is, the ontological politics of meaning-making, are as important as epistemological questions about what counts as knowledge (Haraway, 1988; Collins, 1990; Stanley, 1992; Harding, 1993; Stanley and Wise, 1993). Such questions and arguments are crucial to research on widening participation because they demand careful attention to taken-for-granted research practices that might serve the interests of some social groups whilst excluding others.

Research that examines who has the right to higher education, and who does not, must pay close attention to the questions about how knowledge is produced in research, through particular writing practices and who is the subject and object of such practices.

## Towards a transformatory research praxis

A transformatory research praxis places at the centre of concern the dialogical relationship between theory and practice. As Lather explains, the 'requirements of praxis are theory both relevant to the world and nurtured by actions in it; theory that emerges from "practical political grounding"' (1991: 11–12). The concept of praxis is crucial in moving beyond instrumentalist discourses of widening participation because it demands that practice is shaped by a strong theoretical framework that offers the analytical resources for the project of disrupting deeply entrenched inequalities in higher education. Simultaneously, it requires that the researcher subjects her theoretical perspectives to interrogation by engaging closely with practitioner-oriented knowledge and understanding.

Praxis demands that explicit connections are thus made between research and practice, including deeper-level engagement with theoretical and conceptual perspectives, and tools that help illuminate complex operations of inequality in higher education. In this framework, widening participation is understood in relation to the practices and histories of inequality and misrepresentation. Research praxis aims to create challenging, imaginative and creative spaces for researchers and practitioners to work together to critically reflect on, interrogate and further develop their work. This poses the urgency of creating spaces of dialogue to inspire the methodological and pedagogical imagination in ways that explicitly challenge inequalities, misrecognitions and exclusions.

A transformatory approach demands methodological approaches that are able to address issues of inclusion and exclusion within the overall design of research, aiming to develop opportunities for research praxis. Furthermore, research must be accessible to a wide audience, including scholars in the field, but also those who are committed to developing transformative practices of, and for, widening participation. There is an extensive body of critical, feminist and post-structural research and literature that illuminates and exposes the complex ways in which inequalities in education are produced and reproduced through our everyday practices (e.g. Apple, 1986, 2006; Burke and Jackson, 2007; Crozier and Davies, 2007; Crozier and Reay, 2008; Ellsworth, 1992; Mirza, 2009; Reay, 2001; Reay and Ball, 1997; Reay *et al.*, 2001; Skeggs, 1997; Torres, 1998, 2009; Torres and Rhoads, 2006; Youdell, 2006). Importantly, this body of work shows that the reproduction of inequalities is not always intended or explicit. The processes and practices by which educational inequalities are reproduced are often subtle, insidious and unwitting (Burke and McManus, 2009). Ironically, the body of work on educational inequalities is often written in obscure and exclusive ways that demand a specialist theoretical knowledge in order to decode the arguments and points being made. This is highly problematic as this body of work offers crucial knowledge and explanations but, due to the academic frameworks in which researchers write, publish and disseminate their work, this is often unavailable to those who could draw on it to make a difference to higher education practices and cultures. A transformatory research praxis requires that such theoretical work should be accessible to practitioners, policy-makers, leaders and managers, as well as academics and scholars in the field.

My key argument is that there is no way to challenge deep-rooted inequalities without engaging with the critical theoretical literature on educational inequalities that offers sophisticated ways of understanding issues of access, participation and inequality in higher education. This includes both sociological work that uncovers the patterns of inequality and under-representation at stake, but also research that digs beneath those patterns to explore questions of why and how they come into being and might be disrupted. This requires questioning inequalities in terms of both redistribution and recognition. Critical, feminist and post-structural theories offer a way to deconstruct how the 'right' to higher education is denied to certain subjects on the basis of their perceived lack – for example lack of the 'right' attributes, characteristics, potential, ability, aspiration and motivation. The ways that the right to higher education is constructed in policy and practice has huge implications for inclusion, access and participation. Those with a particular responsibility for widening participation in their institutions, and indeed all working in higher education, need to have access to the theoretical, methodological and conceptual tools and resources available through research that enable the complexity of the problems and issues related to inclusion, exclusion, inequality and mis/recognition to be exposed at the social, economic, cultural, subjective and discursive levels. Indeed, it is important for all higher education staff to understand their own relationship to the operations of exclusion and inclusion. Research must therefore play a key role in supporting staff through an ongoing process of critical reflexivity and research praxis. Indeed, these principles underpin this book and my approaches to writing it.

For these reasons, I am a strong supporter of practitioner-research, as well as academic research, and also opportunities for collaborative research that engages academics, practitioners, policy-makers and students together through the research design and process. A transformatory research praxis provides a framework for the consideration of research designs that include carefully considered methodological approaches that are sensitive to issues of power in the research process, re/presentation and voice, and processes of inclusion, exclusion, inequality, social positioning, identity formation and mis/recognition. This necessitates that anyone conducting research on inequalities in higher education has access both to the critical theoretical resources and to the range of methods and methodologies available to them. Indeed, researchers conducting work on educational access, participation and in/equality must have a firm understanding of the difference between methods, which are simply tools of enquiry, and methodology, which are the ways in which researchers use those tools. In the English policy context, the widening participation agenda has included the capacity to provide funding to practitioner-researchers, but often without providing any grounding in research training and/or research collaboration that would offer them access to the methodological resources that would strengthen their work and contribution to the field. In my own research experience, I have benefitted enormously from working with WP practitioners and I believe that I have in turn offered to those colleagues access to some of the theoretical tools that have helped us to produce research that has a valuable contribution to make (see for example Burke and McManus, 2009 and Burke and Hayton, 2011).

Collaborative research praxis points attention to a range of tensions that researchers must grapple with. One tension is related to the value placed on academic, peer-reviewed journals in the assessment of research quality. For example, in the English Research Excellence Framework (REF), it is not anticipated that publications in professional journals will be recognized, and this creates the desire to publish only in the highest-esteemed, peer-reviewed academic journals. This encourages research to be written in highly academic (often obscure) ways that might be less accessible to audiences outside a scholarly community and tends to set up an opposition between academic and practitioner forms of research. This creates difficulties for developing the kinds of dialogue and collaboration across theory, policy and practice that a transformatory research praxis calls for.

There are ways around this, however, including: (1) collaborative research with teams that have academics, policy-makers and/or practitioners with multiple dissemination strategies; and (2) creating professional development programmes that make the research and theoretical literature available and accessible to policy-makers and practitioners. Other strategies might include: (3) the organization of forums, seminars, conferences, continuing professional development and accredited courses; (4) embedded mentoring and coaching programmes; and (5) informal and formal discussion groups, committees and working groups – all of which address the important relationship between research and developing inclusive and equitable practices. Such strategies would be designed to create spaces of critical dialogues across research, theory, leadership, policy development and practice.

## Final reflections

In this chapter I have argued that moving beyond hegemonic discourses of widening participation requires research methodologies that have the capacity to address complex relations of power, subjectivity and inequality. Such methodologies must draw on epistemological frameworks that acknowledge the situated and contextual nature of knowledge and its intimate ties to power and authority. Indeed, in such frameworks power is seen as central to processes of meaning-making about higher educational access and participation. Research that draws on critical and feminist methodologies aims to disrupt the normalizing and pathologizing gaze of social science research and policy, in order to 'empower' those who have been historically misrecognized. However, just as importantly, such research frameworks also expose the problematic assumptions of discourses of 'empowerment', conceptualizing power as fluid, dynamic, unpredictable and generative, rather than fixed across stable binary divisions. Thus, the narratives, in social science research and policy, of 'dis/empowerment' and 'dis/advantage' are disrupted and reframed to consider the transformative possibilities of different ways of being and doing within educational sites. Research is seen not only as a mechanism for understanding the structures, processes and practices that create opportunities for, and barriers to, access and participation, but also as a way to open up our sociological and methodological imaginations to other ways of thinking about higher education, and who has the right to it.

I have argued for the power of reflexivity and praxis in methodologies that work towards transformative possibilities. Reflexivity is a powerful methodological tool that places ethics at the heart of research practice, and that demands that researchers interrogate the values, assumptions and perspectives that they bring to meaning-making processes. Praxis emphasizes the crucial relationship between theory and practice, and argues for research that is collaborative and designed to create critical spaces of dialogue. The aim is to bring together theory-oriented and practitioner-oriented forms of knowledge so that research is shaped by practice, and practice is shaped by research. Praxis demands that researchers and practitioners critically interrogate the meanings that they bring to the research process, so that reflexivity and praxis are integrated practices.

Processes of writing within such methodological frameworks are understood as contributing to meaning-making, rather than being a simple reflection of 'findings' through detached and objective methods. The decisions that writers make about how to present their research and understanding to an audience, and who that audience might be, are key in processes of shaping the truth-claims made about higher educational access and participation. Ways of writing might serve to exclude certain subjects and knowledge, and thus form and content are seen as inseparable in such perspectives of writing. Writing is understood to be tied to struggles over claims to author/ity. Notions of voice are located in a wider politics of identity, recognition and meaning-making. Authors are socially situated subjects and the meanings they produce through their writing are constituted through the contested and multiple discourses and narratives at play in different social fields. Such arguments are central to concerns about issues of access, both in terms of accessing different forms of knowledge, some which are given greater social value and legitimacy than others, and in terms of accessing the processes by which a subject might be recognized as an author, as having authority within the field of higher education. Thus redistribution (of the resources available to participate in research on widening participation, for example) and recognition (processes of being recognized as a legitimate researcher and author, for example) must both be at the heart of such processes.

I have presented these methodological arguments in the context of a concern to contribute to the production of a body research that deepens theoretical understanding of the complex ways that inequalities might be reproduced and disrupted in higher education, and that makes certain methodological debates accessible to all those who are committed to widening participation and to research for transformation. In the next chapter, I will discuss the methodological frameworks of the research that I have drawn on in this book and the methodological issues that I have considered in writing this book.

# 5 Researching widening participation

This chapter will outline the methodological framework for the book, discussing the approaches taken to collect and analyze data, the ethical dimensions, the epistemological underpinnings, as well as the writing practices adopted. The book will draw on three of my current and recent research projects, an Economic and Social Research Council-funded project on men accessing higher education, a Higher Education Academy-funded project on transitions to Masters-level study and a qualitative study of admissions practices to art and design undergraduate courses funded by the National Arts Learning Network (NALN). I will also draw on small-scale new research, involving interviews, journal reflections and email discussions with a group of widening participation managers and practitioners across England (funded by a Higher Education Academy National Teaching Fellowship Award).

The different sets of data will provide insight into both student experiences and the perspectives and difficulties faced by an emerging professional body created by a national policy commitment to widening participation. The data will be drawn on to illuminate the conceptual and theoretical themes framing the book but will also be used to stimulate reflection and to create a more interactive format to the text. This chapter will pick up on the themes outlined in the previous chapter in relation to the methodological and ethical implications of researching widening participation in the context of 'real research' conducted for this book. This will offer concrete examples of some of the issues and dilemmas researchers face when attempting to shed light on a complex social and cultural set of issues, which circulate around a specific educational policy and social justice agenda.

## Men accessing higher education

This project was inspired by my experiences of raising three sons and observing the different ways in which their gendered identities and negotiations profoundly affected their educational experiences and aspirations as learners. Before this project, I had focused primarily on the dynamics of gender and educational access in terms of women's experiences (see e.g. Burke, 2002, 2004) and I began to have a sense of dissatisfaction with my level of engagement with gender across different formations of masculinity and femininity. I strongly felt as a researcher that I could not understand gender in great depth unless I engaged with the ways that both masculinities and femininities are constructed in relation to educational aspirations, access and participation. Furthermore, I felt increasingly frustrated in meetings I attended about access to higher education by the assumption being made repeatedly that women were no longer of concern as a group. I wanted to find a set of intellectual arguments to address the increasing desire to focus on men as a group, often disregarding the needs of women students. It occurred to me that I could not do this satisfactorily unless I studied men's experiences as well as women's, and developed a stronger handle of gender across femininities and masculinities. In Chapter Six, I draw on the data from my Economic and Social Research Council-funded research on men returning to study, which aims to understand the ways that gendered identities shape and impact on men's experiences of access courses and their educational aspirations.

As women's participation in higher education has dramatically improved, there has been a growing concern about men's participation rates. A recent report claims that men are now educationally disadvantaged and that this could have far-ranging implications for men's future social position (HEPI, 2009). Feminist scholars have pointed out that, after centuries of exclusion from higher education, it is striking that, as soon as women demonstrate achievement, there is a strong political outcry that refocuses the agenda on the needs of men. This oversimplifies the complexities of inequalities in higher education, posing women's recent achievement in simplistic terms of a battle of the sexes. The report by the Higher Education Policy Institute in England focuses on GCSEs as the primary site of 'men's disadvantage', whilst research on gender and education has revealed that privileged constructions of masculinity might cause (some) boys and men difficulties in developing student dispositions. From an international perspective, it has also been pointed out that:

> Although in many countries women are now in the majority at first degree level, they are not in all, and in some countries the proportion of women has declined since the 1990's – a pattern that has occurred historically at different times in different places.
>
> (Leathwood and Read, 2009: 46)

The claims being made about women's rising position in higher education (HE) have emphasized particular statistics, whilst ignoring complex gendered patterns within universities, including important intersections with age, class, dis/ability, ethnicity, race and sexuality. A recent report by the Equality Challenge Unit in the UK has in large bold text '41.6 per cent male, 58.4 per cent female' on the cover of its report (ECU, 2008). This sets alarm bells ringing about a growing gender gap in higher education, in which women are seen to be doing far better than men. Yet, the breakdown of the statistics in the body of the report shows a far more complex picture. For example, subjects continue to

be gendered, with science, engineering and technology subjects being constituted of a predominately male student body and women making up the
majority of the student body in subjects allied to medicine and education.
This becomes increasingly significant, as it is the (male-dominated) science,
technology, engineering and mathematics (STEM) subjects that are being
protected from the current cuts to funding in higher education. The gender-
ing of subject choices revealed in the ECU report is confirmed by wider literature. For example, on a global scale, women represent less than a quarter of
students on average in engineering, manufacturing and construction and only
about a third of students in agriculture and science (UNESCO, 2008 cited in
Leathwood and Read, 2009). Of all female undergraduates, 35.9 per cent study
part-time, compared with 28.7 per cent of male undergraduates, according to
the ECU report (2008). The gendered constitution of academic staff exposes
further complexities in relation to the men-in-crisis discourse. Although women
make up 42.3 per cent of academic staff, only 17.5 per cent of heads of department
and professors are women. A total of 41.8 per cent of women work part-time,
compared with 26.9 per cent of men and, of academics earning over £50,000,
21.6 per cent are women and 78.4 per cent are men (ECU, 2008: 2–4).

Over the past decade, feminist scholars have extensively critiqued mainstream
explanations of boys' underachievement at school, which tend to pose boys
and girls as in competition and opposition through the narrative of a 'crisis of
masculinity'. Epstein *et al.* (1998) identify three main perspectives running
through the crisis-of-masculinity narrative. The 'poor boys' perspective constructs
boys as victims of the education system, due to the perceived feminization of
education and schooling. This perspective best characterizes the position
taken by HEPI in its recent report (HEPI, 2009). The 'failing schools failing
boys' perspective blames poor and ineffective school management for boys'
underachievement. The 'boys will be boys' perspective constructs boys as
biologically less disposed to studying than girls, although maintaining boys'
natural intellectual ability (Epstein *et al.*, 1998). Frosh, Phoenix and Pattman
explain that, by the late 1990's, boys' underachievement was largely understood
in terms of a lack of positive male role models in schools, boys' problematic
behaviour in classrooms, and the impact of feminism (Frosh *et al.*, 2002). The
recent attention to men's 'under-representation' in HE builds on such
assumptions and dangerously recasts a battle of the sexes. This not only
undermines the importance of girls' and women's achievements in recent
years, which should be celebrated, but implies that women's success must
be read as a direct threat to men's social position and status. This ignores
the important, rigorous and sophisticated analyses contributed by feminist
scholars to deconstructing gendered discourses, subjectivities and relations and
to developing a rich and nuanced understanding of the discursive constitution of
masculinities within educational sites and the effect of this on boys' schooling.

Questions raised by feminist scholars draw attention to the interconnections
between masculinity and other formations of subjectivity, which profoundly
shape their dispositions to learning (Archer, 2003). The tensions exposed by

feminist research between some formations of masculinity and school culture raise 'questions about the possibilities of bringing together white working-class masculinities with educational success in inner-city working-class schooling' (Reay, 2002: 221–22). Such questions shift the focus away from damaging constructions of a sex war and towards the important development of sophisticated levels of analysis that will shed light on boys' and men's complex relationship to education and learning. A central question of the ESRC study that I draw on in this book is: How do men construct and make sense of their masculine subjectivities in relation to their aspirations to become HE students?

Five case study institutions, providing Access to HE and Foundation programmes, were selected across London. These programmes offer an alternative entry route into higher education for those students who have not gained traditional qualifications. All the men categorized as 'home' students and participating in access programmes at the case study institutions were invited to take part in the study. Of these, 39 men agreed to participate in in-depth individual interviews, followed by small group interviews, designed to elicit data about the men's journeys through education, from their earliest memories of schooling to their present experiences of their access courses. The interviews focused on the men's relationships, significant memories and turning points, their aspirations and decision-making processes and their sensibilities and experiences as students. The analysis explored the relationship between the formation of masculine subjectivities, which was shifting across space and time, and men's dispositions and aspirations as students. My analytical approach treats the men's accounts as part of the broader transformations of the self, linked to difference, and the shifting interplay of history, culture and power. The explorations of the men's memories of their school experiences were not an attempt to simply recover the past, but to develop accounts that allow an examination of 'the different ways we are positioned by, and position ourselves within, the narratives of the past' (Hall, 2000: 222).

Two research officers, Soile Pietikainen and Tom Wooden, conducted most of the fieldwork, although I also conducted some of the interviews. Two of us are women, white and positioned as middle-class, which raises particular questions about the significance of the research relations in constructing the interview accounts. It further raises issues about the analytical perspectives I have imposed on the data in this book, although this is also shaped by the specific theoretical frameworks I drew on, both to formulate my research questions (thus framing the interview accounts) and to make sense of the data. The data then are not analysed as reflecting an objective reality but as discursive and partial accounts of the men's memories and experiences, which are produced in the specific situation of an interview. My own subjectivities and autobiographies are important in multiple ways, not only in shaping my analysis, but also in why I came to this research in the first place. My research analysis has been shaped by my personal struggles for inclusion and recognition as a viable student-subject, as an 'Access student', as well as my experiences of migration and of mothering three sons.

Although all the men taking part in the study were categorized as 'home' students, they represented over 20 different countries, with migratory experiences emerging as a key theme. The men's ages ranged from 18 to 54 and their socio-economic backgrounds were fluid and changing as they moved across different national and cultural spaces.

I worked with my research team to formulate conceptualized levels of interpretation that made links with the critical sociological literature and a feminist post-structuralist analytical framework to address the key research questions, which included:

- What are the processes that lead men, who have previously dropped out of education, to return to education?
- What forms of masculinities are privileged inside educational institutions and how does this impact on the men's identities as learners and participants in educational processes?
- How do different and competing formations of masculinity shape, facilitate and/or constrain educational participation and experiences?
- What do the life stories of the participants reveal about the interconnections between masculinities, educational participation, institutional practices and policy discourses of widening participation?

As a research team, we carefully considered the sensitivity of the focus on life histories and narratives. The men were never encouraged to speak about issues that caused them discomfort or pain. However, some men did disclose abusive and traumatic experiences in the interview. In one instance, following disclosure of major trauma, the emotional well-being of the interviewee was a concern and we therefore referred this young man to an appropriate agency for support.

Other ethical issues raised by the project included questions about power relations in the research; for example what are the power relations at play between a (female, middle-class) researcher and a (male, working-class) participant? Attention to this demonstrated how research relations are shifting and unpredictable; the researcher does not always 'hold' the powerful position in the research, but power is negotiated over, for example over what is said and not said, who 'leads' the interview and then of course finally who analyses and writes up the research. In this way, to a certain extent the researcher firmly holds a position of power in the research process (and most specifically it is the Principal Investigator who holds the greatest power in this sense).

## Art for a few: exclusions and misrecognitions in art and design HE admissions

This book also draws on data from a National Arts Learning Network (NALN)-funded study on admissions to higher education. I conducted the study with my colleague, Jackie McManus, who is the Head of Widening

Participation Programmes at the University of the Arts London. This is an important relationship to highlight, which supports my concern for developing a dialogue between theory and practice. Working with Jackie was one of the most rewarding research experiences I have had because we were able to share our commitment to widening participation from the perspective of both an academic researcher and a WP practitioner.

The aim of the research was to examine admissions practices in the selection of students for art and design courses in five different case study higher education institutions across England. The research took a qualitative approach, designed to uncover the complexity of processes of admission and to deconstruct the key assumptions underpinning the selection of students. A qualitative approach enabled the collection of detailed data of everyday practices and the analysis of the assumptions, values and perspectives that admissions tutors bring to the selection process. The methods included a review of admissions policies, prospectuses and websites and in-depth interviews with admissions tutors about their perspectives of the admissions system and process, as well as observations of actual selection interviews with candidates. We chose to both interview and observe admissions tutors because as Atkinson and Coffey (2002) argue they are 'equally valid ways of capturing shared cultural understandings and enactments of the social world' (Atkinson and Coffey, 2002: 811), rather than because we favoured one method over the other. However, access to observations of actual selection interviews with candidates put us in a highly privileged position as researchers, having access to a social site of decision-making at a crucial moment in access to higher education, which is not ordinarily available to researchers or indeed to anyone outside the interviewers and interviewee(s). We treated this privilege with great care and consideration, understanding the sensitivities of such an approach. Strict confidentiality and anonymity have been maintained throughout the research process, including throughout dissemination of the research.

Out of the nine English institutions invited to take part in the study, five colleges of art and design agreed to participate. Two are in large metropolitan areas, one in a cathedral town, one in a rural area and one in a large town. Three out of the five were 'selecting' rather than 'recruiting' institutions. All of the 'recruiting' institutions readily agreed to participate in the research, whilst all but one of the 'selecting' institutions initially refused, citing overwork, ethical concern for applicants and a need to 'get our house in order first' as reasons for non-participation. One institution declined the invitation to participate because their staff were 'overloaded', but later asked for a copy of the research team's proposal so that an administrative staff member could internally review their admissions processes. We declined on ethical grounds. The one 'selecting' institution that readily agreed to participate did so at the insistence of a senior manager who was concerned that their admissions tutors were *'trying to make everyone middle class'*.

Admissions is clearly a sensitive subject, and confidentiality was crucial to the ethical considerations of this research. We aimed to develop a 'responsible research relationship' with participants (Mauthner *et al.*, 2002), which considered ethical issues and the sensitivities and power relations of the research process. This included an explicit verbal and written research contract with participating admissions tutors, guaranteeing confidentiality for them and their institutions, clearly explaining that the research would be published and that involvement was entirely voluntary. Additionally, admissions tutors were asked to explain the presence of the observer to the interviewees, emphasizing that this person would not be involved in the interview, or decision-making process, and that they would be happy to leave if the interviewee objected to their presence. None of the applicants objected to the researcher's presence, a likely reflection of the (im)balance of power relations.

In total ten members of staff were interviewed and 70 selection interviews were observed. The data were analysed by drawing on the conceptual insights of critical sociological theory, which supports close attention to the complex workings of inequality and misrecognition.

The principal field researcher kept a reflexive research diary detailing her thoughts, feelings and reactions to field work, including the interviews with admissions tutors and the observation of admissions interviews, because:

> To deny our being 'there' misunderstands the inherent qualities of both methods – in terms of documenting and making sense of social worlds of which we are a part … . The complex relationships among field settings, significant social actors, the practical accomplishment of the research, and the researcher-self are increasingly recognised as significant to all those who engage in research of a qualitative nature (whether that be participant observation, interviewing, or some combination of the two).
>
> (Atkinson and Coffey, 2002: 812)

The fieldwork raised particular ethical dilemmas in relation to the positioning and the construction of the researcher, as both the 'detached' observer and 'insider'. At times the researcher was positioned by the admissions tutors as 'one-of us', a colleague who shared the implicit assumptions underpinning the admissions process, and this appeared to often render her invisible in the interview room. This became particularly problematic for the researcher who struggled with reconciling the admissions tutors' recognition of her as a fellow professional, and colleague, with the reflexivity of her own identity (i.e. who she thought she was, and where she positioned herself) and the tutors' mis/recognition of applicants as worthy or un-worthy of a place on a course.

## Facilitating transitions to M-level study

The book draws on semi-structured individual and group interviews with students undertaking Masters-level programmes at two different higher education institutions, as well as their journal reflections of their learning and transition experiences. This is part of a larger research project funded by the

Higher Education Academy and led by Professor David Scott on different forms of transition to Masters-level study in higher education, including transitions for students from traditionally under-represented backgrounds. As part of a larger study, 15 students were interviewed at different points in the academic year and kept reflective journals of their experiences. The data analysis draws on post-structural theories of power, difference and subjectivity to deconstruct the complex workings of inequalities and misrecognitions, which shape students' transitions, experiences and identities. Such perspectives were combined with the body of work that develops an understanding of academic writing as social practice, emphasizing the centrality of methodological concerns in understanding writing practices and students' experiences of these (see Chapter 8). Through my analysis, I argue that an understanding of transitions in relation to widening participation in postgraduate level study must be underpinned by close attention to difference, inequality and power. Such a conceptualization is not only important in developing an appropriate methodological framework for understanding WP but also in making sense of students' transitional experiences of learning and writing in postgraduate-level contexts. I will draw on examples from the research participants' accounts of their transitions to illuminate my points about methodological considerations.

The question of how I conceptualize widening participation in the context of this particular project, and of postgraduate study, has been particularly challenging and has raised some important issues for broader debate. I am part of a large research team for this project and we inevitably bring different and competing perspectives of what we mean when we are referring to WP. For example, some members of the team understand this as needing to focus on students who enter their Masters courses with non-standard qualifications. Although I agree that this is an important aspect of concerns to widen participation, a specific focus on non-standard qualifications seems to me to lose the complexities of the processes of accessing HE, particularly in terms of cultural contexts, power and subjective construction.

This view of WP has led to the recruitment of research participants who do not have standard entry qualifications but might have accessed their courses by virtue of their experience in the field of education. They might have a senior management responsibility, for example, and have decided to study at M-level to develop their professional and theoretical understanding. Importantly, many of the participants in the study (although they might not have a standard undergraduate qualification) have successfully completed a postgraduate certificate in education (PGCE), enabling them to develop a familiarity with postgraduate level education and with the institution itself before embarking on the Masters, and giving them a sense of confidence. For example:

> I'd already studied my PGCE there, so I was aware of some of the systems. And then I just found out about the course. I managed to get through to the course tutor, the course leader, you know, almost immediately, who

clarified anything for me. So it was really quite an easy process, and then I attended the interview and assessment. So it was all quite easy.

(Christine, interview 1)

Interestingly, the research participants with such transitional backgrounds have largely presented a highly confident self in their first interview accounts, where they seem to have quickly mastered the practices of postgraduate study and easily fit in with the community of learning on their course. Their accounts have presented then a transition into M-level study that is constructed as smooth and easy, with key concerns being external to the course – for example, juggling multiple responsibilities and demands. Their accounts are very different from the kinds of accounts emphasized in the body of literature on widening participation, which tends to focus on student experiences just before or during undergraduate-level study. Rather, for these MA students, there appears to be a sense of confidence and belonging, for example:

> Following last weekend's signature pedagogies session, I was so much more confident about delivering this than I would have been previously. What is particularly interesting is the contrast between the theories of teaching and learning studied at level 4 and those at level 7. This class will also be part of my research for Researching & Improving Professional Practice and it was fascinating to observe their engagement with theory relating to signature pedagogies.

(Mary, reflective journal)

Mary presents herself as a confident and competent student, who has experience of value to bring to her learning. She talks about her understanding of theories of teaching and learning in quite confident ways, for example being able to contrast different theories and to observe the engagement of her peers with these theories. This suggests an included and 'masterful' subject positioning in relation to the others on her course.

My own conceptualization of widening participation differs significantly from the one I have described above – I am interested in understanding widening participation in terms of difference and inequality, power relations and complex identity formations. I therefore focus on the implications of being constructed and indeed institutionally classified as a different kind of student throughout the different transitions through higher education – including postgraduate study. For this project, such a conceptualization has led to the recruitment of students with quite different sets of experiences than those above, who tend to present a less confident self because of a keen sense of not fitting in, with an emphasis on the feeling of being different. Such students might or might not have non-standard entry qualifications but have a strong sense of marginalization or exclusion from the community of learning to which they don't necessarily feel they belong. For example:

I thought I'll update you on my trip to the library. As I arrived I was determined to get help so I approached one of the staff at the library counter and explained that I was new and that I had some problem using the library at home. With a big smile the lady directed me to one of the computer desk and asked to follow the instructions. She added that it was straightforward and usually students find it very easy to use and she pointed to some leaflets which were self explanatory (according to her). At that point I felt too shy to express my despair to have more support. So I used the computer, obviously got confused and ended up annoying the student next to me who was more helpful. I am probably 'thick' and computing is definitely not my strength.

(Aisha, reflective journal)

Aisha presents a sense of student subjectivity around themes of exclusion, not understanding the practices of higher education and feeling an outsider. She presents a self in despair and draws on the deficit discourses of widening participation – as the confused, annoying and 'thick' student.

The ways that we conceptualize WP thus have significant implications for the methodological framework of our research and for the kinds of data collected and analysis produced. This also has significant implications for policy and practice. If students from 'non-standard qualifications' appear to have smooth transitions into M-level study, this supports the view that access to postgraduate study is not a major concern for widening participation policy. However, if students from traditionally under-represented groups (who might have standard qualifications) continue to struggle to feel included in the cultures and practices of higher education at postgraduate level, then this suggests widening participation policy must pay close attention to issues of access to, and participation in, postgraduate level study.

One of the ongoing dilemmas of conceptualizing widening participation is the ways that it then constructs students: sometimes reproducing deficit subjectivities and homogenizing students who are constituted as different and as problematic. This tends to exacerbate rather than disrupt inequalities at play in higher education and tends to focus the problem on individual students who are constructed in deficit terms. Yet, it is important to understand widening participation in terms of persistent patterns of inequality, which relate to embodied intersections of social differences of, for example, age, class, ethnicity, race and gender.

## Widening participation practitioners' identities and experiences

During its period in UK government, New Labour made a significant commitment to diversification, expansion and widening participation, in the attempt to address the under-representation of certain social groups in universities (DfES, 2003a; DfES, 2003b; HEFCE, 2006; HEFCE, 2008). This included a considerable investment in resources, including that of human resources and a growing professional body dedicated specifically to WP and related issues of diversity, access and equity in universities. Yet, with this new labour force in higher education, there has been a dearth of research that contributes to understanding the nature of this work, including the constitution of new professional roles and identities and the location of such workers in universities. Without any concrete understanding of the proliferation of this new labour market in higher education it is difficult to ascertain the impact of this work on diversity, difference and social justice in the context of the widening participation policy agenda. It is thus important to develop research to understand the nature of these new and emerging roles and their impact on the different strategies and practices of, and for, WP across the country. This project, undertaken specifically for this book, aims to understand the experiences, perspectives, identities, roles and positions of those working in higher education with a specific responsibility for widening participation. The research aims to address the following research questions:

1. *How different WP leaders and practitioners construct their professional identities.* What is the relationship between the institutional role and the classed, gendered and racialized positioning of the individual? In what ways do WP professionals understand their work and how does this affect the different national and institutional policies and strategies they support and promote? How is this shaped and constrained by national and institutional policy and practice?
2. *How this professional body shapes, reinforces and/or contests hegemonic discourses of WP.* What meanings do WP professionals bring to their work and to the competing discourses of WP? How is this related to the discourses at play in the university and more widely, i.e. in higher education policy and literature? Where do they locate their work institutionally? What do they experience as constraints in making WP possible? What do they experience as the opportunities and achievements in their work? What are the resistances, challenges and counter-hegemonic discourses at play in their accounts of their work?
3. *How to relate the analysis to relevant theoretical literature and to inform WP policy and practice.* In what ways does the body of theory and literature on widening participation help illuminate the key patterns and themes emerging from the data? In what ways might the analysis of the data contribute to refining the systems, structures and strategies being developed to widen participation in higher education?

The research involved in-depth qualitative methodological approaches to explore the experiences, identities, approaches and perspectives of seven WP managers and practitioners. The research aims to contribute a 'fine grained, hermeneutically grounded' study of WP (Prichard and Trowler, 2003: xiv). The WP managers/practitioners were interviewed by my Research Assistant,

Andrew Wilkins, about their backgrounds, their journeys into the role, their experiences of the role, the way they understand their professional identity and how they think others construct and position them in and outside their institution. The interviews were designed to elicit data about participants' sense of professional identity and how this might be connected to wider discourses at play within the institutions in which they work, examining the intricacies of individual experiences (Gerson and Horowitz, 2002: 200). Taking a qualitative approach helps to expose some of the difficulties, limitations and constraints of the current framework around WP, and to open up a dialogue about opportunities to develop and refine strategies to challenge exclusions and inequalities in higher education that are subtle, insidious and complicated (Morley, 2003; Burke and Jackson, 2007).

The analysis of the data aimed to map out key themes and patterns emerging from the data with regard to the practices, roles and backgrounds of participants. The interview data were subjected to a critical, sociological and post-structuralist analysis, to shed light on the conceptual themes of identity, diversity, positioning, authority, status and power (e.g. Anderson and Williams, 2001; Currie *et al.*, 2002; Morley, 2003). A concept of social justice that seeks to address the tensions between a politics of redistribution and a politics of recognition (Fraser, 1997) has been used as a significant analytical tool to make sense of the experiences of, and practices taken up by, WP teams in higher educational institutions in the context of a specific and directive national policy agenda that operates around particular regulatory measures and expectations. Data have been subjected to both data reduction and data complication processes (Coffey and Atkinson, 1996), drawing on a critical and post-structuralist theoretical framework to identify key themes and to conceptualize the data in relation to the research aims and questions. As in Projects One, Two and Three above, examining issues of identity, experience and institutional micropolitics has the potential to be highly sensitive, and so the interests of the participants and attention to the sensitivities of their negotiations within institutional spaces have been prioritized. Chapter Nine of the book draws on the data from this project to explore the professional identities, experiences and practices of WP managers and practitioners.

## Final reflections

In this chapter, I have provided an overview of four of my research projects on widening participation, which will be drawn on in Part Three to explore key issues and bring to life some of the abstract theoretical and methodological points discussed in Parts One and Two of the book. I have drawn on data from my research in this way to show the relationship between theory and practice and to demonstrate the powerful ways that research might illuminate complex inequalities and misrecognitions, which helps us to move beyond instrumentalist, neoliberal and utilitarian discourses of widening participation. My aim in this chapter has also been to build on the discussion presented in

Chapter Four by using the examples of specific research on and for a trans-formatory approach to widening participation. I have tried to illuminate the themes of reflexivity, praxis and ethics raised in Chapter Four through my discussion of the issues raised by specific research encounters, dilemmas and experiences. In the next Part of the book, I will draw on this research to critique key discourses at play in widening participation policy and practice: barriers, fair admissions and raising aspirations. In the final chapter of this Part, I will consider the importance of the identities, perspectives and practices of WP managers and practitioners, in reimagining widening participation.

# Part 3

# Widening participation strategies and practices

This part will focus more specifically on the key strategies and discourses emerging in and shaping policy, making connections to wider global concerns and socio-political contexts. The aim of the section will be to provide a comprehensive critique of the values and perspectives shaping policy and practice and demanding major national investment, leading to the key policy discourses of raising aspirations, fair access and lifting barriers. This part will consider both the opportunities presented by these discourses as well as the problematic assumptions behind them and the ways that each of these might exacerbate rather than challenge complex educational exclusions. The chapters will include the accounts of students, practitioners and managers through data from previous and new research involving interviews with students and practitioners, as well as an analysis of policy texts and speeches made by key policy-makers in the widening participation field. All three chapters will keep in the frame an examination of the implications of changing economic, political and social contexts on policies and practices of widening participation in relation to challenging discourses of difference.

# 6 Raising aspirations

## Challenging discourses of deficit

> Poverty of aspiration is as damaging as poverty of opportunity and it is time to replace a culture of low expectations for too many with a culture of high standards for all.
>
> (Gordon Brown, 31 October 2007)

A central theme of contemporary WP policy is 'raising aspirations', leading to focus on developing activities designed to target those lacking aspiration but with potential to benefit from higher education. The 'raising aspirations' discourse constructs the main problem for widening educational participation as those individuals and communities who fail to recognize the value of participating in higher education. Material poverty and social inequality are reconstructed as poverty and inequality of aspiration (Morley, 2003). This chapter will deconstruct 'raising aspirations' to expose the underlying and problematic assumptions of this hegemonic discourse as well as the opportunities it produces for WP. The chapter will argue that 'raising aspirations' does not pay ample attention to the complex processes of identity formation, which are situated and produced within the discursive fields and practices of schools, colleges and universities. It will examine the interconnections between a subject's aspirations and their social positioning, drawing on data from my ESRC-funded qualitative study of men accessing higher education, to examine the ways that their aspirations are gendered, classed and racialized. I will explore the cultural, economic and political contexts in which certain subjects are constructed, and construct themselves, as having/not having potential or ability or indeed not choosing to participate in higher education for a range of valid reasons (Archer and Leathwood, 2003). In order to illuminate a post-structural reconceptualization of aspiration formation, this chapter draws in particular on the men's accounts of their aspirations to participate in higher education, to illuminate the complexities of aspiration formation.

## Hegemonic discourses of raising aspirations: policy, research and practice

Despite an increasing number of young people entering higher education in England, the participation rates are considered to be low by international standards (OECD, 2005). Furthermore, there is evidence to suggest that young people from certain socio-economic backgrounds are disproportionately less likely to access post-compulsory education (Blanden and Machin, 2004; Machin and Vignoles, 2004). In an effort to encourage more young people from under-represented backgrounds to participate in further education (FE) and higher education (HE), the New Labour Government implemented the Excellence in Cities (EiC) programme in various phrases from September 1999 and the Aimhigher: Excellence Challenge (AHEC) in September 2001 (see DfES, 2006a: ch. 1). The New Labour Government highlighted 'both economic reasons and reasons for social justice' (DfES, 2006a: 3) as incentives for widening participation to FE and HE for 'disadvantaged groups' (or 'non-traditional entrants'). Improving the global economic position of England in the emerging 'new economy' (DfES 2001: 12) appears to be the main driver facilitating polices aimed at widening access to FE and HE. This is despite consistent warnings that 'there has been no correlation between increases in the age-participation ratio and improvements in productivity or GDP growth' (Ryan, 2005: 90). Alongside the economic imperatives shaping these education policies, the New Labour Government identified expanding HE opportunities as a lever for improving employment, productivity and 'narrow[ing] social class gaps in educational achievement' (DfES, 2006a: 4).

These polices reflect attempts by the previous New Labour Government to raise the aspiration of certain young people, particularly 14–19-year-olds, but also to increase opportunities for mature adults and part-time learners. The AHEC programme, for example, incorporated a number of policy strands that centre on raising educational aspirations, achievement and attainment: (1) creating greater links between universities, schools and colleges; (2) increasing funds to HE institutions to assist and facilitate outreach programmes aimed at recruiting disadvantaged young people; (3) providing better information and marketing; (4) providing better financial support, such as bursaries and maintenance grants, to assist poorer students who need help covering university expenses and living costs; and (5) creating an admissions process that is transparent and fair and which minimizes barriers for applicants from poorer backgrounds (DfES, 2006b). Coupled with this has been an emphasis on further parental involvement (DfES, 2005) which the then New Labour Government deemed necessary as part of its programme of support for facilitating young peoples' learning and educational aspirations. The introduction of Parent Support Advisors to schools for example was implemented in an attempt to assist parents and children from disadvantaged backgrounds, with the aim to 'increase parents' confidence and willingness to engage with their child's school and learning' (DfES 2006b: 7). The then New Labour Government also used £900 million in 2005–08 to increase personalized learning in schools as part of its effort to raise educational attainment: a system of teaching and learning that aims to organize 'schooling around the needs, interests and aptitudes of individual pupils' (DfES, 2006b: 23; also see Leadbeater, 2004, 2006). In this way, the New Labour Government's commitment to

widening access to higher education for young people from poorer backgrounds can be traced to a number of key policy initiatives at the level of
compulsory schooling, which have as their key aim raising educational
achievement and attainment as well as educational aspiration more generally.

The New Labour government report, *Aimhigher: Excellence Challenge: A Policy
Evaluation Using the Labour Force Survey* (DfES, 2006a), used data generated
from household survey information to estimate the impact of these initiatives
on the educational outcomes of young persons aged 16 to 20 across various local
education authorities (LEAs). It concludes, rather tentatively, that 'the policy had
a significant positive impact on the participation decisions of those from disadvantaged backgrounds' (DfES, 2006a: 17). The report also concludes that
the policy design of the AHEC programme, with its various strands, does not
lend itself to a straightforward comparison of the impact of AHEC with the
EiC programme that preceded it. In other words, the initiatives outlined
above need to be analyzed in isolation for a fuller, richer and complex picture
to be presented.

Baxter, Tate and Hatt (2007) draw on interviews and focus groups with
young people who have taken part in Aimhigher initiatives in the South West
of England, and teachers and Aimhigher coordinators involved in planning and
implementing Aimhigher activities for young people. Their study highlights
the positive response articulated by young people targeted for Aimhigher
initiatives and events, such as summer schools, university visits and gifted and
talented schemes. The young people they interviewed expressed a positive
affirmation of the way in which they had been targeted and included in these
schemes, and how such inclusion was translated into positive feelings of self-
confidence and self-worth. 'Participation in Aimhigher is not viewed as a
stigma, a sign of deficit, but as a bonus, an advantageous opportunity, in
which many want to participate' (Baxter, Tate and Hatt, 2007: 277). Such a
view is echoed in a report to the then Minister of State for Higher Education
and Lifelong Learning by the Higher Education Funding Council for England
(HEFCE) in which the feedback from parents, teachers and pupils on WP
interventions (e.g. summer schools) as devices for raising aspirations were
overwhelmingly positive: 'The returns register changed attitudes and increased
interest in entering higher education, with positive responses typically accounting
for more than four-fifths of participants' (HEFCE, 2006: 47). However, the
evidence on whether WP interventions raise attainment levels in the long term
is relatively weak and more difficult to ascertain, according to the HEFCE
report. Too many schools, it seems, were cautious about making claims in this
area. On the subject of the impact of WP interventions on promoting greater
access to HE, the report highlights the lack of causal connection between WP
programmes and participation rates of entrants from traditionally under-
represented backgrounds. The HEFCE report acknowledges: 'The recruitment
outcomes of its WP interventions can only be partially known' (2006: 54).

There is also a body of research that is concerned with how educational
aspiration among working-class children and parents is mediated by their

attachments to locality and the feelings of belonging and social inclusion that underpin those attachments (see Ball *et al.*, 1995; Gewirtz *et al.*, 1995; Reay and Ball, 1997). Connolly and Neill (2001) for example explain how educational aspirations are informed by a politics of belonging that mediates local experiences and community attachments. Drawing on qualitative data generated by interviews with 11-year-old Catholic children attending a primary school in an area of Belfast divided by Republican and Loyalist communities, Connolly and Neill (2001) observe how young children formulate educational decisions and imagine educational possibilities in the context of local politics and the commitment they have to their local area and community. Similarly, Reay *et al.* (2001) observe how working-class HE applicants often stress the importance of locality and community in their decision-making process and the sense of security, comfort and familiarity generated through these localized expressions.

More problematic is the way in which widening participation initiatives attempt to target and recruit potential applicants through a superficial examination that effectively pathologizes non-traditional entrants as a homogenous group with a singular voice and a similar set of needs and interests. Woodrow (2001: 24) suggests that the problem stems from the lack of distinction informing widening participation strategies and targeting practices:

> we are jumbling up young people from low-income backgrounds, ethnic minority groups, refugees, single parents, unemployed people, women returners, those who are rurally isolated and so on into a single category under the label of 'non-traditional'.

Other researchers argue that higher education institutions should avoid promoting the raising aspirations discourse, which effectively pathologizes working-class children as lacking, and instead focus on the practices and cultures of higher education institutions, and develop pedagogies and curricula that address the expressed needs and interest of working-class applicants and students. There are a number of examples where aspiration-raising initiatives have been shown in fact to reinforce rather than overcome cultural and socio-economic divisions (Slack, 2003). Jones and Thomas (2005) highlight the predominance of the aspiration-raising discourse in widening participation programmes as premised on a narrow utilitarian conception of potential entrants, in which those entrants are constructed as lacking both culturally and educationally. The hegemonic discourse of aspiration-raising which underpins the Aimhigher framework is thus problematic in the ways that it tends to reproduce deficit constructions of 'disadvantaged' communities. The aspiration-raising discourse constructs 'aspiration' as decontextualized, disembodied and linear (Burke, 2006). Rather than focusing attention on the reproduction of historically embedded inequalities, located in wider social relations and structures, the focus is on inequalities of aspiration, placing attention on those who are seen to lack the appropriate aspirations against the normalized middle-classed subject.

The practice of 'raising aspirations' involves processes of identifying 'disadvantaged' individuals with potential. Such processes are seen to be objective and fair and unconnected from wider social inequalities. Gillborn and Youdell (2000) demonstrate in their study that the construction of ability within schools continues to be a highly classed, gendered and racialized process (Gillborn and Youdell 2000). The notion of 'potential' is also highly subjective and rests on assumptions about ability and on privileged ontological dispositions (i.e. those coded as middle class, white and heterosexual). Raising aspirations is largely constructed as an individual self-improvement project, facilitated by the new WP professional body, which occurs outside social relations and the micropolitics of educational organizations. Within this framework, the complex social and personal histories in which particular forms of knowledge, experience and capital have been privileged, and particular bodies have been coded as knowledgeable, are ignored. Rather, knowledge and knowing is constructed as objective, apolitical and detached from the legacy of the misrecognition of the cultural capital, literacy practices and knowledge of historically marginalized groups (Apple, 2006).

Furthermore, the discourse of raising aspirations tends to locate problems of deficit in individuals, families and communities who are pathologized through atheoretical and unproblematized notions of 'social exclusion' (Gewirtz, 2001; Skeggs, 2004). Raising aspirations is connected to the neoliberal policy discourse of social exclusion, which has been critiqued extensively by sociologists (e.g. Gewirtz, 2001; Archer *et al.*, 2003) to expose the ways that it leaves complex operations of power unexamined. Shifting the attention to 'exclusion' and away from structural inequalities and discursive misrecognitions operates as a mechanism to re/privilege particular cultural practices, dispositions and values, as well as notions of 'potential'. The heterogeneity of British society is framed in terms of 'diversity' and yet the complex differences and inequalities behind diversity are silenced. Importantly, critical sociological work emphasizes that identities are produced within the discursive sites and practices of schools, colleges and universities (Mac an Ghaill, 1994). Excluded identities themselves are constructed, performed, named and produced within schools and universities (Youdell, 2006). The emphasis on individual aspirations misses out the significant interconnections between a subject's aspirations and their classed, racialized, (hetero)sexualized and gendered identities, ignoring the social, spatial and cultural contexts in which certain subjects are constructed, and construct themselves, as having or not having potential. Aspirations are formed through social relations and identity positions and are negotiated and renegotiated within the social contexts in which the individual is situated; they are not linear in formation but cyclical and reflexive (Burke, 2006). Aspirations are tied to classed, gendered and racialized identities and subjectivities in complex ways that require close, critical and qualitative analytical attention.

Gavin Brown (2009) argues that aspirations are formed at emotional levels and expressed through spatial practices. Policy emphasizes the need for people to take responsibility for their own futures, overlooking systemic class-based inequalities, and focuses instead on inequalities of aspiration. He draws on the arguments made by other sociologists, such as Beverley Skeggs (2004), that through the methodologies employed for targeting widening participation resources, such as through postcodes, class becomes constructed through stereotypes of place (he cites 'Essex girls' as an example of this process of classed construction) (Brown, 2009: 13). How aspirations are connected to spatial relations and practices is complicated and tied to the politics of 'place beyond place' (Massey cited in Brown, 2009: 14): the complex process of making 'connections between one's experience and those of distant others' (Brown, 2009: 14). These points are important in unpacking the social production of aspiration formation, as tied in intimate and complex ways to subjectivity, space and time.

In order to understand the complex ways in which aspirations are formed through social identities, I draw on the growing body of literature that points to social class, and its intersections with gender and 'race', as a key site of social exclusion in higher education (Mahony and Zmroczek, 1997; Thompson, 2000; Reay, 2001; Reay *et al.*, 2001; Archer *et al.*, 2003). This literature conceptualizes class as discursive and cultural as well as structural. Class identities are fluid and always in process, and this insight reveals the complex ways that other social identities and inequalities, such as gender, ethnicity and race, intersect with class identities to re/produce structural inequalities and discursive misrecognitions (see also Chapter Three). The men in my ESRC-study on masculinities (see Chapter Five), for example, self-define their class positions, although many of the men are highly ambivalent about this. Classed and gendered identities are discursively constituted, drawing on the conceptual tool of 'discourse' to capture the ways that identities and aspirations are continually re/fashioned through changing social contexts, meanings, practices, subjectivities and relations. Discourses constrain and create the kinds of spaces we live in and the ways we give meaning to our experiences and aspirations. They shape our decisions and worldviews and are interlinked with competing sets of cultural practices and shifting power relations. It is important to recognize also that discourses not only operate 'through normalization, surveillance and discipline' but also through 'desire, pleasure and complicity' (Raphael Reed, 1999: 94).

It is thus important to address the complicated ways that educational aspirations are discursively fashioned through classed, gendered and racialized power relations, spatial and embodied practices and contradictory subjectivities. For the men in my ESRC study, regulatory and competing discourses make available a range of contested masculine subjectivities within and outside educational fields. The formation of masculinity, and its intersections with other social differences, profoundly shapes aspiration and this is an ongoing social process of becoming and of producing identities (Hall, 1992: 287–88): the subtle, shifting and active recognition of self and other. Masculinity as a concept highlights 'differences in power and experience between groups of men' (Archer, 2003: 14) and supports a sociological analysis of the ways that aspirations are socially contextualized and embedded in gendered relations, practices and politics of difference across age, class, ethnicity, race and sexuality. As 'configurations of practice', masculinities are produced through contradictory social, cultural and institutional relations and positionings, which include 'differences and hierarchies among men' (Connell, 2005, 23). Within different social contexts, such as schools, colleges and universities, men are 'incited to adopt certain practices of "masculinity" and, hence, to display themselves as incumbents of certain categories of masculinity on particular occasions' (Martino, 1999: 240). The men participating in my research gave accounts of their educational aspirations, which reveal 'how centrally class as well as gender is implicated in psychic processes' (Reay, 2002: 223), and a detailed analysis uncovers the interconnections between the auto/biographical, cultural, discursive, emotional and material in the re/fashioning of gendered aspirations across personal and social histories.

## The production of gendered, classed and racialized aspirations

In the remainder of this chapter, I will draw on interviews with the men participating in access and foundation programmes from my ESRC masculinities project (see Chapter Five for a discussion of the research and methodological framework). My aim is to use the data to deconstruct the complex processes by which aspirations are formed and reshaped, through competing discourses at play and complex identity practices, in relation to others and in a range of different sociocultural contexts and spaces. My analysis of the men's accounts will show how the men's aspirations are produced through their embodied, performative and contextualized subjectivities.

The men taking part in this research expressed high levels of aspiration, which is not altogether surprising considering these are men who successfully accessed education through different alternative-entry programmes. However, the ways in which they articulated their aspirations requires close analysis to reveal the connections between their individual aspirations, complex decision-making processes negotiated with others, policy discourses and classed, gendered and racialized identities and practices. The processes by which the men re/constructed their aspirations in the interviews involved taking up, rejecting, challenging and remaking identities across space and time at local, cultural and global levels. The processes were also closely tied to structural and material im/possibilities as well as the different sets of capital un/available to the men. A myriad of positive and negative influences shaped the men's shifting and contradictory aspirations and decisions including family, community, friends and teachers, as well as national and religious identities.

## Contradictory aspirations

There are many examples of contradictory aspirations in the men's accounts, influenced by family, friends and uncertain and shifting identities. The expression of contradictory aspirations highlights the ongoing, discursive process of aspiration formation, which is tied to subjective construction, or processes of becoming. For example, Dragon, born in Pakistan, is an 18-year-old student participating on a Science and Engineering Foundation Programme (SEFP) at a London university. Dragon is significantly influenced by his parents' perspectives and expectations and also by his national and religious identifications. His early aspirations are attached to his strong sense of loyalty to his family and the hegemonic discourses around being a man in his local community. His response below constructs an imagined heterosexual, responsible family man who conforms to the expectations of his extended family. He talks about his own plans in relation to the wider community to which he identifies, explaining that 'we' usually marry at the age of 24.

> Interviewer: If you can recall two years back, when you were 16, what would you have imagined yourself doing at 26?
> Dragon: I would imagine doing my job and hopefully married as well. Because we usually get married about 24. And just a normal house, a car as well ...

In expressing his aspirations in the interview, he constructs different versions of himself that are able to fit in with both his Pakistani and English identities. He plays with different versions of manhood in his account: being a businessman, a dentist, a doctor and these are tied in with the varied contexts of his everyday life moving in and out of different cultures and expectations. Some of these are attractive to him due to the embodied identities that such masculinities carry, such as being a businessman and wearing a suit. Other aspirations are shaped around what he believes is available to him or not, the level of competition involved and the kinds of careers his family would desire for him.

> Interviewer: What was your dream job, before starting your A-levels, what did you imagine ... ?
> Dragon: Before it was just a business manager, because I went into the City and saw these businessmen with their suitcases and suits, and coming out of big buildings, and I thought – yeah, this is something I want. But before coming over here, because doing science engineering its biology engineering as well, so maybe I can do this and try for medicine, or dentistry, which I was really interested in, but dentistry is hard competition. I would have to actually do this and then a degree in biology or something, a science subject, and then apply. And still there might not be a guarantee of me getting in, which is why I left that.

In the context of his national identities as a Pakistani man, his hopes for the future are modest and safe, careful not to rock the boundaries of his community and family. He imagines himself primarily as a husband and father, able to support his family through a secure job.

Interviewer: What about now, if you think yourself ten years ahead, what do you see?

Dragon: Just a normal person with a job, hopefully, and a wife and kids and nothing too much.

Yet, in the discursive context of the interview, and the specific prompts used by the interviewer, he also expresses contradictory dreams that are challenging to these hegemonic versions of being a man within his community.

Interviewer: What would be a dream come true, in jobs?

Dragon: Oh I'll be very rich, going around to countries with my job and be a very important person. Not like a politician or anything, but close to that. And have a massive house, probably in America. I visited America and the houses over there are really nice. Very big. And one more thing which I want to try to make possible, is to become a cricketer. I'm a really huge fan of cricket. I'm not actually in any clubs at the moment and people say I should join. And I'm OK, I can play good as well. Not really good. But just good. So that's one of those dreams I think is achievable with a bit of practice.

Dragon plays around with discourses of success and heterosexual masculinity, having a huge house and being 'a very important person', such as a cricket celebrity. He is drawn back and forth between 'dream' and 'realistic' aspirations in the interview situation and he fashions his 'realistic aspirations' around being modest, responsible and unselfish, characteristics he associates with what it means to be a Muslim man.

Interviewer: OK, now you've described to me the big dream. What would you realistically expect of yourself?

Dragon: I think a job that just pays well, just to manage my family and house. Expenses and ... maybe just occasionally holidays and things. That's fine. Because really my religion does say that you don't really need much, and if you do have much you just give, so you are equal to everyone. So I just don't want too much. Just enough will be fine.

## Relational aspirations

The men's accounts also highlighted that aspirations are relational; that is they are formed in relation to others, in relation to constructions of gendered subjectivity and in the context of fluid, contradictory and unpredictable power relations that shift across space and time. Relations within the family are a central space for the formation of aspirations, and mothers play a key role in aspirational re/shaping. However, a critical sociological analysis helps illuminate the social and relational dimensions of decision-making and aspiration, rather than simply focusing on individual mothers and families. Such an analysis takes account of the complex power relations within families and the gendered relationship between mothers and sons. It also highlights the fragile line that mothers walk when they are supporting their children in making the 'right' educational choices and decisions, a thin line between regulating and policing decision-making processes and being nurturing, caring and supportive.

Ali, a 19-year-old SEFP student originally from Iraq, speaks specifically about his mother's important influence in processes of decision-making about his choice about what and where to study. In his account, his mother is unable to strike the almost impossible balance of simultaneously being a friend and a responsible parent. Ali describes the double-edged sword of parental expectations, and relates his difficulties with A-levels as an effect of the pressure his mother exerted over his schoolwork. Ali defines his family's background as middle class, and his account fits closely in with wider expectations of (middle-class) parents and sociological literature on the relationship of middle-class parents to their child's education (Power *et al.*, 2003).

> Ali: I would say my mum, she had a big influence, because I always had to do ... she asked me if I had done my work or had not done my work, how am I doing in the school, am I doing fine? [ ... ] even though when somebody insists that you have to do the work you start to hate it. That's one of the reasons now I find it a bit hard with A-levels, to keep up with my work, because always I've been told – we came all the way from back home, here, for you to study and to be better. And that put more pressure on me. And when you pressure someone he wouldn't do as good as he wants.

Later in the interview, though, Ali talks about his admiration for his mother, who was able to overcome what he describes as a set of catastrophic events, and through her own determination made the decision to come to England to escape the 'constant pain' (Ali's words) of living in invaded Iraq. He explains that his mother comes from a wealthy background and became a single mother after the death of his father. Concerned for Ali's safety due to the war, she made the 'tough decision' (Ali's words) to move with the children to England. Ali explains that his mother had specific aspirations for him to pursue a career in medicine, while Ali wanted to go into physics. Although he was not motivated to study, he put effort into his GCSEs because it would have been 'cruel' in his eyes to have done any differently considering the sacrifices his mother made to seek refuge in England for his safety.

> Ali: Yes, even though I was trying to do something in physics I didn't tell my mum. She always wanted me to be a doctor, or something prestigious. So I had to just say – OK. That's when I really tried ... actually from GCSE I started to drift away from my studies, trying to avoid the

subject, because my mum, she tells me to go and study. I tried to avoid it. So when it came to doing the other subjects, it would be a bit cruel if I said for my mum, because it was for myself. But I would say for mum, because I know she got through so much hassle to get us here. But I thought it would be rewarding, even though I didn't make it. Still I passed.

Ali explains how he came to decide to pursue engineering, which involved sensitive and careful negotiations with his mother. Engineering, he explains, fits in better with his 'personality' than medicine, and he seems to take up neoliberal discourses around entrepreneurialism, ambition and self-determination. This again exposes the complex processes involved in aspiration-making, which, in Ali's case, is linked to his mother's perspectives, her auto/biography and its relationship to his experiences, his self-identifications and hegemonic discourses around acceptable careers for young men in England.

Ali appears to position himself in relation to neoliberal discourses of success and determination. He constructs himself as immune to any social constraints because he has a goal and so he is able to overcome anything through his individual determination and self-belief. In this way, he might be seen as the ideal 'widening participation student' who constructs himself in relation to discourses of meritocracy and sees success as available to all men who work hard, adapt to 'British culture' and are willing to give 'whatever it takes' to succeed. Ali explains:

> First of all, when I came from Iraq, for me it doesn't make a difference wherever I go. Wherever I go I feel home, for some reason I don't know. People say they are homesick and stuff, but for me I just adapt to it because I have to. Because I've got a goal, which is to be successful. So whatever it takes, I will.

## Respectable aspirations

The men in my study construct their aspiration to access HE around idealized formations of masculinity, which are entwined with the desire for respect and respectability. Skeggs has illuminated in her work on formations of gender and class that struggles over respectability are central in processes of recognition and subjective construction (Skeggs, 1997, 2004). In her study, she shows the contradictory positioning of working-class women and their uneasy relationship with femininity due to their class positioning. Notions of 'respectability' provide the women with an 'interpretative trope for them to construct their own version of femininity distinct from stereotypes of the working-class slattern' (McNay, 2008: 170). Similar to the women participating in caring courses in Skeggs' 1997 study, respect emerges in the men's accounts of accessing higher education as a key theme:

'Because, as you know, basically when you've got an education you are more respected' (Ali).

Of course, the men in my study occupy a different social location than the women in Skeggs' study. Their gendered positioning offers them a relatively privileged social location but, simultaneously, the working-class, migrant and ethnic minority men have an uncertain relation to discourses of 'respect'. Although the men are positioned across different and competing subjectivities, they all share a particular understanding of what it means to be university educated and respectable, including not doing physical work and having a well-paid job, whilst not being too wealthy but being 'comfortable' and having the resources to support a family. Their constructions of masculinity resonate with traditional heterosexual, white and middle-class values of the male breadwinner who provides a stable financial basis for his wife and children.

> I hope I will be settled with a proper profession and have a family. Yeah, I am looking forward to it. I am really concerned about my future. I know it is almost getting late, but it is not too bad, too late. At least if I attain this level and try and achieve a bit further, I could have a comfortable life, that is all I want, and that is what I am looking forward to.
> (Sammy, aged 48, Black African, working class, Access to HE course)

The men distance themselves from working-class subjectivities, and their aspirations to become HE students seem to be linked to the desire for being recognized as a respected subject. For example, in Gladiator's account, the constitution of respectability relies on a distancing from physical labour:

> [Being a student] feels good. Because working is not good. Working is very hard and physical, compared to learning. I don't know, I've always had this thing, when I walk along the road, as either being common or intellectual, just the two groups. And I know it sounds horrible, but I don't like mixing with the common or, I don't know, choose people. So I've always wanted to be in the higher learning class, so being amongst all these students here is great.
> (Gladiator, aged 19, Italian, 'comfortable', Science and Engineering Foundation Programme)

In refusing to name class, Gladiator's account highlights that 'class formation is dynamic' (Skeggs, 2004: 5): 'Class (as a concept, classification and positioning) must always be the site of continual struggle and re-figuring precisely because it represents the interests of particular groups' (Skeggs, 2004: 5).

Higher education is a site of class struggle, intensified perhaps through policies of widening participation that emphasize accessibility to students from class groups historically under-represented in university spaces. In those spaces, seen largely as neutral (once admission has been achieved), 'the systems of inscription and classification (which work in the interests of the powerful)' are hidden (Skeggs, 2004: 4). It is not surprising, then, that the desire for respect and respectability is a central theme in many of the men's accounts of accessing higher education.

> It's kind of respect as well. You are considered more in society, if you've got good education you are OK.
>
> (Dragon)

Respectability is closely tied in with the desire for financial stability in the men's accounts, invoking hegemonic constructions of masculinity as the male breadwinner. Higher educational participation for many of the men represents an opportunity to gain security. This illuminates the struggles at the structural and discursive levels for respectable subjectivities of class and gender and the ways this is linked to the men's aspirations to participate in higher education.

## Diasporic aspirations

Over half of the men participating in the study have complex experiences of migration, and their aspirations are formed between and across competing discourses about forms of masculinity and aspiration in different familial, national and cultural spaces and contexts. In some of the men's accounts, 'British culture' is idealized and contrasted to their 'home cultures'. To theorize their accounts of migration in relation to aspiration formation, I draw on the concept of 'diaspora'. This concept illuminates the complex ways in which the men reconstruct their traumatic experiences in terms of hope and possibility, across different cultural spaces and expectations.

Diaspora is both a social condition and process, which helps to explore 'the destabilizing effect of transition and movement of the individuals' cultural certainties' (Anthias, 1998: 565). Importantly, diaspora emphasizes the formation of subjectivity as constructed in and through difference, where the diasporic subject is positioned as the 'Other'. Jackson argues that the diasporic subject participates in education with the understanding that 'they have been admitted under sufferance as long as they conform to dominant constructions of what it means to be a learner, and what counts as knowledge' (Jackson, 2007: 10).

Skiddo is a 30-year-old Access to Health Studies, Nursing and Midwifery student from an African background at an East London further education college. Born in Cameroon, he is self-defined working class. At the time of interview, he had been living in England for about five years and came as an asylum seeker with his pregnant wife. In Cameroon, he worked with his father in his business but at the age of 26 experienced a traumatic event as a result of his family's political perspectives.

> Because [my father] was in the opposition party. He was one of the members, so during the election process the ruling party were targeting

those from the opposition who had got businesses and got houses, they were burning houses down. That was what happened. And that is why he was killed.

Soon after, he fled to London, and took work as a porter in a hospital, which was how he became interested in pursuing a career as a nurse.

> I quite enjoyed it, where I was working, I was part of a team. And the nurses there were so good and lovely, and they encouraged me. I don't know why. They keep telling me, why don't you do this and that? I never really had the interest. When I was talking to patients who come, when they come there, feeling bad, and they go away feeling better and you see the joy on their faces. And I imagined being a part of that, it seemed a wonderful thing to do. That was when I developed the interest.

The nurses' recognition of Skiddo as a potential nurse is important in reshaping his aspirations, and in his pursuit of inclusion in a new cultural context. Through their encouragement and recognition, Skiddo becomes inspired to explore a new direction in his life. He also identifies the emotional work of caring, often socially constructed as a feminine disposition to labour, as a key aspect of his aspiration to become a nurse. His account suggests moments of recognition and inclusion, which he describes in the familiar phrase of being 'part of a team'. His motivation is constructed in emotional terms of 'feeling bad', 'feeling better' and 'seeing joy on their faces'. He also describes his experiences of his course in emotional ways. When he is asked what he has learned in his access course, he answers in terms of gaining broader values as a father, specifically values of love and respect. Yet his account also resonates with Gewirtz' critique of New Labour policies that are focused on working on the marginalized to become more like white, middle-class parents (Gewirtz, 2001).

> At home? You can never compare them because what I have learned here is respect and love, and you don't have that from the teachers there. If I was back home the love that I have for my daughter, I don't believe I should have now, because there you just believe everybody is looking after themselves. Some parents, they don't even see their kids for days, weeks, but they live in the same house, get out in the morning, come back in the night, and don't even check to see if they are asleep well. Too many things I have learned I can never compare them, because it depends on the society. It is not a bad thing for them, but it is just a way of life in that part of the world.

Although there are generational and trans/national differences in the men's accounts, related to their experiences of moving across different cultural contexts and relations, there are also important and notable similarities. Like Ali above, Skiddo takes up neoliberal discourses of flexibility, individualism and adaptability in describing his decisions and aspirations but also ideal-type student-dispositions. Both Skiddo and Ali explain their decisions through familiar narratives of positive thinking, working towards a goal, staying focused and moving forward. They both take up neoliberal discourses in making sense of their migration experiences and in coping with the challenges that face them, both as students and as living in new cultural environments. He talks about self in dis/continuous terms of leaving behind, forgetting the past and looking ahead. Again, Skiddo's account resonates with Brah's (1996) concept of diaspora, both in terms of coping with traumatic events and with embracing hope and possibility. He holds on, however, to remnants of the businessman subjectivity, which might operate to enable Skiddo to take up discourses traditionally associated with femininity, such as caring for others. Skiddo's account highlights the ways in which aspirations are formed through the 'articulation of normative understandings' (Bird *et al.*, 2009: 49).

> I would say I am the type of person, I adapt to any situation and any environment very quickly. When I left my country I left everything behind me, but I never thought about who I was and what I left, and stuff. I just think there is a challenge ahead of me. So I would say when I left there I forgot what I used to do. I would think that part of being a businessman inside me, probably might do something part-time like that. But now I am focused on doing what I want to do now.

Skiddo positions himself as the masterful, included subject, irrespective of his diasporic experiences as a refugee and his current location as the student marked by discourses of disadvantage, migration and difference. Although the kinds of discourses Skiddo draws on have resonance with the success narratives of neoliberalism, he also re/locates himself firmly in relation to the traditional tribal values of his home community:

> Skiddo: Bamlake, Bamlake is a very proud tribe. So I am proud to be a Bamlake. They are business inclined and hard working. Most people from this tribe are always doing well.

In this way, Skiddo constructs his aspirations as related directly to the tribal community to which he continues to have a strong sense of belonging and reactivates narratives of the continuous self. Skiddo's adherence to the tribal values of Bamlake challenges the English policy focus on the role of individual parents and helps to shed light on the strengths that refugee and minority ethnic students bring to access courses from their experiences of broader forms of support offered beyond immediate family relations.

## Othering, student divisions and gendered aspirations

Policy in England that explicitly addresses widening participation clearly lays out the agenda: the main strategy will be to create new kinds of courses for new student constituencies. For example the 2003 White Paper, *The Future of Higher Education*, reads:

> Our overriding priority is to ensure that as we expand HE places, we ensure that the expansion is of an appropriate quality and type to meet the demands of employers and the needs of the economy and students. We believe that the economy needs more work-focused degrees – those, like our new foundation degrees, that offer specific, job-related skills. We want to see expansion in two-year, work-focused foundation degrees; and in mature students in the workforce developing their skills. As we do this, we will maintain the quality standards required for access to university, both *safeguarding the standards of traditional honours degrees and promoting a step-change in the quality and reputation of work-focused courses.*
>
> (DfES, 2003a: 64, emphasis added)

In this excerpt, WP is being explicitly linked with concerns about 'safeguarding the standards of traditional honours degrees'. The text implies that opening access to new student constituencies has a negative effect on traditional university spaces, which need to be protected against the entry of 'non-traditional' students. It also assumes that the appropriate level of participation for those new student constituencies is work-based degrees rather than traditional honours degrees. This leads policy in the direction of creating new and different kinds of courses for new and different kinds of students without addressing that these differences are shown to be classed, gendered and racialized by research in the field (HEFCE, 2005; Reay *et al.*, 2005). New social inequalities are thus formed through the very policy that claims to be committed to social justice. In this way, the WP policy agenda is not able to challenge the status quo or redress the legacy of the under- (mis)representation of certain social groups in traditional forms of higher education, which carry with them status and esteem. As a result, enduring hierarchies, privileges and inequalities remain untouched whilst new forms of unequal social relations are being created (Burke, 2002). This logic constructs 'WP students' in particular ways, leaving notions of deficit in place. Traditional student identity is subtly held in place so that the traditional university undergraduate is reconstituted as the ideal-student subject, the measure of quality and standards against which other student identities are formed. The 'WP student' is constituted as 'Other', deserving of higher education access but usually to 'other' kinds of courses and institutions.

A strong sense of Othering, division and difference runs through the men's accounts, significantly shaping their subjective constructions and aspiration formations. In the following quote, Ali illuminates the processes by which students construct themselves around institutional status, categories and divisions, such as being a first-year student or studying Engineering, and this contributes to the possibilities for peer relationships and student identifications. This is always linked in with gendered subjectivities, not least because the subject areas themselves are gendered as masculine areas of study. Ali talks about this in terms of a feeling of discomfort in forging friendships beyond the groups he is deemed to belong to.

> Ali: People tend to separate themselves into groups. You see people all people doing the same. They are going to be on one side or another. I find it, I think the students make it hard for themselves, how they socialize with people. They don't have to categorize themselves from the point of view of first year, second year, third year, or fourth year, or if you are doing medicine, engineering, or doing maths. So it's not as comfortable to talk to someone doing something else as it is comfortable when you talk to someone who is doing the same thing.

Ali's discussion highlights the ways that institutional categories and divisions shape student identities in relation to others, in terms of being the same or being different. Furthermore, their encounters at college and university repeatedly serve to situate them as different from the 'traditional' student body. Ali explains how he came to decide on a foundation degree:

> My teacher in the college. My tutor. She told me to be realistic. She told me I was good. But she didn't think I was good enough. So she told me not to apply for big degrees. Why not apply for foundation? Even though I find it repeating myself. Repeating what I already know.

Bruce talks about his experiences of the foundation degree in terms of his desire to be recognized as a university rather than a college student. This is clearly important to Bruce and he expresses his disappointment that the course mainly takes place at the College site, rather than at the University.

> Interviewer: Has there been anything that's disappointed you about the course?
> Bruce: Well, I think the course that I intended to go to was a university-based course. So a lot of it is the perception that I thought I was going to be at the University, where most of my time was actually spent here. I think this semester we just had ... we was here every day, like all the days we have to come and we had to be at the College, so ...
> Interviewer: Yeah. So that was a little bit disappointing?
> Bruce: Yeah. I wanted to get the feel of university life, so ...
> Interviewer: Because, I mean, the way it's marketed it's not quite so clear, is that right, that ... ?
> Bruce: It's marketed as the University but when you come to it you actually go to the College, that's what really ...
> Interviewer: So when you do go to the university, I mean, how often do you go or ... ?

Bruce: This semester we haven't been once for lessons. But the first semester we had we'd go there.

Interviewer: Right, okay. So you don't see that much. ... In terms of being at the university and being here, what are the differences do you think?

Bruce: Well, you get restricted access. And there was just the ... the vibes that you get off the people that work here, they treat you like a young kid: 'Oh, you can't do this.' Make you wait in queues. I understand you've got to wait but it's the attitude they bring it across. In your head you're saying, 'I'm a university student but I have to put up with the same things that a 16-year-old does.' So it's slightly unfair. See, where with me it is a social thing, because I'm still young, I'm only 19, so it is a social thing. I want to get to know a few more people.

(Bruce, aged 19, white English, working class, Foundation
Sports Science)

Bruce's experiences of the foundation course highlight a number of key issues for understanding participation in higher education in relation to complex social inequalities and aspiration formation. Bruce desires to be recognized as a legitimate university student, yet his status on the foundation degree seems to position him as an outsider of the university community. He feels undermined and compares this to being a teenager; there is a strong sense of disempowerment in his account. He claims his access to the university to be restricted, and this not only makes it difficult to conduct research for his studies but also to forge friendships with other university students. He appears to feel marginalized by the status of the course he is taking, which directly impacts on his sense of identity as a university student. Inequalities of age and class are at the heart of Bruce's account, and gender plays out implicitly again in terms of subject choice. The foundation degree in sports science is constituted mainly of male students and fits in easily with assumptions about appropriate educational aspirations for working-class men.

## Final reflections

Drawing on interviews with men participating in access and foundation programmes, I have argued that widening participation policy is too narrowly focused on simplistic notions of 'raising aspirations', which are embedded in problematic deficit and individualist discourses. This not only leaves hidden intricate operations of power, privilege and inequality but also constructs certain groups as lacking and inferior as compared to a core community of 'included' citizens who are seen as having the 'right' kinds of values, skills and aspirations.

The interviews explored aspiration-making across time, by examining the men's auto/biographies and memories, and across space, by considering the impact of changing cultural and geographical contexts and competing masculine formations. In highlighting classed, generational, national and racialized differences, I have argued that individual aspirations are discursively constituted formations, always contextualized and produced within complex social relations. The men's decisions and aspirations are produced through their masculine identities and intricate re/negotiations with others, in relation to changing trans/national discursive fields.

This chapter argues for a theorized and nuanced approach to understanding formations of aspiration that accounts for identity, context and social relations. Policy developments that aim to tackle social exclusion and injustices must take into account the discursive nature of aspiration-making. Utilitarian and instrumental approaches to WP are stuck at the attitudinal level, unable to capture the complexity of decision-making about educational participation. It is crucial to understand that aspirations are not constructed exclusively at the individual level but are tied in with complex structural, cultural and discursive relations, identities and practices. The accounts of men students accessing higher education in London institutions illuminate the complexity of aspiration forming, which is relational, spatial, negotiated and contextualized.

# 7 Fair access

## Challenging discourses of fairness and transparency

In this chapter, I interrogate another hegemonic discourse at play in current WP policy: 'fair access'. This discourse is premised on the assumption that, through 'transparent' sets of criteria, procedures, rules and regulations, admissions tutors and other educational professionals are able to make fair decisions about accepting some candidates onto a course over others. It is problematic that such decisions are seen as outside wider social relations and contexts assuming that candidates apply to higher education on a level playing field. The assumption that candidates can be selected on 'merit alone' has been extensively critiqued within the sociology of education, which has exposed the flaws of mainstream concepts of 'merit' and meritocracy, as well as the assumptions often made about ability and potential. For example, Gillborn argues that ability is constructed as inherent and fixed rather than socially constructed and tied to classed, gendered and racialized values and perspectives (Gillborn, 2008). This chapter seeks to expose the ways that inequalities are hidden within the discourse of 'fair access', drawing in particular on data from the NALN-funded study of admissions practices in the context of art and design undergraduate degrees. It will argue that the discourse of 'fair access' ignores the operations of selectivity (Williams, 1997), which are embedded in specific cultural values and assumptions, and often serve in the interests of historically privileged groups. Wider social discourses that legitimate certain sets of cultural capital ensure that candidates are identified and identify themselves as deserving or undeserving, and this significantly affects decisions and choices (Webb, 1997; Williams, 1997; Reay *et al.*, 2001; Reay *et al.*, 2005). In this chapter, I argue that those entering higher education from 'different' backgrounds are often seen as potentially contaminating of university standards and as a result a key policy strategy is to protect the quality of higher education by creating new and different spaces for those new and different students (Morley, 2003).

## Meritocratic discourses of 'fair access'

The notion of 'fair access' has its roots in liberal concerns to promote access to higher education to individuals from disadvantaged backgrounds who are deemed to have high levels of potential and ability (Kettley, 2007: 335). This concern has been expressed at different moments and in different ways throughout the twentieth century, from the first half of the twentieth century to the Robbins Report, which presented the meritocratic principle that HE should be provided for all those who have achieved the appropriate entry qualifications and who wish to pursue such courses (Kettley, 2007: 337). The underpinning meritocratic principle has not changed, with a similar line of argument expressed most recently, that higher education should be available to all who have the potential to benefit, regardless of their social background. This meritocratic view of access has been extensively critiqued over many decades for failing to engage with the complexity of the relationship between social inequalities, educational achievement and life chances. Meritocracy is premised on the belief that all individuals who work hard, and have the pre-requisite ability, can succeed within a fair and democratic system (Young, 1961). However, the notion of meritocracy does not address the differential social positions that different individuals occupy, providing some privileged groups with the valuable cultural and material resources necessary to 'play the game' and succeed. A lack of attention to how some groups have unfair access to the cultural tools needed to get ahead tends to individualize 'failure', explaining it in deficit terms, of lacking ability, determination or aspiration. Furthermore, 'there is no neutral definition of "merit"; however it is defined, it will benefit some groups while disadvantaging others' (Karabel, 2005: 3). In the US context, Jerome Karabel exposes that admissions to the three highest status universities has been 'a history of the recurrent struggles over the meaning of "merit"' (2005: 3).

Morley and Lugg (2009: 41) explain that 'in a meritocracy, with the door wide open, via increasing strategies to widen participation, the causes of disadvantage are located within under-represented groups'. Thus, widening participation might be understood as a technology of differentiation and stratification, rather than a social justice intervention.

> International debates on the ideology of widening student participation policies question whether they are a force for democratization or differentiation (David, 2007). Initiatives are perceived as a form of meritocratic equalization and/or as a reinforcement of social stratification processes. Those with social capital are often able to decode and access new educational opportunities. Those without it can remain untouched by initiatives to facilitate their entry into the privileges that higher education can offer.
> (Morley and Lugg, 2009: 41)

Rodolfo Leyva (2009) traces the implicit logic behind meritocratic discourses to the historically entrenched relationship between social Darwinism and neoliberalism. This logic tends to naturalize social inequalities on the premise that the socially 'fittest' groups, those who demonstrate economic and educational success, gained their superior social position and advantage through their evolved ability, intelligence and merit. Leyva connects this logic to the ideas of Herbert Spencer, a prominent sociologist and public intellectual of the nineteenth century, who drew on Darwin's theory of natural selection to explain social stratification in Western societies (Leyva, 2009: 367). Spencer used this framework to pose an 'evolutionary' distinction between industrial and non-industrial societies, arguing for the political superiority of non-interventionist states and individualism. This later developed into a neo-liberal political agenda, underpinned by the 'misnomer that evolution meant progress [ ... ] thus less state intervention meant that unregulated market-forces would lead humanity to even greater progress' (Leyva, 2009: 367). Individual underachievement and non-participation in HE are thus understood largely as the result of lack of ability, potential, effort and motivation. Yet critiques of meritocracy and neoliberalism confirm its intimate entanglement with social inequalities.

> Neoliberalism cannot be abstracted from race and gender relations, or other cultural aspects of the body politic. Its legitimating discourse, social relations, and ideology are saturated with race, with gender, with sex, with religion, with ethnicity, and nationality.
> (Duggan, 2003: 16 cited in Leyva, 2009: 369)

Morley and Lugg argue that a key problem of widening participation policy, underpinned by the logic of meritocracy, is that it usually focuses on one dimension of social exclusion, such as social class, thus homogenizing the targeted social group and overlooking the 'relationships between socio-economic and sociocultural categories and identities' (Morley and Lugg, 2009: 42). They point to intersectionality theory as a valuable framework to analyse how 'multiple identities interact in experiences of exclusion and subordination (Crenshaw, 1989; McCall, 2005; Davis, 2008: 67). Within social relations of systemic inequality, differing forms of oppression may be mutually reinforcing' (Morley and Lugg, 2009: 42).

## Discourses of admissions policy

In recent years, admissions policies and practice have become an explicit focus of national policy in England, with new regulatory technologies in place, such as the requirement for institutions to submit an 'access agreement' to the Office of Fair Access (OFFA). In 2003 the New Labour Government commissioned a report on admissions practices in higher education, chaired by Steven Schwartz, to examine 'the options that English higher education institutions should consider when assessing the merit of applicants for their courses, and to report on the principles underlying these options'. Schwartz concluded that some groups continue to be under-represented in higher education and that admissions are a key factor in who participates. Admissions processes shape understandings about who is seen as having the right to higher education and who is not. The final report on admissions, published in 2004, high-lighted five central principles for a fair admissions system: (1) transparency; (2) the selection of students able to complete the course as judged by their achievements and potential; (3) reliable and valid assessment methods; (4) minimizing barriers for applicants; and (5) creating a professional system underpinned by 'appropriate institutional structures and processes' (Schwartz, 2004: 7–8). The Schwartz report claimed that there was no evidence of poor admissions practice in universities, but that there was a need for greater transparency of entry requirements and selection processes, thus conflating transparency and fairness, a notion that has acquired considerable currency in hegemonic discourses of HE admissions. Yet, making admissions processes and practices clear and transparent does not render them 'fair' if they continue to discriminate against certain class, ethnic and gender groups (Burke and McManus, 2009).

In 2004, the Office for Fair Access (OFFA) was established to ensure that the forthcoming introduction of tuition fees would not deter people from entering higher education for financial reasons (see Chapter One for a detailed account of WP policy developments in England). All universities and colleges that planned to charge tuition fees above the basic national level were required to first submit an access agreement to OFFA for approval and similar regulatory frameworks will continue to exist under the Coalition Government's new funding regime. OFFA states that it 'helps to safeguard fair access by approving and monitoring access agreements' (OFFA, 2009). It explains that 'fair access' means 'removing the barriers to higher education, particularly financial barriers, that students from lower income and other under-represented backgrounds face' (OFFA, 2009).

The concept of 'fair access' enshrined in policy thus embeds the concept of 'barriers', which I will critique in detail in Chapter Eight of this book. However, it is worth making the point now that the focus on barriers over-shadows concerns with sociocultural dimensions of access, concentrating primarily on material and concrete issues (such as financial matters), largely ignoring the cultural and discursive practices that produce complex mis-recognitions and exclusions in processes of judging who has 'potential' for a particular course of study. It also fails to account for the more complex aspects of funding and economic inequalities, which are linked both to past and future inequalities across a range of social relations and contexts.

Concerns about higher education admissions continue to be high on government widening participation agendas, and notions of transparency and accountability run through such policy concerns. For example, in a speech made at the 2008 HEFCE annual conference, John Denham, then Secretary of State for the English government body responsible for higher education policy, states that:

> We have to look for ... measures that will re-assure the public ... based
> on the fundamental principle that universities decide whom they should

admit. The answer lies ... in openness, transparency and accountability. It lies in each university having a published admissions policy; being able to show that it has measures in hand to equip all those involved in admissions to implement the policy accurately and fairly; and in each university being able to assure itself that this is being done.

(John Denham, 2008)

The emphasis is on notions of transparency and accountability with reference also made to a principle of 'openness'. Yet, in this chapter I will show that such notions are highly problematic, both in terms of their underpinning assumptions but also in terms of the practices being taken up in admissions.

Neoliberal technologies of regulation are central to the discourses of 'fair access'. For example, in summer 2009, HEFCE and OFFA required higher education institutions to submit a WP strategic assessment, bringing together WP strategies and admissions policies and procedures. The guidance on how this document should be produced contains a strong emphasis on admissions and further embeds hegemonic discourses of 'fair access':

> Although admissions remain an important aspect of institutional autonomy and academic autonomy and academic freedom, institutions should provide a high-level statement focusing on the principles of the institution's admissions policy, providing assurance of consistency, professionalism and fairness.
>
> (HEFCE, 2009: 8)

Further mechanisms to regulate the discursive practices of 'fair access' have included the creation of an independent body for admisisons: Supporting Professionalism in Admissions (SPA). This is in response to the Schwartz report's recommendation that a 'central source of expertise and advice' (SPA, 2008:3) was needed to support higher education matters on the 'continuing development of fair admissions' (SPA, 2008:1). Although the Schwartz report (2004) addressed that there are varying understandings and interpretations of 'fairness' at play in higher education, SPA draft guidance on admissions policies does not define what constitutes 'fairness'. Indeed it emphasizes the promotion of 'transparency' as a key concern, reinforcing the conflation of 'fair access' with 'transparency' (Burke and McManus, 2009).

The notion of 'fair access' extended in English policy discourse beyond concerns with access to higher education to consider issues of access to the professions. In July 2009, the report, *Unleashing Aspiration*, was published, outlining the key findings of the Panel on Fair Access to the Professions, chaired by Alan Milburn. A key argument made in the report is that, 'Despite a sharp growth in professional employment opportunities over recent decades, access to the professions is becoming the preserve of those from a smaller and smaller part of the social spectrum' (Milburn, 2009, p. 14).

However, a meritocratic view is sustained as the report argues that increasing fair access 'is about making current access routes fairer and ensuring that those young people who succeed in gaining a top job do so on the basis of talent and merit alone' (Milburn, 2009: 22). The report strongly argues against positive discrimination, and asserts that policies must ensure that 'all get the fair chances and support they require' (Milburn, 2009: 23). The hegemonic and enshrined meritocratic view, which is a legacy of twentieth-century policy, is thus held in place, despite the significant concerns voiced in the report that 'birth, not worth, has become more and more a determinant of people's life chances' (Milburn, 2009: 5).

In response to the Milburn report, Director General of The Russell Group of Universities, Dr Wendy Piatt, said:

> Academic achievement is the key factor in determining whether a student will go on to university and subsequently thrive in their chosen career. Once a pupil from a working class background has managed to overcome all the barriers they have faced and achieved the grades they need to go to university – they are just as likely to do so as their middle-class peers. Financial considerations do not play a significant role in access to higher education. In fact under the new system of deferred fees, loans and grants there has been a huge rise in applications to English universities. There-fore, we would be wary of any recommendations that involved reducing fees as it will not address the core problem – namely under-achievement at school. [ ... ] We agree that better information for potential students is a priority, particularly for pupils from families who haven't been to university, or who have less knowledge about higher education. Russell Group universities are making concerted efforts to ensure that teachers, par-ents and pupils receive the better information, guidance and encouragement to apply to their courses.
>
> (Piatt, 2009)

In Piatt's response, the main issue for fair access is articulated through the metaphor of barriers. The onus of overcoming barriers is placed on the indi-vidual before entry to higher education through the academic achievement of necessary (A-level) grades. Although academic attainment at secondary school level remains a major determinant of access to higher education, Karabel's (2005) detailed analysis of the history of admissions to selective institutions in the USA demonstrates that the processes of selection are far more complex and political than just academic attainment. The politics of selection are tied to shifting definitions of merit, which enable key gatekeepers to maintain control over who is seen as having the right to (elite) higher education. The notion of merit is implicit in Piatt's statement. Although she suggests that barriers are important, she sees financial barriers as less significant, arguing against any reduction of fees. She picks up on the theme of 'raising aspira-tions' through her reference to 'encouragement' as being of importance. Transparency, through reference to 'better information' and guidance, is also a central theme of her response.

## Critiquing 'fairness' and transparency'

Policy concerned with access to and widening participation in higher education has overemphasized notions of 'fairness' and 'transparency' without close attention to the meanings shaping these notions. Furthermore, 'fairness' and 'transparency' have often been conflated in policy talk, assuming that the act of making something transparent will also make it fair. For example, in the attempt to develop fair mechanisms for admissions, the aim to make criteria for acceptance transparent is seen to make it fair. This not only misunderstands the relationship between fairness and transparency, but also glosses over the problematic and contradictory nature of both fairness and transparency.

Of course, it is important that the advice, information and guidance provided to potential applicants is as clear and accessible as possible (Burke and Hayton, 2011). However, transparency is a problematic notion, as it constructs language as a simple conduit to express meaning, rather than as discursively produced and embedded in competing cultural meanings and assumptions. Language is open to multiple constructions of meaning, shaped in relation to complex sets of sociocultural dimensions, including competing identities, subjectivities, epistemologies, contexts and values. In deconstructing discourses of transparency, Strathern asks the critical question: 'what does visibility conceal?' (Strathern, 2000). This is a useful question for deconstructing discourses of transparency in admissions. What are the technologies of visibility in the admissions process, and how do discourses of transparency operate to conceal power relations, exclusions and misrecognitions in selection and assessment processes? Susan Orr argues that the concept of transparency implies that total explicitness is attainable (Orr, 2007: 646), making invisible the tacit practices shaping assessments, judgements and selections. Writing things down, for example in creating clear application guidance and admissions criteria, is confused with transparency in admissions policy (Orr, 2007: 646). Post-structural theories help deconstruct such confusions; language constructs and produces contradictory meanings rather than reflecting a concrete reality that can be straightforwardly communicated. This disrupts the notion that information is simply transmitted from person to person; rather, meanings are constructed discursively and in relation to different and shifting historical and cultural contexts.

Such theoretical insights are important in understanding why transparency is impossible to fully achieve in the development of technologies of admissions. Admissions criteria will always be subject to the discourses and contexts in which they are constructed and then reconstructed by those who read them in different ways, according to the identities, understandings, values and contexts they bring to their reading(s). This is shaped by complex and intersecting sets of social differences, so that for example notions of 'experience' are always open to classed, gendered and generational re/mis/interpretations of what counts as 'experience'. Thus, the practice of transparency does not simply equate with the practice of fairness in complex processes of selection and judgement about what 'experiences' are to be recognized as relevant, valuable and legitimate to the individuals making the judgement.

Notions of fairness are also problematic, particularly as they rest on conflations between fairness and equality. Treating two different applicants from different sociocultural backgrounds fairly might mean treating them differently, rather than equally. For example, if one candidate comes from a highly privileged background and has had access to the most privileged forms of cultural and social capital, whilst another comes from a very poor background, with little or no access to the forms of social and cultural capital valued by universities, then being fair might translate into treating the two candidates differently in the admissions process. The experience the two candidates might draw on in their applications will probably reflect their different sociocultural backgrounds, making it impossible to treat the applications the same in any straightforward way. This raises challenging political, moral and ethical questions about the project to widen educational participation, and necessitates a deep interrogation of the underpinning principles guiding this project. How do institutional policy frameworks help admissions tutors understand their responsibility in making fair decisions and judgements in these contexts? If it is simply guiding them to ask the same questions in the same way to a candidate regardless of their sociocultural background, this could be argued to be unfair. On the other hand, if it is asking the admissions tutors to take up positive discrimination practices in favour of the candidate from the disadvantaged background, is this also unfair? Such complex and difficult questions are crucial in developing an ethical agenda for access to, and widening participation in, higher education, if we are to genuinely engage with the challenges raised by legacies of historical under-representations and exclusions from universities, which after all, are a primary site of the reproduction of life chances.

As I have argued, the discourse of 'fair access' ignores the operations of selectivity, embedded in specific cultural values and assumptions, which serve to reinforce social inequalities. Wider social discourses that legitimate certain sets of cultural capital ensure that candidates are identified and identify themselves as deserving or undeserving and this significantly affects decision-making processes (Williams, 1997; Reay *et al.*, 2005). Although Access to Higher Education courses have been significantly expanded over the past decade and brought into the mainstream through the efforts of the Quality Assurance Agency (QAA) to standardize Access courses, A-levels continue to be constructed as the preferred route into traditional honours degrees (Bekhradnia, 2003) in an increasingly stratified and differentiated higher education system. This could be exacerbated by the tariff proposed by the Browne review, which would take a simplistic approach to counting points and be in danger of ignoring other forms of entry than A-levels but would determine the allocation of loans (Burke and Hayton, 2011). The preferences of certain qualifications and entry routes are thus institutionalized through policy texts such as the *Future of Higher Education* (DfES, 2003a), which gives Access courses one brief mention, and this has particular implications for how applicants from Access courses are viewed by higher education institutions, particularly higher status universities. Research has exposed that Access students have often been characterized by problematic assumptions that they require special help, lack skills and require more resources (Bowl, 2003; Burke and Hermerschmidt, 2005).

Yet, students themselves contest the normalized construction of A-levels as the ideal route into higher education. My research on students accessing higher education through non-standard courses reveals that students do not accept A-levels as the best route into and preparation for higher education. John, who has taken A-levels and is now on a foundation programme, explains:

> But the Science and Engineering Foundation Programme, you know, it gives you an introduction to university because it's like the same. You have all these subjects that relate to university. So it's like a much better course than just sitting a test as for example A-levels.
>
> (John, interviewed in 2004, in Burke, 2006)

Sadie, a Return to Study student taking A-levels as part of her programme argues that examinations make students feel that they 'must be awful' and yet, she explains, it is the assessment method, rather than the student's ability, that is responsible for letting students down:

> I do think exams are unfair. Some people just get on with them and don't pain over them, but they do let you down. Which is why I try to do my best in my coursework, try to make up my grade … I know, even if I revised every day from now to my exams, I wouldn't do any better than if I left it to a couple of months before, because I blank anyway when I get in there. It does gradually come back, but then you've run out of time. And your writing's all messy and you've got spelling mistakes and … things like that. It's awful. I hate them. I know you've got to have them, but I don't think they show who you really are. You can end up getting a grade you don't deserve. There'd be a lot more people out there doing well in education and moving on, but they just don't get recognised in exams. And then they feel 'gawd, I must be awful' but they're not really. You just panic too much. And that's what I'm dreading, that I'll know in myself if I don't do that well, I'll know it's not me.
>
> (Sadie, interviewed in 2000, in Burke, 2002)

Sadie's account exposes the ways that conventional assessment practices regulate exclusions, mis/recognitions and subjectivities: 'There'd be a lot more people out there doing well in education and moving on, but they just don't get recognised in exams.' Both Sadie and John contest the logic that A-levels are the best preparation for higher education. They expose that the traditional pedagogical and assessment approaches do not necessarily support access to higher education and this is not about issues of transparency or overcoming barriers, but about more complex issues of subjectivity, experience and inclusive pedagogical practices. Sadie's account highlights the emotional dimensions of being misrecognized through educational practices deemed to be fair and transparent.

## Classing/classifying the student-subject

Applying to university requires the individual applicant to subject herself to a range of institutional technologies of assessment, which are entangled in complex relations of power. Technologies of assessment in the admissions process might include (depending on the subject or discipline): the application form, the personal statement, the selection interview, the selection task, the entry criteria and the use of grades or marks to judge an applicant's merit, ability and potential and her suitability for a particular course. Through such technologies, the subject is individualized, categorized, classified and incited to disciplinary practices of self-surveillance. Such processes of subjection are complicit in the re/construction of unequal classed, gendered and racialized positonings and subjectivities and the marking out of difference. Widening participation discourses are underpinned by discourses of deficit, in which the different and 'Other' subject is named and identified in terms of what she is seen to lack. In the English policy context, social class is a primary measure of difference and the need for regulation, through the mobilization of pathologizing subjectivities (Skeggs, 2004).

In their analysis of the operations of class inequalities, Hey and Evans (2009) confront discourses of deficit and lack underpinning supposedly equity-oriented policies such as widening participation by drawing analytical attention to questions about working-class achievement and success. Placing power at the centre of analysis, constructions of class are reformulated in terms of being/becoming a classed subject and being in the authoritative position to be the classifier. Taking a critical approach to Bourdieu's theoretical framework, as both a useful frame for the analysis of class inequalities but also as one that reconstructs class inequalities, they scrutinize the personal statement as a key technology of English admissions processes. The personal statement is a space of the reconstruction of the self, to be used by the classifier as a way to read the subject. They argue for institutions to denaturalize their specific class cultural privileges and to offer counter-hegemonic discourses that 'do not mark incapacity as inherent in some groups' (Hey and Evans, 2009).

Morley (2003), Leathwood (2005) and Burke and Jackson (2007) argue that widening participation is often associated in policy texts with anxieties about 'dumbing down' and the lowering of educational standards. Leathwood points out that assumptions are often made that 'more must inevitably mean less "able", and that the "new students" now being admitted to HE are "unsuitable" as "university material"', a perspective underpinned by evident class prejudices

(Leathwood, 2005: 313). This has led to a moral panic about lowering standards and to a general mistrust of GCSE and A-level exam results, resulting in the use of additional admissions examinations in some universities (Leathwood, 2005: 313).

## Fair access? Processes of exclusion and mis/recognition in art and design

In attempting to illuminate the complex ways that misrecognitions are produced through technologies of admission, I now draw on my research on art and design admissions with Jackie McManus (Burke and McManus, 2009). The research illuminates the complexity of selection processes in the specific disciplinary context of art and design. The research, funded by the National Arts Learning Network, examines the practices and perspectives of admissions tutors, drawing on post-structuralist concepts of subjectivity and power, to shed light on subtle processes of mis/recognition, as well as Bourdieu's concepts of capital and habitus. The methods included in-depth interviews with ten admissions tutors, as well as 70 observations of actual selection interviews with applicants, across five case study institutions (see Chapter Five for further details). We also analysed national and institutional policy documents on admissions as well as the materials and information available to applicants through the higher education institutions or UCAS. In the specific context of art and design, certain technologies of admissions are important in the selection processes, including the submission of a portfolio.

> The strong emphasis on the portfolio for admission to art school makes it a very different matter from the typical admission to university ... the portfolio process is complex and pupils from deprived areas where admission to art school is a rarity are often ill equipped to develop a portfolio of high standard. Further, they typically do not have access to adequate facilities and materials, either at school or at home.
>
> (UUK, 2002: 49)

Although the production of a portfolio is essential to the application and assessment process (McManus, 2006), our documentary analysis found that there is very little information provided to candidates about this in the pre-application advice and promotion materials. Indeed the admissions tutors themselves often struggled to articulate what they were looking for in the interviews we conducted with them:

> It is quite difficult to be really specific about it, and it sounds like a cop out to say you know it when you see it but you do. It becomes fairly obvious after a while. I know what I am looking for and it stands out a mile.

The interviews suggested that the admissions tutors shared a tacit understanding of what they think should be in a portfolio, projecting this implicit expectation onto the applicant. The admissions tutors saw the portfolio as a valid and reliable tool of assessment, which aided them in the objective and appropriate selection of candidates with the potential and ability to complete the course. The admissions tutors implied that the portfolio is an instrument of measurement about a candidate's innate level of potential, ability and talent, often constructed as 'creativity' in their accounts of the admissions process. They used the portfolio to make judgements about who the candidate is: a sign of being the right kind of student for the course. Knowing what should be in the portfolio was itself a sign of being right for the course. Although there was no explicit guidance, candidates were expected to know (instinctively) what a 'good' portfolio consisted of. The cultural capital and identity formations the candidate must demonstrate, perform and master in their portfolio is tied in with (middle) classed, (white) racialized and (masculine) gendered subjectivities, as the following quote from an admissions tutor highlights:

> Originality, experimentation, diversity, an open mind, exploration, even if the work, at this point in time, we were talking about pre-higher education, even sometimes if the work itself is a bit raw around the edges, but you can see someone is really trying to explore and experiment, if they have the motivation to do that then you can do an awful lot to help them to learn what they need to learn on that programme. If somebody has got a closed mind it is that much more difficult.

The admissions tutor cites a number of characteristics historically connected to white, middle-class and masculine-centred dispositions, for example open-mindedness, motivation, originality, experimentation. Although the admissions tutor suggests that this is a tall order in terms of the educational level of the candidate (pre-higher education), he expects to see these characteristics in the portfolio even if they are 'raw'. Again, this implies a sense of innate ability, which has the potential to be developed, rather than as connected to social and cultural habitus, background and subjective construction (i.e. who is seen as an ideal candidate and according to whose criteria).

It was during the interview that the importance of habitus and the conversion of cultural into symbolic capital were most apparent. Furthermore, the interview was a space in which subjective construction played out in ways that reinforced classed, gendered and racialized inequalities and misrecognitions about who is (not) seen as having potential. There was a distinct preference for a particular kind of privileged cultural capital, acquired through familial and academic background, which is arguably coded historically as white and middle-class forms of habitus (Bourdieu, 1984). There was also a process of (dis)identification in which certain forms of embodied, performative and discursive subjectivities were mis/recognized.

In our observations of selection interviews, we identified a pattern of the privileging of certain forms of cultural capital, habitus and subjectivity to the exclusion of others. For example, we found that the majority of applicants had portfolios that were assessed as 'mid-range' by the admissions tutors; in other words these portfolios were judged as neither exceptional nor unexceptional. This enabled some applicants, predominantly those who were from white, middle-class backgrounds, to talk their way onto the course by demonstrating the possession of symbolic cultural capital, capital which is valued and can be traded in the field/market of art and design higher education for a place on a course. Such candidates were able to 'do' or perform particular forms of subjectivity that enabled them recognition as applicants with 'potential'. It was standard practice to construct the interview around a series of canonical questions and acceptable answers that arguably reflect particular forms of middle-classed habitus (McManus, 2006) and subjectivity. A fashion admissions tutor explained why he always asks applicants what they were reading:

> If someone is reading Vogue but also Jane Austen and they are going to exhibitions of ceramics, and all this sort of thing, it means they are interested in more than one thing, and their work will have all different elements to it when they join us.

A graphics/digital design foundation degree admissions tutor describes what he asks interviewees and why:

> What is your favourite book? And explain why. What is the best film you have seen recently, and why? Have you been to any galleries, exhibitions, theatre, recently? What is the best advert on television and which is the worst? And are there any contemporary artists, in a broader sense, it could be a designer, or an author, director, musician or something like that, that you particularly admire? So we are trying to find out what they are aware of, you know, and how critically they are ... their understanding of a particular genre. We are not asking them to be experts in every single aspect of art, but what we need to find out is if they have a particular interest in one particular area at this moment in time with digital, maybe film or something like that. So it is about kind of trying to understand their critical analysis thought process.

A textiles admissions tutor gives her reasons for persistently (sometimes six or seven times in an interview) asking interviewees questions about their influences:

> It helps us assess how outgoing the student is and how prepared they are to look over and above their own little area. So how prepared they are to go out, into the environment. And it is about communication as well, so they can maybe talk about, articulate and talk through ideas from other designers or artists. And sometimes that question invites them to talk about how that artist has influenced them, so we can start to make connections

between the critical, the wit and the contextual aspect of the work and their own practice.

It is important to note the age group of most of the applicants (the majority were 17 and 18 years old) in relation to the expectation that they talk in a highly analytical and critical way about their work, and the work of famous artists and designers, before they had even started their degree courses. In the rather daunting context of an interview, significant judgements are made about the candidate's ability and potential and life-chance decisions are made about a candidate's future. Such judgements and decisions are largely made in relation to a set of questions underpinned by the assumptions, values and perspectives of hegemonic and privileged social groups. We argue therefore that it is not surprising that many candidates from black and/or working-class backgrounds were simply not able to respond to these questions in ways that enabled them the forms of recognition necessary to secure their place on the programme of study and thus were often rejected (Burke and McManus, 2009).

There were many examples of the subtle ways in which this played out in the interview. For example, Alan, an 18-year-old from a 'notorious' inner-city council estate was asked to name a contemporary artist whose work he liked:

> Interviewer: Tell us about a contemporary artist whose work you admire.
> Alan: (after a brief silence): Salvador Dali.
> Interviewer: He's dead.
> Alan: Pardon?
> Interviewer: I said contemporary. Salvador Dali is dead.

Alan was able to name a 'modern' artist, but not a 'contemporary' artist and was not offered a place on the graphics foundation degree for which he had applied. It could be argued that the words 'modern' and 'contemporary' are almost interchangeable in everyday, rather than technical, language. Alan's misunderstanding of the language used, we argue, is deeply connected to the processes by which he is misrecognized as not having potential.

The observation data expose the ways that racialized and gendered subjectivities inform admissions tutors' judgements in the selection process. For example, Nina, a black working-class young woman from a poor inner-city area, applying for a Fashion Design BA, was asked at the beginning of her interview about the influences on her work:

> Interviewer: What influences your work?
> Nina: I'm influenced by hip-hop?

In response to Nina's answer, the body language of the interviewers visibly changed and they appeared to disengage from her. She explained further that she'd like to design sports tops. After Nina left, the admissions tutors immediately decided to reject her.

They discussed how they would record this on the form they were required to complete:

> Interviewer one: Why should we say we're rejecting her?
> Interviewer two: Well she's all hip-hop and sport tops.
> Interviewer one: We'll say that her portfolio was weak.

Yet, when the interviewers reviewed her portfolio before the interview took place, they had not deemed it as weak. Following her interview, they recorded on their form that Nina's portfolio was below average, noting also that the clothes she wore to the interview were not fashionable and that she lacked confidence. They also noted their dissatisfaction with Nina's intentions to live at home whilst studying, suggesting this was a sign of immaturity.

The candidate interviewed immediately after Nina was from an affluent spa town, expensively dressed, and cited famous artists and designers amongst his influences. In the interview discussion, he confirmed that he would 'definitely be leaving home because it is all part of the experience.' The young man was offered a place in spite of having considerably poorer qualifications than Nina, including having failed GCSE art.

Nina was not recognized as a legitimate subject of art and design studies because she cited a form of fashion seen as invalid in the higher education context. Nina embodied black racialized ways of being, which were seen as signs of immaturity and lack of fashion flair. Furthermore, her intentions not to leave home were read off as signifying her inappropriate subject position. The male, middle-class, white-English candidate knew how to cite the discourses that would enable him recognition as a legitimate student-subject. The admissions tutors' judgements were shaped by implicit, institutionalized, disciplinary and racialized perspectives of what counts as legitimate forms of experience and knowledge.

Classed, gendered and racialized formations of subjectivity, which are embodied as well as performative, profoundly shape selection processes. Such judgements are made in the context of struggles that the tutors themselves are involved in with relation to their own institutional, embodied, performative subjectivities. This is tied in with the derogatory discourses of 'dumbing down' and 'lowering standards' and the desire to be recognized as 'world class'. This is implicitly underpinned by debates about knowledge and skills and work-based, vocational provision, as marked out as less prestigious than courses and institutions seen as academic and high status.

> Success of individuals and of schools, FE colleges and HE institutions is still measured against traditional models: all school children being examined at the same age, regardless of their preparedness; A-levels in traditional 'academic' subjects being the most acceptable for entry into many universities, 'vocational' routes seen as suitable only for those who cannot achieve in 'academic' routes. Full-time under graduate study, preferably

away from home, is the most valued and many employers only recruit graduates with high A-level scores from their shortlist of traditional universities.

(Copland, 2008: 4)

Paul Goodwin, Cross-Cultural Curator at Tate Britain, writes about the paradox and contradiction between the considerable contribution of black and immigrant cultures to the arts and creativity. He argues that this represents the global commodification of black urbanism and the continued 'marginalization' of black and immigrant groups:

Black and migrant urban culture – styles fashions, music, arts, cultural productions – are in many places a driving force, among other factors, in the so called 'renaissance' of culture in metropolitan areas – New York, London, Paris, Tokyo etc. Notions of urban 'cool', and 'hipness' as in the jazz age are being re-defined around the global traffic in black culture fuelled by the phenomenal rise in hip-hop and its related industries. Yet at the same time, black communities in these same cities are living in on-going conditions of squalor, extreme poverty and social and economic marginalization.

(Goodwin, 2009)

So, although black urban culture, and in particular hip-hop, has contributed significantly to the arts, the black community has not benefited from the commercialization of their urban culture. In Gilroy (2004) a black fashion designer who uses the name Karl Kani (can I?) to question his social location and black racialized subjectivities, sheds further light on the exploitation of black urban culture, and the exclusion of those who create it:

People see black people as trendsetters, they see what we're on and they wanna be onto the same thing, figuring it's gonna be the next big thing. They try to take things away from us every time. Slang we come up with ends up on T-shirts. We ain't making no T-shirts.

(Fashion designer Karl Kani, cited in Gilroy, 2004: 241)

Mathia Diawara (1998) argues that black working-class masculinity has become coded as 'cool' through representations produced across a range of popular culture, including film and music. Although attached to black bodies signifying 'cool', this signifier can be 'transported through white bodies' (Diawara, 1998: 52 cited in Skeggs, 2004: 1). However, Skeggs points out that such signifiers become fixed on black bodies whilst they are 'excluded symbolically from performing "whiteness"'. Skeggs explores the ways that 'some cultural characteristics fix some groups and enable others to be mobile' (Skeggs, 2004: 1). In this way, applicants such as Nina, who are marked and coded by black racialized subjectivities, are constrained by citations of music, fashion and art (such as hip-hop) that are also fixed by codes associated with 'blackness'.

## Final reflections

This chapter has critiqued the discourses of 'fair access' at play in the selection, recognition and exclusion of higher education students. It has traced the discourses to the long-standing political commitment to meritocracy, the idea that success comes from hard work, effort and ability rather than social privilege and advantage. The chapter has shown how meritocratic views underpinning discourses of 'fair access' serve to exclude, marginalize and misrecognize applicants from those groups traditionally under-represented in higher education, including students from poorer backgrounds and minoritized ethnic groups. Analysis of contemporary English policy documents on admissions revealed that 'transparency' is a central concept in shaping WP policy, strategy and practice. However, the concept of transparency is a significantly problematic one, as it understands written text as a straightforward process of the communication of information. Post-structural insights illuminate that language is discursive and is not a straightforward conduit of meaning. Rather, language constitutes meaning, and is open to multiple, contradictory and contested interpretations. For example, the data from the Arts and Admissions project (Burke and McManus, 2009) shows that admissions tutors present multiple versions of the characteristics they are seeking in potential students for their courses, and are simultaneously vague about their expectations. The data drawn on show the complexity of selection in the specific disciplinary context of art and design, which is not a straightforward process of applying fair and valid sets of criteria but a subjective process tied to the values, identities and perspectives that admissions tutors bring to the judgements they make. Recognition of potential, ability and creativity is profoundly shaped by subjective constructions, which are tacit, implicit and tend to favour the ontological and epistemological subjectivities of privileged social groups. My analysis also highlights the importance of a politics of redistribution, which would enable less privileged young people, for example interested in the field of art and design, to have access to the same resources, support, guidance and opportunities available to young people from privileged backgrounds. This analysis demonstrates that both a politics of redistribution and recognition are central to widening participation in higher education. It also illuminates that there are both material barriers to accessing higher education, as well as subtler, complex processes tied to power and subjectivity.

# 8 Lifting barriers

## Conceptualizing inequalities and misrecognitions

'Barriers' is a prominent concept in both WP policy texts and in literature on WP (e.g. Thomas, 2005; Gorard *et al.*, 2007). The concept is helpful in exposing some of the difficulties and challenges that students from tradition-ally under-represented groups might face in terms of broader national and institutional structures and policies (such as funding and financial support) and other practical issues relating to infrastructure and mechanisms of support (such as the accessibility issues of higher education institutions or need for childcare provision). However, this chapter will argue that the concept of barriers is also limiting in many important ways. This chapter will subject the concept of barriers to critique, considering the ways it is used in policy and practice, the different meanings that researchers bring to the concept and the limitations of the concept for thinking through the complexities of operations of inequality and misrecognition in shifting cultural, political and economic frameworks. Alternative conceptual perspectives will be suggested that are able to address the concerns raised by the discourse of 'barriers' but are also able to examine the politics of access and participation, in terms of academic, disciplinary and institutional practices, as well as the processes of subjective construction, in which certain subjects can be recognized as (potential) students in higher education. In particular, attention will be paid to the problematic analogy of the 'barrier' in a context in which local, national and global conditions are under constant change and are unstable rather than fixed.

## Barriers to participate in higher education

The concept of the barrier has become a central focus in much of the policy and practice of widening participation. For example, the Higher Education Funding Council for England (HEFCE) commissioned a large-scale review of existing relevant evidence on widening participation in higher education (Gorard *et al.*, 2006). The findings were published in a book called *Overcoming the Barriers to Higher Education* (Gorard *et al.*, 2007). This book emphasizes the concept of 'barriers' as a way to understand the issues connected to the widening participation policy agenda in England, particularly focusing on the period of the New Labour Government and its explicit commitment to WP (see

Chapter One for an outline of New Labour WP policy). The book makes a number of important points in relation to identifying key barriers to widening participation and highlighting the significant challenges we continue to face. For example, the authors point out that, despite the investment of the New Labour Government of about £2 billion between 1997 and 2004, there had been a decrease in HE participation of young entrants from lower social classes (Gorard *et al.*, 2007: 4 citing Sanders, 2006), raising questions about precisely what the 'barriers' to HE participation might be. They argue that there are two principle issues that government policy must address: (1) 'because educational participation has benefits for society as a whole, these benefits must be "internalized into each individual's decision-making"'; and (2) the 'barriers which prevent people from participating in education who would benefit from doing so must be removed' (Gorard *et al.*, 2007: 51).

However, the identification of these principles is underpinned by particular (problematic) assumptions that are worth teasing out for closer scrutiny. The first is that the individual should in some way be worked on to ensure that if she or he has potential to benefit, then that person should internalize the shared perspective of what those benefits are for wider society. In this way, their formulation of this key principle might be interpreted as connected to wider neoliberal discourses of regulation and governance over individual selves and their desires (e.g. their desire for particular forms of 'benefits'). The second is that barriers are identifiable through research and evidence and thus can be 'removed'. Finally, in referring to people 'who would benefit' from educational participation, they imply the notion of an innate core self, that either 'has' potential or not (see Chapter Three and Chapter Seven for my critique of this notion). This potential, furthermore, can in some way be 'known' or 'measured' to ensure that those individuals can access education without barriers blocking their way.

Following on from these two key principles, Gorard *et al.* (2007) argue that there are various forms of barriers, which need to be removed to support WP. One such barrier is cost, which includes the shift of cost from the state to students and their families. As they importantly highlight, there is 'evidence that there are financial motivations behind some young people's choice not to participate in higher education', and particularly not wanting to end up in debt, or 'debt aversion' (Gorard *et al.*, 2007: 53). Research shows that the cost of higher education is a significant concern for those from economically poorer backgrounds (e.g. Van Dyke *et al.*, 2005) and the dramatic move in England towards the substitution of public funds with individual fees will inevitably exacerbate such concerns (Carpentier, 2010). At a time of continued economic turbulence and rising unemployment, a degree is not a guarantee of employment and there is no assurance of a graduate premium on earnings. Furthermore, the labour market remains classed, gendered and raced, with female graduates and those from working-class and minority ethnic groups continuing to earn significantly less than average (Milburn, 2009).

Financial cost is thus one key dimension of the highly complex processes of decision-making, selection, choice and accessibility connected to higher educational participation. However, my concern is that the notion of barriers tends to concentrate attention rather narrowly, sometimes ignoring the complexity of such processes. For example, a key focus of attention is on the willingness of an individual to go into debt, or not. The notion of 'debt aversion' implies that being willing to accept debt for the sake of gaining a university degree is the appropriate disposition to debt. Yet, the willingness to accept debt as an inevitable part of the pursuit of 'success' is tied to particular (white, middle-class) values and dispositions, as well as certain (neoliberal) political and cultural conceptions. The issues relating to debt and 'debt aversion' are also connected to wider social relations, for example, the position of certain social groups in relation to the labour market and the differential and unequal levels of risk thus attached to going into debt. Furthermore, the debate about cost as a barrier detracts from wider questions about higher education as a public good, as well as questions about who has the right to higher education. Interestingly, when the UK Coalition Government recently explored the possibility of universities being allowed to offer additional places for higher fees, there was an immediate and strong public expression of disapproval. The principle that the right to higher education should not be connected to the ability to pay was so powerfully invoked that the Coalition Government withdrew its proposal by the end of the same day that it had been introduced.

As well as cost, other key barriers identified by Gorard *et al.* (2007) include: time and travel, motivation and institutional barriers. Barriers of time include the time demanded by partners and children, which tend to take up women's time more than men's (Abroms and Goldscheider, 2002: cited by Gorard *et al.*, 2007: 61). In discussing 'barriers of transport', they draw on research by Dhillon (2004), to argue that flexible learning provision with local learning centres offers ease of transportation and provides an incentive to participate in higher education (Gorard *et al.*, 2007: 61). In relation to 'motivational barriers', they argue that 'barriers of any kind are harder for the less motivated prospective student' and that the 'influence of lack of motivation to learn may be underestimated by literature concentrating on the more easily visible barriers such as cost and entry qualifications' (Gorard *et al.*, 2007: 62). Institutional barriers they describe as largely relating to the 'procedures of the providing organizations', including for example advertisement, entry procedures, timing and scale of provision and level of flexibility (Gorard *et al.*, 2007: 63).

Such 'barriers' suggest that there is more to access to, and participation in, higher education than the simple 'removal' of barriers, including individual motivational factors and institutional procedures. However, attention to the ways that inequalities play out in higher education beyond 'barriers' is also important, including an analysis of complex relations of power, cultural and discursive misrecognitions and the ways that the legitimization of particular epistemological perspectives also validates certain subjects as potential HE students. Gorard and his colleagues explain that, although they find the concept of 'barriers' an 'elegant' one, '[r]emoving the apparent barriers to participation is not as easy as it sounds', which 'casts doubt on the value of the concept of barriers as an explanation for non-participation' (Gorard *et al.*, 2007: 63–64). They argue that the 'solution to educational inequality may not be found in education at all' arguing for a 'life course view of participation' (Gorard *et al.*, 2007: 65). I agree that it is important to understand educational inequalities in relation to wider social inequalities, for example in relation to class, gender and race, and to think through the life course in terms of reconceptualizing widening participation. However, it is also crucial that we pay attention to the subtle operations of inequality that are at play within and between educational sites, including colleges and universities. Although always connected to deeper and wider social injustices, this book argues strongly for a transformatory approach to widening participation, that begins from an understanding that a key aspect of the problem of educational inequalities is embedded in the very structures, discursive and cultural practices of education, which tend to privilege the knowledge, experiences and subjectivities connected to historically white racialized, Anglo-American-centric, masculinist and middle-classed perspectives of pedagogies, learning and being a student. However, although I critique and problematize 'barriers' as a concept, there is no doubt that the current financial crisis and the significant cuts to public funding will exacerbate material inequalities and that we might be witnessing the end of widening participation, as constructed by the New Labour Government in the English context.

## Material inequalities and the end of WP

At the time of writing, England is facing unprecedented cuts to the public sector. This is echoed in other national contexts with an economic crisis on a global scale. In England, some universities will face up to 90 per cent cuts in their funding over the next few years and students will see their fees tripling from the current £3,200 to up to £9,000. The focus on spending in the STEM (science, technology, engineering and mathematics) fields means that universities specializing in the arts, humanities and social sciences are particularly vulnerable to these cuts. Universities that recruit a high proportion of the students associated with WP are in jeopardy if fees rise to the levels predicted, as those students are highly unlikely to be able to afford the significant costs of higher education. The MP for higher education, David Willetts, argues that

> What matters is that – as well as the choice to attend university – people have other choices too. On A-level results day at UCAS, I listened to young people who had phoned in, fearful that their life chances had been wrecked because they hadn't got a place at university. But they need to be confident that there are other options as well. We cannot have a

society where university is the only route to a well-paid job and a career. That is bad for social mobility. We are committed to ensuring young people have a wider range of options to choose from: apprenticeships; places at FE college; part-time study; online learning; an ordinary degree first, and then honours – and not necessarily at 18 either. The bottom line is more options and better advice.

(Willetts, 2010)

Although I have argued that we need to interrogate the assumption that HE participation is the best trajectory for young people seen as having the 'potential to benefit', we must do this with great caution and detailed attention to educational inequalities. As the system becomes increasingly selective because there are fewer places and less funding available, it also means that those who come from historically under-represented backgrounds in HE are less likely to have access to the material and cultural resources needed to 'play the game'. Taking up the other options cited by Willets comes of course at a social cost in a context where those from the highest income and professional groups are more likely to have a good honours degree from a high-status university. Willetts acknowledges the great benefits of gaining an under-graduate honours degree: 'Graduates, are – on average – more healthy, more active in the community and more likely to be engaged in the education of their children.' (Willetts, 2010) Yet it appears that, increasingly, the right to higher education will be lost to those who do not have access to the range of capital necessary, including economic but also social and cultural capital in demonstrating their 'right'. However, I will argue in the remainder of the chapter that this is not simply about 'barriers' but about the complex ways that inequalities and misrecognitions play out in the interests of hegemonic habitus, subjectivities and social positions.

## Disrupting the discourse of 'barriers'

In this section I want to disrupt the discourse of barriers to argue that this concept might be contributing to the stabilizing of long-standing inequalities. This is because it constructs issues of educational access and participation in largely superficial terms, which are seen as posing the possibility of simply 'lifting' or 'overcoming' these without examining the deeply embedded processes of privileging certain social groups and epistemological perspectives above others that lie beneath those 'barriers'. Attention to processes of gate-keeping, exclusion and access to privileged forms of knowledge and knowing, for example, demands that we look beyond 'barriers' to the mechanisms in which some groups have access to 'powerful knowledge' and social positioning whilst others do not. Furthermore, attention to the processes by which some groups are able to continue to claim a position of authority over knowledge, truth and knowing is crucial to understanding the privileges that remain beneath and beyond the 'barriers' that are in place.

The notion that motivation, or lack of it, is a key barrier, for example, places again the onus on those constructed as 'deprived' or 'disadvantaged', rather than on the social conditions, discourses and practices by which 'motivation' might be expressed and recognized within the discursive fields of education. The appropriate practices of 'motivation' are not simply straightforward self-expressions of desire and aspiration. Rather, practices of motivation are tied in with access to privileged forms of knowledge and knowing, including knowing the ways that self-motivation might be recognized by those who have the institutional position to recognize it. This is tied in with complex formations of identity, which are embodied and performative; motivation must be 'done' in the 'right' ways by the 'right' kinds of bodily and academic practices in order to gain access to (high-status) higher education. This requires particular forms of being a person, and is tied in with middle-class, white subjectivities and dispositions. The power to be recognized as a 'motivated student' does not reside entirely with the individual because the recognition of 'motivation' is always tied to social practices and embodied identities. The concept of 'barriers' is unable to speak to such complexities and therefore masks the complicated processes by which inequalities are reproduced and, ultimately, the right to higher education denied. Only certain kinds of 'motivated' persons might be recognized as having the right to higher education and this demands the embodied performance of particular ways of being and doing 'student'.

The notion that 'time' is a barrier is another example of the ways in which inequalities might be masked by the concept of 'barriers'. This is not to argue of course that these 'barriers' do not exist in many cases; for example, the lack of childcare provision to cover the period of scheduled classes on a university course might act as a 'barrier' to the educational access and participation of those with childcare commitments during that same period of the week. However, this is merely one aspect of the complexities of time, and tends to conceal the more subtle ways that time is deeply interconnected with inequalities and access to, and participation in, higher education. In the context of neoliberal discourses of 'individual choice' the clashes posed by childcare and university schedules might be perceived as either individual choice (i.e. to have children) and/or poor time management skills. In this framework, the problem lies with individual choice and decision-makers and the 'barriers' of time are constructed as relatively straightforward. The individual might overcome those barriers, for example, by drawing on supportive family members (e.g. grandmothers) to provide childcare. Another solution might be seen for the university programme to offer classes that are scheduled within the school day. If this is not available, that individual might be re/constructed as a problem. In my research with Jackie McManus on access to art and design courses (Burke and McManus, 2009), for example, the admissions tutors often cited such issues as being a reason to avoid taking such candidates on their course, because they were seen as students who would struggle and need additional support. Such conceptualizations of time though ignore the gendered and classed nature of time and the social and institutional inequalities that shape the possibilities for 'overcoming' such 'barriers'.

Time might also be understood in more complicated ways, beyond discourses of 'barriers', in relation to Bourdieu's concepts of capital. For example, Mills and Gale, drawing on Bourdieu's work in the context of Australian schooling, explain that those groups 'whose cultural capital is not always highly valued in schools, frequently find their access to dominant forms [of cultural capital] restricted to time in school'. (2010: 75). This concept of 'restricted time' draws attention to Bourdieu's argument that 'cultural capital cannot be transmitted instantaneously; its accumulation requires an investment, above all of time' (Mills and Gale, 2010). This highlights that time is more than a simple 'barrier' to do with organizational issues of timetabling or time management but is a deeply entrenched form of exclusion that ensures access to 'highly prized capitals' for some social groups and not others (Mills and Gale, 2010: 76).

Mills and Gale (2010: 75–79) explore the relationship of parents to schools in Australia and interrogate the common assumption that some parents 'don't care' about their children's schooling. This is connected to deficit discourses that assume that some individuals lack interest, motivation and the right kinds of values, which is often implied by the discourse of 'barriers'. They argue that the level of parental involvement in children's schooling is not about lack of motivation, interests or values but connected to complex reasons, including 'that it is the culture of the dominant group which is embodied in schools; a culture in which not all parents are equally knowledgeable' (Mills and Gale, 2010: 77; see also Crozier and Davies, 2007).

## Thinking beyond barriers to participatory pedagogies

The concept of barriers has tended to fix attention to lifting financial, time or geographical barriers to ensure that students from under-represented backgrounds are able to access higher education. I have outlined the limitations of such a conceptual framework above, in the way that 'barriers' ignores deeper-level inequalities that cannot simply be 'lifted' or 'overcome'. Barriers that are recognized at the level of actual participation in higher education, after entry to university, tend to be conceptualized in terms of the need for remedial provision, such as academic language support or additional study skills classes. The focus of attention thus tends to be on individual students constructed as 'weak' and in need of additional help, usually provided outside their programme of study, with their writing skills.

Yet, inequalities are maintained through such a focus of attention, not only because the problem of widening participation is constructed largely in terms of discourses of individual student deficit. The remedial approach to the teaching of writing also tends to focus on the *mechanics* of writing as a set of techniques or skills, without engaging students in discussions about writing as methodology (Burke and Hermerschmidt, 2005). I argue that such approaches to the teaching of academic writing not only contribute to the reproduction of exclusion and misrecognition but also are deeply pedagogically flawed. The struggles of writing, both intellectually and emotionally, are made absent, collapsing writing into a set of skills and a linear process rather than the iterative, subjective, emotional and complicated process it often is. For example, reading is often taught in terms of different methods of reading, such as skimming and scanning. The complex interrelationship between reading and writing is not given full attention, including processes of 'being critical', drawing on the relevant literature and developing a logical and coherent argument. How students make decisions about what to read and what literature to draw on in their writing is not considered in relation to wider power relations: how does the student position herself in relation to 'the field' and the voices in the literature that carry with them status, power and authority? In what ways might the student bring in the voices of others to give legitimacy and authority to her own voice and in locating herself as the author of her text? Such decisions and approaches are central to the process of developing an authorial voice, one that is recognized by others as valid in relation to disciplinary frameworks and shared assumptions, often left unspoken, about what counts as knowledge and 'being critical' within that community of practice. Such approaches have the effect of re/locating issues of access and participation with the individual student's writing, rather than understanding that particular literacy practices may narrow who can be recognized as a legitimate author/student in higher education. The teaching of writing tends to construct the written text as separate from ontology and epistemology. This ignores the production of text as a discursive process that is constitutive of knowledge: knowledge about the social world and knowledge about ourselves and our position within it. Modes of assessment that rely on written text and yet assume that student writing is decontextualized and separate from disciplinary and social practices and relations play a key role in re/producing exclusions and inequalities. This pushes the focus beyond 'barriers', which often lead to deficit perspectives of the 'problem' of widening participation, towards a concern with pedagogical approaches in relation to writing and the production of meaning-making and subjectivity.

I argue that we need to disrupt problematic and narrow concepts of 'barriers' and instead focus on developing pedagogies in higher education that acknowledge the complex processes by which writing is produced by students. This involves the pulling together, rather than separating out, of pedagogy, curriculum and assessment, so that how we learn and teach is connected to what we learn and teach, and how we then assess what has been learned and taught. Writing and other academic practices, such as reading and speaking, must be considered in relation to the development of pedagogies for widening participation. For example, it is important for teachers and students to have the critical spaces to re/consider the implications of different writing practices, conventions and frameworks in higher education. Teachers and students could collaboratively examine the conventions underpinning privileged and regulatory ways of writing and representing knowledge to unearth taken-for-granted assumptions about what counts as knowledge and who counts as knowing. Rather than be separated out from subject or disciplinary knowledge, writing in this framework is recognized as part of the process of constituting meaning. Writing is a key part of the learning process rather than simply an objective tool of assessment to measure achievement. Writing is a 'method of inquiry' (Richardson, 2000), a pedagogical tool and research practice that creates meaning and ways of knowing and understanding. This develops a reflexive practice, bringing together the 'autobiography of the question' and the notion of writing as a method of inquiry:

> I consider writing as a method of inquiry, a way of finding out about yourself and your topic. Although we usually think about writing as a mode of 'telling' about the social world, writing is not just a mopping-up activity at the end of a research project. Writing is also a way of 'knowing' – a method of discovery and analysis. By writing in different ways, we discover new aspects of our topic and our relationship to it. Form and content are inseparable.
>
> When we view writing as a method, ... we experience 'language-in-use', how we 'word the world' into existence (Rose, 1992). And then we 'reword' the world, erase the computer screen, check the thesaurus, move the paragraph, again and again. This 'worded world' never accurately, precisely, completely captures the studied world, yet we persist in trying. Writing as a method of inquiry honours and encourages the trying, recognizing it as embryonic to the full-fledged attention to the significance of language.
>
> Writing as a method of inquiry ... provides a research practice through which we can investigate how we construct the world, ourselves and others, and how standard objectifying practices of social science unnecessarily limit us and social science. Writing as method does not take writing for granted, but offers multiple ways to learn to do it, and to nurture the writer.
>
> (Richardson, 2000)

Understanding writing as part of the process of learning and meaning-making, rather than as a reflection of what one knows, radically alters teachers' and students' pedagogical approaches to writing in higher education. Writing is not seen as a barrier but as a pedagogical tool. Issues of power become foregrounded as students have the opportunity to consider how certain texts and certain writers represent their knowledge claims and how these are recognized as il/legitimate and in/valid. This moves away from hegemonic approaches to the teaching of writing, such as bringing in models of 'good essays' to explain to students what 'good writing' looks like. Such an approach suggests to students that there is only one way of writing in higher education and misses the opportunities for students to develop the critical perspectives required to develop their writing and sense of authorial voice.

It is useful for students to have the opportunity to work with pieces of student writing but in a way that emphasizes writing as methodology. In this framework, students might analyse different examples of writing, not to place them as 'good' or 'bad', but to consider more sophisticated questions about the written text and its production. For example, how does the writer/reader locate herself in the writing? If she uses the first person, what effect does that have on the claims that she is making? How does the writer draw on other writers exploring similar lines of enquiry? Which voices are dominating and which are subdued or erased? How does this link to the writer's theoretical and/or methodological framework(s)? What is the relation between form and content in the text? In what ways is the writer developing a critical analysis and position? These and other questions begin to expose the complexity of writing practices, how writing is always connected to relations of power and author/ity, how formations of identity underpin the text and its claims to knowledge and the epistemological perspectives privileged in and through the text (e.g. positivist, post-structuralist, feminist, etc). Such pedagogies are able to deal with questions of method and skill whilst also paying attention to wider issues of methodology and process. This creates a space where students are able collectively to decode the practices of writing, so that it is no longer mysterious and unknown to those who have not had access to the forms of literacy most privileged in academic spaces.

## Writing as a form of exclusion

Importantly, hegemonic discourses about 'good academic writing' contribute significantly to the creation of the boundaries around access to, and participation in, higher education, and this is increasingly linked to notions of a skills-based society and the 'knowledge economy'. In this context, access to HE has been identified as a key policy imperative, expressed through the hegemonic neoliberal discourse of 'widening participation'. However, the politics of knowledge production in relation to discourses of 'skill' and 'knowledge economy' is largely hidden within this policy discourse. Research conducted within universities is seen as of major strategic importance in policy on higher education in terms of the 'knowledge economy' (DfES 2003a). However, the implications of an increasingly hierarchical, diverse and differentiated higher education terrain – for example institutions seen as 'research-intensive', and recruiting a mainly 'traditional' student body, and those seen as teaching-intensive, recruiting a larger proportion of 'non-traditional' students – is not being explicitly addressed. Who is seen as worthy of HE access and to what forms of HE (Reay *et al.*, 2001; Reay *et al.*, 2005)? Who is associated with 'knowledge' and who with 'skill'? Who is able to participate in producing knowledge and in what contexts (Burke 2002; Burke and Jackson, 2007)? Different forms of writing (and reading) that students participate in are tied to such issues and questions. Furthermore, different forms of literacy determine the kinds of institutions that students might aspire to and this is made explicit in higher education policy texts (e.g. DfES 2003a). Standards, quality and access become entangled in problematic ways, without clear consideration of the assumptions behind what counts as 'quality', 'high standards', and how and why this is inextricably linked to issues of access, participation and in/equality (Burke and Jackson, 2007).

Students constructed as 'non-traditional' through policy discourses are caught up in the politics of knowledge and identity, and the literacy practices that are privileged are often unfamiliar, alienating and intimidating. I argue that this is far more complex than the notion of 'barriers' is able to acknowledge; this is about complex processes of misrecognition and exclusion. Such limited frameworks for understanding students' engagement with academic and pedagogic practices reinforces exclusionary forces, not only at the structural level, but also at the emotional level, in which students talk about 'not being good enough', or not fitting in (Skeggs, 1997; Reay, 2001; Burke, 2002; Bowl, 2003; Reay, 2003). This does not just play out in ways that disadvantage certain student groups but also produces inequalities among academics, who are similarly classed, gendered and racialized. The privileging of the masculine, white racialized, English-speaking and middle-class authorial voice is one of the 'myriad ways in which women are undermined and excluded from access to resources, influence, career opportunities and academic authority' (Morley, 1999: 4). However, such dynamics also work to exclude men from backgrounds traditionally under-represented in higher education.

Students are expected to meet the specific conventions of the academy, although these conventions are themselves contested and heterogeneous across a range of different and often competing contexts. Particular constructions of 'academic knowledge' regulate what can be claimed and who can claim certain meanings in their writing. Knowledge that is seen as 'subjective' or 'personal' is often at risk of being discounted and there are certain rules of the game that must be adhered to if a student is going to succeed in higher education. 'Other' bodies of knowledge that the student might bring to their work are often invalidated if the student does not construct that knowledge to fit in with the expectations of the relevant discipline and academic context. For example, students must often frame their understanding in terms not of practical or professional knowledge but in relation to academic knowledge, the literature or 'the field' that will then validate the points they want to make. In speaking 'the field', the complex processes that might constitute 'the field' are silenced – who is seen as 'in' and who is seen as 'out' of the field. Complex processes of selection and regulation are rendered invisible through hegemonic discourses of writing as 'skill' or 'technique'. For example, referencing is largely taught in higher education as method – 'how to' cite, 'how to' construct a bibliography. However Burke and Hermerschmidt (2005) argue that referencing is a social practice, which involves meticulous processes of selection, editing and 'orchestrating the voices' (Lillis and Ramsey, 1997) in a contested 'field' of study.

Teresa Lillis argues that the writing frameworks and conventions privileged in higher education require students to participate in very particular kinds of literacy practice. Those students who are unfamiliar with these practices are often misrecognized as intellectually inferior or lacking ability. She also points out that this practice 'involves and invokes particular ways of meaning/wording, and can consequently serve to exclude others' (Lillis, 2001, 40). This highlights that academic writing is not simply a barrier to accessing higher education; it is a form of exclusion and misrecognition and shapes judgments about who has the right to higher education. However, writing is embedded in contested power relations and different social and disciplinary contexts and therefore can be a practice of resistance and subversion as well as exclusion and misrecognition. The essay is constituted through particular modes of representation, produced through the authorial voice, which demonstrates 'criticality' and develops a coherent argument that substantiates its claims through referencing 'the relevant field'. Assumptions are made about what 'criticality' is, what constitutes the relevant field and the forms of writing that create a recognizable and coherent argument. In my book with Sue Jackson (Burke and Jackson, 2007), we argue that writing practices in higher education might operate as forms of exclusion but also, and sometimes simultaneously, as forms of resistance. As new modes of writing are being developed in higher education in the context of widening participation, such as the learning journal and the portfolio, spaces are opened for the possibilities of resistance to privileged epistemological frameworks that uphold notions emerging from positivist frames of reference, such as 'objectivity', 'rationality', 'validity' and certain ways of being critical. In our book, we attempt to draw on such forms of resistance by writing in 'Other' ways: using, for example, fictional narratives and vignettes to highlight the struggles over access to learning and being recognized and legitimated in formal educational institutions. This was a deliberate strategy to resist the conventions of the academic voice and to present our ideas in forms other than the essay (although we write in conventional academic ways in the book too). It also enabled us to show the different literacy practices that subjects engage in within formal educational contexts, including, for example, composing emails and writing minutes, as well as reflective journal writing.

Mary Evans conceptualizes writing as a 'survival strategy' which has 'allowed individuals to occupy a conventional private space while constructing a radical world of the imagination' (Evans, 2004: 129). She explains that: 'writing is not just about the conscientious fulfillment of professional expectations; it can also be about protest' (Evans, 2004: 129). However, writing does not only act as a form of resistance, as Evans acknowledges. Writing can be a key gate-keeping device, ensuring that particular forms of epistemology carry status and privilege, giving legitimacy to certain knowers and those students recognized as having the right forms of linguistic capital (Burke and Hermerschmidt, 2005). As argued above, writing is inextricably connected to complex relations of power and formations of identity (Ivanic, 1998; Lea and

Street, 2000; Creme, 2003). The essay is a 'gendered practice-resource', operating around a binary framework, which 'provides particular ways of meaning-making' (Lillis, 2001: 129). The binary framework of the essay 'privileges particular dimensions of meaning-making over "others"' (Lillis, 2001: 129). Lillis explores, through an analysis of her interviews with women students from 'non-traditional' backgrounds, the desires of women writers and their longing for connection and involvement.

> It is no accident that these categorizations of 'other' – for example, emotion, evocation, informality – are precisely those dimensions of meaning that those historically constructed as 'others' should desire. The women writers seem to accept the dominant conventions in constructing their texts, but resist them in their thinking about what their texts are, or might be.
>
> (Lillis, 2001: 129)

Academic writing involves struggles at the intellectual and emotional levels and it is ultimately about author/izing the self, the production of an authorial and authoritative voice. It involves complex selection processes, which are deemed to be 'objective' and are talked about simply in technical terms of 'referencing' and 'editing' but are actually about 'orchestrating the voices' of contested fields (Lillis and Ramsey, 1997), while also crafting an authorial voice that is recognized as authoritative by (legitimated) others. Audience is central in the process and assumes an ontological link between self and other. Writing in higher education requires complex decoding of tacit understandings and conventions that often remain mysterious to those on the outside of academia. Academic writing therefore is an exclusive practice, serving as a gate-keeping mechanism.

In my research on students' transitions to Masters-level of study funded by the Higher Education Academy (see Chapter Five for details), I developed an intervention and explored this with a group of students. The intervention was a writing workshop that drew on the theoretical insights discussed above and was situated in a 'writing as social practice' framework (Lea and Street, 2000; Lillis, 2001; Burke and Jackson, 2007). In the workshop, the students worked with pieces of writing to ask questions of the text and to try to understand what it might mean to 'be explicit', 'be critical' and 'orchestrate the voices' through referencing practices. They also used Laurel Richardson's idea of 'writing as a method of enquiry' (Richardson, 2000) to explore their experiences of writing and to develop their writing plans and material. A key aim of the workshop intervention was to move beyond a 'barrier' approach to widening participation, which tends to conceptualize academic writing as a set of skills and techniques with the need to provide remedial and additional support to students perceived to have 'problems' with their writing. Rather, I aimed for the workshop to take an inclusive pedagogical approach that acknowledged the complicated processes that writing entails for all students, including the intellectual and emotional struggle of crafting and producing a piece of writing for assessment. I deliberately organized this as a workshop embedded in the course, rather than as additional support for students identified as 'needing help' with their writing. The workshop emphasized the importance of the different contexts in which writing is produced and also the identities and perspectives that profoundly shape the student-authors' experiences of, and approaches to, writing. After the workshop, I interviewed the students in groups about their experiences of writing and of the workshop intervention. In the discussion they raise a number of key issues in relation to writing experiences and processes and consider the value of the workshop intervention. Mark, who feels quite confident about his writing, explains the significance of the workshop being embedded in the course, rather than as an additional option:

> Mark: I think writing is one of the things that I feel able at, so that I wouldn't perhaps have chosen to go to an extra course, but it is actually really useful in enlightening me to the different styles of academic writing that were needed for this particular course. So it is perfect that it is embedded into the course.

Gary explains that the workshop would have been useful to him as an undergraduate to help explore 'thought patterns' and ways of structuring his writing:

> Gary: I would have liked something like this in my undergrad. It would have directed me so much better ... something actually in the course saying this is how we do it, this is how we expect the writing to be, because again I think the writing is very personal to a subject and like my writing now is very different to what I was doing in my undergrad and even in what I was doing in my PGCE. Like there are very different styles of writing and so it would have been useful. This {workshop} was excellent because I have actually realized what I need to do in terms of my dissertation and how I need to structure it, maybe what thought patterns I need to have instead, and obviously having that clear guideline will hopefully help.

In referring back to the anxieties she expressed about writing earlier in the group interview, Beth talked about the fear that she might be laughed at if her writing is not of the standard expected by her tutors at Masters-level:

> Beth: I think it is really important actually to embed it and wish that it had been earlier on for me. I think it would have helped with the anxieties that I was talking about at the start. You know they are just going to laugh when they get these essays; it is just not at all the standard that they are expecting. Because if you have never worked at that level before, you don't know at all whether you are achieving the standard ... .

In the second group interview, Tina talked about the importance of our deconstruction of key concepts in writing methodology, for example 'being explicit' and 'being critical'. She explained that these were ideas she often took for granted herself and that would be useful not only in her own writing but also in her teaching of writing to her sixth-form students. She implies that she will take up a more critically reflexive position in her teaching and writing practices:

> Tina: I really liked the bit where you were talking about all the different ways of interpreting, be explicit and be critical, because I am an English teacher, so I find the writing bit okay and I mark people's essays all the time, so I find that bit fine, but I think as a teacher I write, 'be explicit' and it is quite useful to see it like that and I can imagine me writing a similar thing and then going back to that checklist and just sort of, it is that meta-cognition isn't it, I guess? Because I can always be too comfortable with what I am doing and it is making me think a bit more carefully I think.
>
> PJB: Well, actually that hopefully is where the connection between the research and the practice comes, because hopefully some of this will be helpful to your practice that way.
>
> Tina: Well I could see myself giving those bullet points to my students, to my sixth form, to check against.

Two of the male students, Matt and Tony, in the second group interview also talk about the issue of student accessibility to concepts and ideas in relation to different higher education teachers and their pedagogical practices. It is notable that accessibility is equated to 'dumbing down', a derogatory discourse used frequently in everyday talk about the anxieties of widening participation:

> Matt: I mean for me, the way you deliver things is much more dumbed down academic speak and clarifies things for me than some of the other lectures that we have and I come away thinking, 'I know what these words mean now' and it actually does mean something to me, whereas in a lot of other sessions we have had, I go home with a headache thinking, 'What has happened?' But on your last session, I had a eureka moment; finally I get this.
>
> Tony: Do you often think though that is sometimes the way it is presented at times, you have got nothing to put your hat on? You can't hang your hat on anything. Because actually it is not saying, 'This is it'. Sometimes, well me personally I want to know that that is it. Okay, some things are not as black and white as that, but I think people sometimes just make problems and say, 'Well what does this mean?' Well what do you think it means? I think that is what you did quite clearly today.

The students are referring to pedagogical practices that move beyond the notion of barriers to inclusive, interactive and participatory pedagogies, which aim to involve the students in deconstructing key discourses in relation to their 'thought patterns', perspectives and experiences. In this way, they have a sense of connection to those ideas; what seems distant and abstract and inaccessible now, the students suggest, had resonance with their own interests and subjectivities. Writing as a methodology allowed them to further explore these connections, building a sense of confidence as authors of their writing and learning. The students highlight the vulnerability attached to academic writing, through which the right to higher education is often judged in relation to standards that require the complex decoding of unspoken expectations. Concepts of 'being explicit' and 'being critical' are often the explicit expectations shared with students and yet these are not straightforward writing 'skills' but rather complex social practices located within particular disciplinary and academic contexts.

## Final reflections

This chapter has argued for the importance of shifting the focus from 'lifting barriers' to a critical and reflexive framework, which takes seriously the complex dynamics of power and inequality. Such a framework is underpinned by a strong commitment to social justice and emphasizes the need to carefully consider the deep-rooted nature of educational inequalities and develop sophisticated tools and strategies to disrupt these. The focus in such a framework moves away from individual deficits and disadvantage to attention to socially embedded and historical formations of inequality and misrecognition that are tied to subjectivities. Tools such as reflexivity and praxis could be taken up, not only by researchers but also by policy-makers, practitioners, managers and students. Attention is being drawn away from the 'targeting' of certain individuals or groups to the need to transform educational structures, practices, cultures and discourses with detailed attention to participation. The concept of participation is thus broadened beyond entry to higher education and/or taking a university course, to who participates in developing educational policies and practices, meaning-making and knowledge production and who is represented and/or silenced in pedagogical processes, relations and practices.

# 9   WP professional subjectivities and practices

This chapter focuses on the processes of subjective construction in relation to those who have specific responsibility for WP in higher educational institutions. This will draw on data from interviews with WP practitioners, as well as their written reflections. Little attention has been paid to the production of new professional identities in higher education as part of the expanding WP market (Burke, 2008). Jones and Thomas argue that WP practitioners tend to work on the periphery of universities, in separate centres and outside academic faculties and departments (Jones and Thomas, 2005). This chapter will consider the ways that these workers themselves might be constructed as 'non-traditional' and even marginal in academic spaces. Those who have specific responsibility for WP in universities tend to have non-academic posts and this might have implications for the ways in which they are constructed within different institutions as well as for the processes of decision-making, allocation of resources and the development of WP strategies. Complex power relations are at play within universities, which are intensely hierarchical institutions, although of course this plays out in different ways across a highly differentiated higher education system. WP professionals within higher education have primary responsibility for developing and sustaining WP strategies within their institutions and in this way WP has its own special space, outside the main work of academic staff. The ways in which the new WP professional workforce is constructed matters and impacts on decision-making processes, including the potential for serious questioning of what WP is, questions such as: what is meant by 'widening participation'?; what are the implications of being constructed as a WP practitioner/student?; who is responsible for WP and how might this shape strategic directions and the allocation of resources?; how is WP related to other key issues such as quality assurance/enhancement and issues of equality and diversity?; and how is WP related to academic practices in higher education such as pedagogy, curriculum and assessment? Questions of identity matter as well in terms of power relations within institutions and the constructions of (lack of) authority that might facilitate or impede processes of change and transformation. This chapter will explore these questions by drawing on in-depth interviews with those who have specific responsibility for widening participation in HE, as well as their reflections of their experiences and identities through written reflective accounts.

## Widening participation and professional identities in higher education

Although there has been a growing body of work on WP and the experiences and identities of students from 'non-traditional' backgrounds (e.g. Parr, 2000; Burke, 2002; Bowl, 2003; Crozier and Reay, 2008), little attention has been paid to the production of a new professional workforce in higher education with specific responsibility for WP strategy and practice. There is a dearth of data available to understand the size and constitution of this new professional body. WP professionals tend to work on the periphery of universities, in separate centres and outside academic faculties and departments (Jones and Thomas, 2005). Activities to 'raise aspirations' have been prioritized in WP policy, yet such activities tend to be detached from the main work of universities and arguably have 'little or no impact on institutional structure and culture' (Jones and Thomas, 2005: 617). If Jones and Thomas (2005) are correct that most WP work takes place at the margins of universities, what are the possibilities for deep-seated patterns of educational inequality and exclusion to be shifted, disrupted and challenged? Those who have specific responsibility for WP in universities tend to have non-academic posts and this has important implications for the ways in which they are constructed within different institutions as well as for the processes of decision-making, allocation of resources and the development of WP strategies. Complex power relations are at play within universities, which are intensely hierarchical institutions, although of course this plays out in different ways across a highly differentiated higher education system (Morley, 2003). WP professionals have primary responsibility for developing and sustaining WP strategies within their institutions and in this way WP has its own special space, outside the main work of academic staff.

The majority of literature on professional identity in higher education focuses on academic identities (e.g. Henkel, 2000, Anderson and Williams, 2001; Morley, 2003). This literature is concerned to understand the impact of a changing higher educational landscape on conceptualizing academic identity and notions of professionalism.

> Higher education is undergoing a series of complex overlapping changes, which are profoundly affecting its organisational structures, traditional practices, and the way in which its institutions and those who work within them are viewed by the public.
>
> (Nixon *et al.*, 2001: 229)

Nixon *et al.* (2001) outline the literature on professionalism and higher education, which presents a crisis of professional identity in universities as a result of expansion, new managerialism, increasingly diverse practices, lack of autonomy and self-regulation and alternative values and aspirations (Nixon *et al.*, 2001: 231). They present an alternative conceptualization of professionalism in the following ways:

> It sees professionalism as the capacity of an occupational group to be extrovert, generous and knowledgeable in its relations with professional colleagues, other professional groups, and 'the public'. It defines professionalism, therefore, not in terms of status and self-regulation, but in terms of values and practices. Why I do what I do is of the utmost significance; as are the deliberative processes whereby I address that 'why'. Without this emphasis on the moral purposefulness of practice, there would be no claim to professionalism.
>
> (Nixon *et al.*, 2001: 234)

Clearly the emphasis on values and practices is significant and important in the context of WP. Indeed, as I have argued in earlier chapters, a transformative approach to widening participation places strong emphasis on the ways that academic practices are tied up with the values, identities, epistemologies and perspectives of hegemonic and privileged social groups (e.g. middle class, white racialized and (hetero)masculinized). However, this concept of professionalism does not go far enough; there is no explicit analysis of power relations and inequalities and how these operate within the complex and subtle micropolitics of higher educational organizations and institutions (Morley, 1999; Burke and Jackson, 2007). Furthermore, little attention has been paid to the production of new professional identities in higher education as part of the WP agenda. There is a range of new professional roles within and outside higher education as a result of WP policy. Yet, WP staff tends to work on the periphery of universities, in separate centres and outside academic faculties and departments.

> Subsequently, widening participation initiatives in utilitarian influenced higher education institutions are more or less 'bolted on' to core work, for example mentoring and guidance activities, learning support mechanisms (via 'study skills centres', etc.) and stand-alone student services (Layer *et al.*, 2003). Whilst research examining student services has identified some examples of integrated student support, many student service departments reported institutional resistance to their integration into core activity (Thomas *et al.*, 2003a).
>
> (Jones and Thomas, 2005)

There has been some research specifically on new and emergent professional identities in higher education that is helpful for thinking about the positioning of staff working specifically on WP (Whitchurch, 2008a, 2008b, 2009). Whitchurch has developed a useful conceptual framework for theorizing professional identities in higher education, including bounded, unbounded and cross-boundary professionals. Bounded professionals are located within specific functional or organizational boundaries, governed by particular rules and resources (Whitchurch, 2008b). Those working within widening participation remits tend to be either unbounded or cross-boundary professionals. Unbounded professionals have a 'more open-end and exploratory approach to the broadly based projects' they are involved in and cross-boundary professionals use boundaries to 'build strategic advantage and institutional capacity, capitalizing on their knowledge of territories on either side of the boundaries that they encountered' (Whitchurch, 2008b: 377).

Although the work of Whitchurch provides a useful framework for thinking about those professional identities that fall outside traditional academic identities, we still require further research to build an understanding of the constitution of the specific WP professional workforce. This would include attention to their location in different higher education institutions and their experiences of being on the front line of widening participation strategies. Such research would shed light on the construction of this new workforce in universities in relation to the impact of their positioning on the approaches and strategies being taken with the aim to widen participation.

From the small-scale study undertaken for this book, which involved qualitative research (see Chapter Five for a discussion of the methods), I will show that the field is highly differentiated and that this has implications for the resources and opportunities available to different constituencies of students in relation to their geographic and institutional location, as well as the different strategies being developed and imagined by WP professionals and their teams.

In the main, it seems that those who are explicitly part of WP teams in higher education tend to be institutionally categorized as non-academic staff. The status of WP professionals has significant implications for their work across their institutions with other members of staff. WP professionals have primary responsibility for developing and sustaining WP strategies within their institutions and in this way WP has its own special space, often outside the main work of academic staff, profoundly limiting the impact of widening participation policies and strategies. The knowledge that WP professionals bring to higher education is likely to be placed at a lower value than academic and disciplinary knowledge, and this might exacerbate the distancing between WP strategy and academic identities in relation to developing institutional cultures and practices for widening participation, including pedagogies, curriculum and assessment. However, there are potential spaces for the merging of different formations of knowledge, which provide the possibilities for imagining new ways of doing. Clegg argues, for example, that newer forms of knowledge are emerging in higher education, 'breaking down traditional assumptions in some areas of universities' (Clegg, 2005: 24).

The concern to merge different formations of knowledge might usefully be connected to the work of Bernstein in his distinction between sacred and profane forms of knowledge (Bernstein, 2000 in Abbas and McLean, 2010: 245). Drawing on Bernstien's concepts of profane and sacred knowledge, Abbas and McLean examine the pedagogic tensions between a 'managerial and market-ised quality agenda', associated with the profane, and 'the redistributive principles necessary to address inequality' (Abbas and McLean, 2010: 246). Although academics are the 'custodians of "sacred" pedagogic discourses', in contemporary higher education fields, which are increasingly shaped by 'new forms of regulation', the profane represents the requirement for higher education to become 'international big business' and is also connected to managerial discourses of quality (Abbas and McLean, 2010: 246). In thinking about the gaps, tensions and conflicts between the profane and sacred, and quality and equality, and the derogatory discourses of WP which often construct WP as undermining quality by 'dumbing down', WP professionals must negotiate and mediate these different knowledge formations and perspectives, and this of course differs according to institutional and national context. I will explore this in more detail, when I draw on the accounts of the WP professionals I interviewed, later in this chapter.

However, my main argument is that it is important to understand more clearly the different forms of knowledge, experience and perspectives that WP professionals bring to higher education and the impact of that on the cultures, values and practices within different institutional spaces. In my own professional work, I designed a course on widening participation policy and practice. The course was motivated by my concern to bring theory and practice more explicitly together in dialogue, to explore the potential of using critical sociological tools to transform practice and to interrogate theory through analyzing the experiences of professionals. This I hoped would open up spaces of dialogue between practitioners and researchers to refine theoretical and professional perspectives in response to the challenges and realities of everyday practice and professional knowledge and experience. During my six years of teaching the course, I was struck by the common expression of a rather relentless denial of institutional authority when the course participants were talking about their experiences of effecting change in their respective insti-tutions. They often referred to their experiences of not being taken seriously within their professional settings, sometimes because of their 'non-academic' status. A common purpose for taking part in the module was that the parti-cipants wanted to find an (academic and authoritative) language/discourse that would allow their perspectives to be taken more seriously by their col-leagues, particularly their academic colleagues. I will explore the implications of institutional positioning and subjective construction further, drawing on interviews with WP professionals.

## Professional identities and approaches to WP

I have drawn attention to the significance of structural inequalities and cul-tural misrecognitions in relation to the construction of identities of those associated with widening participation. Complex, multiple and shifting identities, produced within educational sites, have been put at the centre of consideration. This is in the context of WP policy that privileges economic-oriented concerns and tends to ignore issues of identity, difference and inequality. I have argued that the onus of WP rests mainly on those new WP professionals who are often denied the levels of status, authority and power required to effect change. This is highly problematic in a context where WP is often treated as a separate issue rather than integrated into the development of professional and academic practices across the university. Academic practices themselves are rarely interrogated in relation to issues of multiple and complex social exclusions (Burke and Hermerschmidt, 2005; Burke and Jackson, 2007) and this, I argue, is highly problematic for WP and those given responsibility for it.

It is important of course to note that not only are *student* identities constituted in complex and multiple ways that are always intimately interconnected with wider social and power relations across complex social differences but so too are *professional* identities. In *Reconceptualising Lifelong Learning*, Sue Jackson and I aim to illuminate through fictional narratives the complicated ways that inequalities and misrecognitions are produced and how these are tied in with complex identities, resistances and subjectivities (Burke and Jackson, 2007). WP professionals are constituted in relation to the discursive ways that their bodies and subjectivities are read off (in terms of age, class, race and gender for example) and also in relation to the discourses of WP itself. To further explore these conceptual points, I offer an analysis of interview and reflective accounts of widening participation professionals produced for this book (see Chapter Five for further details about the methodological framework).

Lisa, who is based at a Russell Group university, writes in a reflective piece about the ways she is positioned, not only by colleagues in the wider university, but also by others on the widening participation team she works with. She writes that:

> It was unbelievable to me that people who claimed to believe in WP should treat colleagues who had come from that background in such a bad way. Our big boss used to walk past me on the corridor and not even acknowledge me. I would go to meetings with colleagues in my team who were officially less qualified than me, yet if I spoke, they would talk over me or smile condescendingly then put my ideas across in a slightly different way, the ideas always seemed to be worth more if one of the others put them across.
>
> (Lisa, written reflection, July 2010)

Social class background emerges as a significant theme in the accounts of the widening participation professionals as a form of 'othering' and institutional marginalization. This is about the contradiction within the professional community about who might be recognized as 'one of us' and the signifiers that might contribute to processes of professional subjective construction. Sarah writes:

> Another response to discovering where I originally come from is to assume that I don't know anything – it shocks my colleagues to discover that a working class girl has been to a 'posh' university. Is it any wonder that I feel like an outsider when people are patronising me in one way or another!
>
> (Sarah, written reflection, February 2011)

Despite the forms of symbolic and verbal violence they describe, including being patronized and ridiculed, both Lisa and Sarah express their passionate commitment to the project of widening participation in higher education. Although also a source of marginalization, their passionate commitment to WP is deeply connected to their personal experiences of being positioned in and through social inequalities. Sarah explains that her commitment to WP relates directly to her experiences of accessing higher education as transforming her life chances:

> I suppose my own experience is entirely behind my decision to work as a WP manager in an 'elite' university. My life is so different from that of my peers at school that it actually took me a long time to enjoy any of my successes because I felt so guilty. Education gave me, a working class woman, an opportunity to make choices for myself and a degree of financial independence unheard of in the working class community I come from for men or women.
>
> (Sarah, written reflection, February 2011)

It is interesting that Sarah expresses a sense of guilt connected to her academic and career achievements, and this seems to be connected to the feelings of 'discomfort, ambivalence and uncertainty' that often arise when habitus confronts an unfamiliar field (Reay *et al.*, 2005: 28). Sarah makes a clear distinction between the different forms of transformation that HE participation might contribute to and how this relates to her personal commitment to WP. She is very clear that it is not about transforming the attitudes of working-class people. Rather it is about the possibility of transforming life chances that motivates her professional commitment to widening participation as a project of social justice:

> I went to university because I was interested in studying the subject I studied, but I feel that it actually transformed my life, and made me have a life that is so different from my peers, my working-class peers at school, from my family, and it kind of made me realize what education just gives you. I'm not saying it makes you a better person, I certainly don't believe that, or it's the only thing to do, but I know it's made a huge, massive,

difference to my life, and I really strongly believe that more people should have access to Higher Education. And it's nothing to do with kind of innate intelligence, it's largely to do with background, and I feel really, really, strongly committed to that, so I think that's a kind of general overarching kind of ethos that I feel that spurred me to work in widening participation, and because I've got a professional background in working in education with young people it just seemed kind of perfect, kind of a perfect job, something I wanted to do that would really enable me to be involved on a day-to-day basis in what I believe in.

(Sarah, interview, July 2010)

In the analysis I offer, it is important to keep sight of the complex intersections between social class positioning and gendered subjectivities. The struggles that Sarah and Lisa face in being recognized as professionals in higher education and in asserting positions of authority are produced at the intersections of embodied classed and gendered subjectivities, which are also tied to their racialized identities and politics of mis/recognition. It is interesting to contrast their accounts with Jack, who also comes from a working-class background, but does not speak about experiences of explicit marginalization. As a white English man in higher education, he positions himself quite differently in his account and there is a strong sense of his institutional authority in his role as a manager and leader of WP at a Russell Group university. He takes up the cross-boundary identity described by Whitchurch (2008b), in the ways he seems to use his 'understanding of boundaries to perform interpretive and translational functions across the institution' (Whitchurch, 2009: 2). Importantly, the institutional context in which they work is also central to the construction of their intersecting classed, gendered and professional subjectivities – Jack, Lisa and Sarah all work in elite institutions. Similar to Lisa and Sarah, in Jack's account of his trajectory through education and in the process of becoming a WP professional, his social class background features as central to his experiences and understanding of WP. However, he talks about this in terms of social mobility and the aspiration to 'get myself into careers and professions that my parents never experienced themselves'. Jack does not speak of forms of marginalization; rather, his positioning as a professional in his university is presented as unproblematic, stable and respected. In his account, Jack is a recognized and included subject and his positioning does not appear to be questioned or undermined by his colleagues. He clearly locates himself as a leader and manager in his institution; he explains that 'I head up a team of 23 people'. His positioning as a manager is highlighted for example when he speaks about the achievements of his team in implementing their WP strategy and his confident position as a lead figure in taking this forward:

Greatest achievements are, I think, introducing contextual data in the admissions process, but also having a strategic commitment to this in the first place, actually having a story to tell, a strategy, which is very clear about what we are trying to achieve at different stages of the student life cycle, I think we articulate that well here, whereas I think, particularly in Russell Group institutions it's easy to muddy what you are trying to achieve. So quite honest where we are trying to recruit students to this university and where we are not. I think having a clear strategy is key to that. But I think in terms of policy strategies first, I'd say is important, because everything comes from that. Policy, I think, is what we've done with the contextual data, that's one of the big achievements, also our Access Programme which, as our targeted regional programme for sixth-form students, is the largest of its type in the country, and again that's very successful at getting students into this university.

(Jack, interview, July 2010)

Jack's account seems to be a clear example of Whitchurch's 'cross-boundary professional' in his strong sense of contributing to institutional capacity (Whitchurch, 2009: 2). Sarah, on the other hand, repeatedly uses the metaphor of a battle when she describes her work in taking the WP strategy forward, which involves:

dealing with the micropolitics of the institution. For me, in my experience, that's a difficulty. I think what's happened is widening participation has become a highly competitive space, and it's also one of the few areas of Higher Education that's had any money. So it's become the site of a big battle, a lot of which is ideological, and some of which is about people's careers. I know people at university where I work try and make their careers on the back of WP and they don't really know anything about it. And the university doesn't understand that they don't know anything about it, because the university doesn't know anything about it.

(Sarah, interview, July 2010)

From their accounts, it would seem that Sarah, Lisa and Jack are differently positioned in their institutions and this is connected to the complex intersections of institutional context and positioning, and the constructions of gender, ethnicity and class at play in their accounts, but also in higher education more broadly. Sarah's classed experiences deeply shape her subjectivity as a woman professional, in terms of her sense of identity and in the practices that she takes up in relation to WP:

Everything I do in my job is influenced by where I came from. I've never believed that working class people lack aspirations. We don't do tours of the university or anything like that because I don't see the point, it just re-enforces young people's (accurate) belief that we are just a load of posh people whose lives are nothing like them. I've tried to set up educational programmes and projects where young people become involved with us for months at a time on something that is helping them academically. That way they get to know us, and can make a decision about whether they think they want to apply to the university or not. Most do apply and are successful. It's an amazing experience for me to see students at this university, including on world renowned courses, who came in through a WP programme, especially when they tell me how it's changing their lives. I don't think that HE is the be all and end all, and I certainly don't subscribe to the patronising 'civilising effect' argument, I just think that ultimately it gives you more options in life.

(Sarah, written reflection, February 2011)

Sarah explicitly rejects the raising aspirations discourse as patronizing to working-class young people and relates this firmly to the knowledge she has developed not only through HE study but also through personal experiences. She implies links with colonizing practices, when she asserts that WP is not about 'the patronising "civilising effect"'. For Sarah, the project of WP is one of social justice, transformation and the redistribution of life chances and opportunities. She is clear that WP is not about changing the attitudes and cultures of working-class communities and this profoundly shapes the kinds of activities and approaches she supports and promotes through her institutional role as a leader and manager of WP.

I will now turn attention explicitly to the structures and practices of WP described by the participants in my study across seven English higher education institutions.

## WP structures and practices

As I have argued above, although WP has led to the development of a new professional body in higher education in the English context, with the specific remit to widen participation, there is a dearth of research that explores the impact of this workforce and the structures associated with this work for the direction of WP strategy. My study shows that WP is very differently conceptualized, structured and undertaken across different English institutions, which highlights issues of inequity in relation to place and the different provision, resources and opportunities available to students. In the seven higher education institutions studied, the size of the teams undertaking specific WP work varied from 4 to 38 staff members. Some of the teams were centrally based, arguably giving them more institutional authority and status, whilst others were based in Recruiting or Marketing departments. The institutional location of the main work of WP will have inevitable implications for the development of strategy, the ways that the WP team is able to work across the institution and also the ways that WP is contested and conceptualized within the institution. The concepts of the profane and sacred are valuable here in thinking about the ways that WP professionals navigate between institutional positions strongly connected to the discourses of marketing, quality and recruitment and their commitment also to working with academic staff to re/consider pedagogical and disciplinary practices in relation to concerns with equity in higher education. In this way, WP professionals must position themselves as 'cross-boundary professionals', to draw on their access to different forms of knowledge and resources across the institution in relation to strategic and capacity development. However, complex power relations create im/possibilities for cross-boundary work, through technologies of regulation, class/ification and normalization. For those with a strong sense of commitment to WP as a project of social justice, this cuts deep into professional and personal sensibilities. Lisa describes the ways she is undermined by the dominant culture of the particular department in which she is located, which is immersed in the profane discourses of quality and managerialism:

> I felt that it took me a while to feel confident enough to overcome my own personal issues to gain a strong voice for the WP cohort in my previous jobs and now I feel like I'm being stifled. I feel like I'm being told to get rid of my principles in order to fit into this department and that's never going to happen. It's such a conflict and I don't know people like this so I don't know how to reach them. They have no visible empathy with the groups not traditionally represented in HE and that's the thing I find most difficult to understand.
>
> (Lisa, written reflection, May 2011)

Institutional context is important, but so too is institutional position. Lisa is not in a position of leadership but part of a new team, following the closure of Aimhigher, and is told she must learn to conform to the aims of her Department. Importantly, only one of those interviewed, Chris, has an academic contract as the Associate Dean (Widening Participation), and through his institutional position he is able to actively mediate between the WP Team, a small support team based in Recruitment, and his academic and senior colleagues. The position of Associate Dean carries formal status and enables the flow of counter-hegemonic discourses, resisting utilitarianism and individual meritocratic discourses. It is also noteworthy that his institutional context is a small, high-status specialist higher education institution, which might afford a greater sense of autonomy from mainstream higher education discourses. His perspective of WP is strongly focused on embedding WP across the work of the institution and working closely with academic staff to consider different approaches to admissions and teaching in order to influence and ultimately change institutional cultures and practices. He is able to position himself strongly in relation to an academic subjectivity, but also to work closely with his colleagues in the WP team positioned in Recruitment, enabling him to do strong 'cross-boundary' work, focusing on strategy and capacity-building, and to develop strategies to bridge the intersections of profane and sacred formations of knowledge at play in his institution.

In another large Russell Group university, Jack leads a large centrally based team of 23 staff and focuses more on outreach, although, like Sarah, he is also critical of the mainstream discourses of raising aspirations. Jack's overall approach is a liberal one, working within current systems to create greater fairness for all social groups. In table 9.1, I have set out some of the key differences in the structures, organization and practices of WP across the seven HE institutions in my study. One WP professional takes a liberal orientation to WP. Four of the WP professionals take an explicitly transformative orientation to WP, where the key focus is on changing the culture and practices of the institution rather than the attitudes of individual young people. Two of the WP professionals take an individual meritocratic orientation to WP. In this perspective, the focus is on outreach with young people at an early age, so that they understand the opportunities available to them if they work hard at school. Sheena exemplifies this position in her account:

> in a holistic way, what university can offer, should they choose to go down that route, because at the end of the day not everybody is going, are inclined to go to university, it could be for one reason or another, it could be for cultural reasons, social reasons, or academic reasons, but to show them that they can work hard and raise their game, if they work hard at school.
>
> (Sheena, Interview, July 2010)

Importantly, though, their individual orientations do not necessarily reflect the overall institutional orientations to WP. None of the institutions takes a transformative orientation, four take a liberal one and three take an individual meritocratic one. Interestingly, although individual and institutional orientations to WP differ, the activities undertaken to widen participation are similar, and most of the institutions undertake outreach as the central activity. However, the approaches to outreach differ according to orientation, both individual and institutional. For example, the outreach work that Sheena organizes tends to be one-off university visits and summer programmes, while Sarah has developed ongoing embedded projects led by academics and in partnership with key specialist organizations. Despite these organizational differences, both Sarah and Sheena believe it is important to establish an ongoing relationship with the young people engaged on their outreach programmes. Table 9.1 sets out the different institutional approaches, orientations and structures of WP.

Two institutions, one Russell Group and one specialist, both institutionally oriented to a liberal approach, supported an alternative approach to admissions, involving the use of contextual data. Jack explains this as a radical development in their WP strategy:

Table 9.1 Overview of WP structures and practices

| Institution type | Specialist | Russell Group | New | New | New | Specialist | Russell Group |
|---|---|---|---|---|---|---|---|
| Pseudonym | *Sarah* | *Jack* | *Josh* | *Beth* | *Sheena* | *Chris* | *Lisa* |
| Individual orientation to WP | Transformative | Liberal | Individual meritocratic | Transformative | Individual meritocratic | Transformative | Transformative |
| Contract | Support | Support | Support | Academic related | Support | Academic | Academic related |
| WP team size | 38 | 23 | 6 | 23 | 7 | 4 | 20 |
| Structure of WP | Centrally based | Centrally based | Based in Recruitment | Based in Marketing | Based in Recruitment, Access and Partnership | Based in Recruitment | Centrally based |
| Key partners | Schools, subject-related organizations | Internal networks, managers and heads of units, prospective university students, local authority, schools and parents | Aimhigher – Aspire, local schools and colleges | Local schools and colleges | Local schools, colleges and other organizations | Institutional heads and deans, equality and diversity officer and partner institution, local schools and colleges | Local schools |
| Institutional targeting strategies | Parental history (no HE experience); parents not in professional work | Parental history (no HE experience), geo-demographic indicators, type of school attended | Work with targeted schools | Children from families in socio-economic groups 4–7, care leavers, and children with disabilities | Parental history (no HE experience), with potential to benefit from HE, year 7, geo-demographic indicators | Work with targeted schools, children from families in socio-economic groups 4–7, and care leavers, and children with disabilities | Parental history (no HE experience), work with targeted schools |

Table 9.1 (continued)

| Institution type | Specialist | Russell Group | New | New | New | Specialist | Russell Group |
|---|---|---|---|---|---|---|---|
| Institutional approaches | Outreach, embedded programmes, changing institutional practices | Outreach, contextual admissions practices | Outreach | Outreach and progression agreements | Outreach | Outreach, changing institutional practices | Outreach |
| Institutional orientation to WP | Liberal | Liberal | Individual meritocratic | Liberal | Individual meritocratic | Liberal | Individual meritocratic |

Notes: These are key partners at the time of writing. As Aimhigher is disbanded, new partners and strategies will be developed.

One of the most radical things we've done in the past few years is intro-
duce contextual data in the admissions process, so that we are actually
understanding more about the context and the educational journey a
young person has made, prior to applying to the university, and also that
we can, using a battery of different indicators, build up a kind of a
smorgasbord, if you like, of socio-economic and educational indicators,
additional things, information which is passed on to admissions tutors. So
particularly in sort of tie-break situations where you receive many more
applications than places, to understand that some of our applicant pool
have achieved quite glittering academic achievement, despite all the statistics showing very few people from these sort of backgrounds or schools
progress to university at all, we want to positively affirm that, and highlight that in the admissions process, so that's what, as part of our fair
admissions strategy, this is kind of the intersection, the very important,
and interesting, and I think radical intersection of widening participation
with your admissions policy. So this is something which we introduced
last year, it took a couple of years of planning, to make sure that we are
doing it in a fair and consistent, transparent way, and I think that's a
really innovative part of what we do.

(Jack interview, July 2010)

Chris explains that in his institution they have introduced adjusted grade
criteria into the admissions process, which sets minimum entry points in
relation to the average achievement level in that particular school. This has
been particularly successful in recruiting students from non-white backgrounds and from alternative entry programmes such as Access to Higher
education, and mature students from 'non-traditional' backgrounds. However,
he explains that, as the student constituency has changed, there have been
questions raised about the quality of their students:

In the last five years we've completely changed the kind of make-up of
the programme so the students are now: last year our intake was 50 per cent
from non-white backgrounds; we had only 35 per cent from A-levels –
and the rest were either mature and had done a degree before or were
from an Access – from different backgrounds – but now we're getting
this little voice … 'what's happening to the quality of your students?' …
and that kind of fear that we're not getting the same throughput – that
students might take a little longer – they might think OK I can't kind of
cope with all this at this point in time – you know things that come with
mature students – other commitments that they have and therefore they
might not finish their first year and have to do some of that again in their
second year but you know, I'm comfortable with that. It might be difficult for administrative purposes but its enabling – and thinking about
the student learning across a period of time that is not structured to be
just three years and being flexible about that is what I think we need to

start to be more – but we get marks down if we haven't reached a certain level [of progression and retention].

(Chris, interview, June 2010)

The discourses of quality seem to be in constant tension with concerns about equality, inclusion and social justice in HE (Morley, 2003). In another Russell Group institution, Lisa describes her concern that WP is isolated from the work of the university and that, similar to Chris's account, there is a strong emphasis on individual quality in relation to the students recruited through the WP agenda:

[WP] is very much out on its own, if that makes any sense. They do offer a Scholars project, which is meant to take the 'cream of the WP cohort crop' (a term used by the Head of WP in a meeting!) which means the manager of that project liaises with some academics who then offer guest lectures/masterclasses etc. From an Aimhigher perspective, we found that WP is not embedded in the academic departments at all with many academics still not even understanding the remit of Aimhigher even after almost ten years of work. [My department] is a very insular department, the SMT have repeatedly used the word 'quality' in response to my questions about how WP is incorporated into their admissions strategy ie. I was told the focus has to be on recruiting 'quality' students. I feel this implies that the SMT believe that the WP cohort must include young people who are somehow, sub-standard. I believe this is down to a complete lack of knowledge on the SMTs behalf yet they do not appear to want to learn anything about WP.

(Lisa, written reflection, May 2011)

Lisa is deeply concerned about the impact of the loss of Aimhigher on work on widening participation in the local schools and communities:

[WP] do not have any really strong links in the local community. There is one manager who repeatedly tries to engage the local community but he is regularly not given the time or funding to develop his innovative projects enough for them to fully run. He is instead given lots of US linked projects which the Head [of WP] spends time in the States developing. My very cynical opinion is that without the input of Aimhigher who organised the more locally based initiatives, WP will become much more focused on international initiatives. I believe money/funding is the key driver in the WP strategy as opposed to any sort of real interest in building equity in HE.

Although her own orientation to WP is a transformative one, Lisa works within an institutional context in which WP is clearly on the peripheries and is seen as potentially undermining quality and reputation. This highlights that WP cannot be the work of any one individual or team; it must be embedded in the ethos of the institution and recognized as a long-term project designed to dislodge deeply rooted exclusions and misrecognitions. This requires a serious level of engagement with the large body of research that illuminates and exposes the complex operations and relations of power in educational institutions.

## Widening participation praxis

Throughout this book I have argued for the importance of theory and practice being brought together in dialogue to produce widening participation praxis. The WP professionals participating in the study also emphasized the significance of developing strategies and practices underpinned by a deeper theoretical understanding of the workings of inequalities in education. This did not necessarily link to their overall orientation to WP. This highlights the limitations of my attempts to classify their orientations, as practices and orientations are fluid and iterative and move across and between different and contested conceptualizations of WP.

Sarah and Jack are both strongly committed to drawing on research on educational equalities and widening participation in the development of institutional approaches and strategies to widening participation. Sarah emphasizes the significance of having a theoretical understanding of educational equality and widening participation:

> Sarah: Well, working in a huge university, and nobody understands that issues of equality in education are highly theorized. So they go along making up these programmes off the top of their head without any kind of theoretical understanding.
>
> (Sarah, interview, July 2010)

Sarah is also deeply concerned that, in the new funding framework, universities will be given a greater responsibility in terms of the funds specifically identified for widening participation work. This could intensify conflicts within institutions, as resources become scarcer in other areas. Without a developed understanding of the relationship between WP and complex inequalities, these funds might be misused in ways that further reinforce inequalities and misrecognitions:

> In the new funding regime, universities will have to spend more money on WP. I think that WP will become an even more contested site because there will be a fight over the money. There will be all this money and who is deciding how it is spent? Is it people with no understanding of educational theory – then there will be the argument that all this money has been spent and it hasn't made any difference at all, so the problem must be with the young people.
>
> (Sarah, written reflection, May 2011)

Sarah's concerns are significant; without a sophisticated framework for developing WP strategy, there is a strong chance that additional funds being available in the context of a shrinking budget will be used by those with greater authority and power and not necessarily those with a deep commitment to and understanding of social equality and justice.

Jack also emphasizes the important relationship between theory and practice. He continually draws on research in the field to articulate his professional perspectives of widening participation in his interview account. He draws on this literature to position himself in authoritative ways and this perhaps accords him the recognition he requires to lead the institutional strategy and to manage his team. This positions him as an objective professional, drawing on research evidence, but it also helps him to formulate a rationale behind the arguments he makes for the direction his university should take:

> Interviewer: And are there any key issues that you address, that you are concerned with, personally, or professionally?
> Jack: Yeah, both, I think ... when I say personally or professionally I wouldn't put a lot of the reasons into either of those, I just think they are evident through social research and theory more than anything, rather than they are my own views, or they are part of the work we do. I think they are evidently true from everything that we understand of the social processes, the research that we understand about this. So I think the key issues are that life chances are distributed unequally long before people go to school in the first place, so the idea there is just, you can say it is to do with differences in attainment between different groups, or something happens before that that causes differences in attainment in the first place. I think most research we know about in this area would identify social class or socio-economic factors as being the single and largest most important variable, and that's what the research shows, it's what I personally believe, and it's what, professionally, our strategy aims to address, so I think that ties together, the personal and professional dimension to your question, it being informed by research really.
>
> (Jack, interview, July 2010)

Although both Sarah and Jack highlight the importance of theory and research underpinning practice, their positions on how to use research differ. Sarah takes a redistributive approach and draws on theories of social justice in education to focus on the need to redistribute resources and opportunities to working-class young people who have not benefitted from the socio-economic and cultural privileges of many white, middle-class young people. This takes the form of embedded programmes, which aim to develop long-term relationships with the young people in the university rather than to offer one-off activities that seek to raise aspirations. Key issues that she identified in her account include the importance of the preparation and organization of the work of the

WP team, of changing admissions practices, of working closely with the young people themselves and of changing the university culture:

> We've done a massive amount of work in the organization, we've done a massive amount of work on admissions and what the issues are with our admissions, at the university, so trying to tackle it from all directions really. So we work with young people, because they are competing with other young people who have had every advantage and privilege you can think of, including being taken around the world by their parents. And some of them go to the poorer schools in the city, so we are trying to counteract that. And equally we are trying to change the culture of the university, including its admissions processes.
>
> (Sarah, interview, July 2010)

Jack is less focused on the idea of cultural change, although he also sees this as being important. He is more focused on trying to work within the current frameworks and create spaces within that for widening participation. He is concerned that some of the research places too much responsibility for social inequalities on higher education institutions and that there needs to be more attention to making the current system fairer. He describes this as 'working around the margins', a project he is committed to and passionate about:

> I think, though, that some of the [research], it can perhaps present higher education as the bad guy in all of this as well, which again, I know that's not the intention ... . But the kind of assumption people can make from that kind of research is that the fault lies at the gates of the university. Now that's not to say that there's [not] vast cultural changes that need to happen within higher education, of course there are, and it needs to continue to evolve and adapt to the changing nature of society, and expectations we have of largely publicly funded universities, but I think it's also quite simplistic to say it's universities discriminating against young people. But if you say, well, that's the system we work within, can we make that system yet fairer? Yes, of course, you can, there are things that could be done within universities to make our existing system much, much, fairer, without having to tear apart the whole system itself. But of course some people would say there's a limit to how much you can do, and that's ameliorative, and actually it's a hierarchical system, that's hard-wired into the very notion of higher education, which is selective. Some of our most elite institutions that give young people better life chances, that's kind of set up really, to exclude people from poorer backgrounds who tend to achieve less highly. I've a lot of sympathy with that view. I think it's a similar argument with independent schools, isn't it? They exist, and meanwhile life goes on and I think the existing educational landscape, if you like, can be made a lot fairer, which I think is that kind of work around the margins, very important work around the margins,

which I am passionate about, and our team is committed to do through it's widening participation strategy, because we are, clearly, whilst you can't change the nature of society, there are really important opportunities that can be given, and young people can take those opportunities, and indeed achieve very significant, positive, improvements in their lives, which they could not get if those initiatives, policies, programmes etc., weren't available.

(Jack, interview, July 2010)

Jack's notion of working around the margins is important in thinking through the day-to-day praxis of widening participation within the current frameworks of higher education, which are constantly shifting and fluid. This addresses pessimistic arguments that are often made about the unequal nature of wider society, which at times feels overwhelming to those committed to educational equalities and social justice. Jack's point that, despite this, there are changes that can be made to the existing structures and practices is valuable in sustaining the energy of those given responsibility for widening participation.

## Final reflections

This chapter has analyzed data from my small-scale study of professionals explicitly connected to WP in seven English higher education institutions. I have argued that we need to have a clearer picture of this professional workforce, in terms of identities, structures and practices, to better understand the relationship between this work and what happens in different HE institutions with regard to issues of equality and widening participation. I have argued strongly that the different structures and positions of those associated with WP profoundly shape, and limit, how WP is imagined and conceptualized and how strategies are developed in relation to contested discourses and perspectives.

The accounts of the WP professionals have highlighted the complex ways that WP identities and practices are marginalized in different institutions, as well as the politics of authority, status and positioning that take place at the intersections of difference in the formation of identity and subjectivity. Gender, class and ethnicity, as well as institutional status and location, have an important impact on the politics of representation of WP within HE institutions, as well as the processes of securing available funds and resources. The data have also provided a starting point in tracing the different approaches, orientations and practices in HE institutions, although more work needs to be done on this with a larger follow-up study. However, this initial mapping out of WP work has helped to highlight the differences, hierarchies, conflicts and micropolitics that inevitably shape the institutional ethos in relation to WP and ultimately create different kinds of resources, opportunities and constraints for the students (who are targeted in different ways depending on context). This highlights national inequities in terms of what is available to different students across different regions, places and spaces, and the important relationship between the WP professional workforce and the im/possibilities for widening participation in a hyper-hierarchical HE terrain. Although, under the new funding regime, WP resources are likely to increase, this does not necessarily mean that those funds will be used to challenge exclusions and inequalities. In a context of decreasing funds and resources, it is possible that conflicts and struggles to secure resources will intensify and there is no guarantee that those resources will benefit the social and cultural groups who have been historically misrecognized, marginalized and under-represented in higher education institutions.

There are important themes emerging from the data in relation to moving beyond the current utilitarian, neoliberal and instrumental discourses of WP towards a richer imaginary of transformation. The notion of 'working at the edges' of the current system offers possibilities of doing things differently with the aim of achieving a fairer HE system. Embedding WP across the institution through cross-boundary work, which mediates across the 'profane' and 'sacred', is crucial in moving beyond the superficial WP discourse of working on an individual basis with those students who 'need additional support' or have 'special needs'. An embedded approach to WP is inclusive, and requires the understanding and support of senior management, as well as academic, managerial and support staff, and works together with all staff and students to create transformatory and participatory practices. Embedded approaches are tied to a praxis of WP, which acknowledges the crucial importance of bringing together theory and practice to challenge insidious inequalities, exclusions and misrecognitions in different HE institutions and contexts. This is also connected to material inequalities, and the processes by which scarce resources might become available to different social groups, even those resources that have been specifically identified for WP purposes. This chapter highlights WP as a contested terrain of struggle over representation, positioning, voice and authority, as well as material resources. The current global economic crisis has intensified such struggles and this could pose further complex challenges for widening participation within an increasingly aggressive, competitive and individualist framework. However, the chapter has also shown the passionate commitment of many of those who work in the name of WP within and across higher education institutions, and their dedication to fight for more equitable, inclusive and ethical higher education spaces and practices, drawing on the insights of critical theoretical perspectives to support their work.

# Part 4

# Imagining the future

Despite significant investment in widening participation in terms of funding, resources and personnel, patterns of under-representation continue to persist amongst certain socio-economic groups. Even where students from 'non-traditional' backgrounds have been recruited successfully to higher education, there are patterns of non-completion, and research, both in the UK and other international contexts, highlights that often such students experience a sense of not belonging and exclusion. In this final section, a higher education landscape is imagined that is accessible, inclusive, representative and participatory. Drawing on the insights of critical and feminist theoretical and pedagogical perspectives, Part Four sketches out the possibilities of inclusive higher educational spaces whilst acknowledging that contradictions, struggles and tensions will always exist. However, this part of the book will offer students, practitioners, policy-makers, educational leaders and academics possibilities for carving out more inclusive and dialogic educational and pedagogical spaces.

# 10 Conceptualizing WP differently

This chapter returns to and further develops my earlier discussions about the importance of critical and feminist theoretical and pedagogical perspectives for conceptualizing widening participation differently. Such perspectives place concepts of power, subjectivity and social justice at the centre of analysis, whilst mainstream perspectives of WP tend to ignore such issues. The book has developed a strong argument that despite substantial levels of financial and human investment in the project of WP, persistent patterns of under-representation amongst certain socio-economic groups raises crucial questions about the effectiveness of current frames of understanding and of current practices. I will suggest more radical perspectives, which, when in dialogue with policy and practice, might work more effectively to dislodge and desta-bilize enduring relations of inequality, which continue to be reflected and produced in universities in complex and insidious ways.

## Conceptualizing widening participation as a project of social justice

Throughout this book, I have argued that widening access to and partici-pation in higher education is primarily a project of social justice, which must then attend in detail to complex issues of inequality, exclusion and mis-recognition. The neoliberal framing of widening participation policy, and indeed of education policy more generally, has worked to shift attention away from concerns with social justice to a focus on employability, skills enhance-ment, entrepreneurialism and economic competitveness, as well as to produce a realm of self-disciplining technologies. However, the concern with *widening* participation in higher education to those groups who have historically been excluded from the privilege of university education is ultimately a project of social justice by virtue of its underpinning aim. This requires detailed theor-etical attention to social justice in order to develop the strategies, policies and practices that are able to disrupt and dismantle long-standing inequalities in education and, more specifically for the focus of this book, in higher education.

I have drawn on a range of theoretical perspectives to develop an explicit social justice agenda in relation to projects of widening access to, and participation in, higher education, including feminism, critical and political sociology and post-structuralism. Processes of 'recognition' and 'misrecognition' have been a key focus of the book, as these broaden the focus of widening participation in higher education, including attention to material and structural inequalities and the politics of redistribution, but close attention has also been paid to processes and relations of symbolic, discursive and cultural misrecognition. This approach calls upon a politics of recognition and attention to the workings of difference and inequality.

## The politics of mis/recognition

Theories of social justice that bring attention to the politics of recognition are key to conceptualizing widening participation differently. Nancy Fraser's work, which emphasizes attention to difference, is particularly compelling for developing a different conceptual framework for exploring issues of the right to higher education beyond hegemonic neoliberal and utilitarian discourses of widening participation. Fraser argues for a 'two-dimensional' conception of social justice, which addresses both claims for redistribution and for recognition. Claims for redistribution are concerned with a more just distribution of resources and wealth, and are rooted in the late-twentieth-century Anglo-American branch of liberalism. Claims for recognition involve detailed attention to difference and are rooted in Hegelian philosophy.

> Recognition designates an ideal recipricol relation between subjects in which each sees the other as its equal and also as separate from it. This relation is deemed constitutive for subjectivity; one becomes an individual subject only in virtue of recognizing, and being recognized by, another subject.
>
> (Fraser, 2003: 10)

The two claims, redistribution and recognition, are 'mutually irreducible dimensions of justice' and Fraser argues that 'only a framework that integrates the two analytically distinct perspectives of distribution and recognition can grasp the imbrication of class inequality and status hierarchy in contemporary society' (Fraser and Honneth, 2003: 4). Yet claims for redistribution or recognition are often posed in opposition and in conflict, so that a choice is seen to have to be made between either an egalitarian redistributive approach to social justice or a politics of recognition (Fraser, 2003: 8). Arguing against this opposition, Fraser emphasizes that social justice in contemporary society must embrace *both* redistribution and recognition. She analyses the injustices suffered by different social groups (e.g. across class, gender, race and sexuality) in contemporary societies, demonstrating not only that each social group requires both redistribution and recognition (although some might require recognition as secondary to redistribution and vice versa), but also that axes of domination and subordination intersect with one another, so that 'nearly every individual who suffers injustice needs to integrate those two kinds of claims' (Fraser, 2003: 26). Thus, the dilemma is not which form of injustice to prioritize, but how to combine these into a 'single comprehensive framework' (Fraser, 2003: 9).

Fraser conceptualizes recognition as a key dimension of justice in terms of social status or the 'status model of recognition' (Fraser, 2003: 29):

> On the status model, misrecognition is neither a psychical deformation nor an impediment to ethical self-realization. Rather it constitutes an institutionalized relation of *subordination* and a violation of justice. To be misrecognized, accordingly, is not to suffer distorted identity or impaired subjectivity as a result of being depreciated by others. It is rather to be constituted by *institutionalized patterns of cultural value* in ways that prevent one from participating as a peer in social life. On the status model then, misrecognition is relayed not through deprecatory attitudes or re-standing discourses, but rather through social institutions. It arises, more precisely, when institutions structure interaction according to cultural norms that impede parity of participation.
>
> (Fraser, 2003: 29)

Status in this conceptualization 'represents an order of intersubjective sub-ordination derived from institutionalized patterns of cultural value that constitute some members of society as less than full partners in interaction' (Fraser, 2003: 49). Fraser's conceptualization of recognition has clear importance for understanding widening participation in higher education and for reconceptualizing participation in broader terms that deepen the focus from participation as about gaining entry to higher education to *parity of participation*. A claim for recognition aims to 'deinstitutionalise patterns of cultural value that impede parity of participation and to replace them with patterns that foster it' (Fraser, 2003: 30). Importantly, the status model of recognition challenges notions of 'the good life that is universally shared'. This helps interrogate assumptions about aspirations that do not include higher education participation and questions value judgments that construct higher education as the premium aspiration. This also shifts attention away from individual attitudes and towards institutional cultural practices, supporting a transformatory framework for widening participation in higher education.

Fraser's conceptualization of social justice challenges the assumptions of policy discourses, such as 'raising aspirations', which are underpinned by notions that aspiring to participate in higher education represents the 'right' kinds of values, dispositions and aspirations, particularly for those who 'have potential' to 'succeed'. It similarly challenges assumptions about 'success', that 'success' for example is mainly about gaining a higher degree or progressing in a professional career. Crucially, this perspective of recognition destabilizes normalizing discourses of 'aspiration', 'potential' and 'success'. Parity of participa-tion 'assumes that it is up to individuals and groups to define for themselves what counts as a good life and to devise for themselves an approach to pursuing it, within limits that ensure a like liberty for others' (Fraser, 2003: 31). This might include for example choosing *not* to participate in higher education and choosing to participate in other forms of non-formal learning, such as travelling to other parts of the world to learn from, and participate in, different cultural practices (Burke and Jackson, 2007).

However, this perspective must be underpinned by a critical concept of 'choice' that understands that individuals do not simply choose freely but are constrained by the multiple discourses, structures, resources, subjectivities and policies that frame their decision-making processes. Importantly, the status model of recognition, as developed by Fraser, locates the problem in social relations and not individual or interpersonal psychology (Fraser, 2003: 31). Fraser explains that:

> When misrecognition is identified with internal distortions in the structure of the self-conscious of the oppressed, it is but a short step to blaming the victim [ ... ]. Conversely, when misrecognition is equated with prejudice in the minds of the oppressors, overcoming it seems to require policing their beliefs, an approach that is illiberal and authoritarian. For the status model, in contrast, misrecognition is a matter of externally manifest and publicly verifiable impediments to some people's standing as full members of society. To redress it, again, means to overcome subordination. *This in turn means changing institutions and social practices.*
>
> (Fraser, 2003: 31, my emphasis)

An example of this from the research data presented in this book is the way that applicants to art and design degree courses are misrecognized on the basis of their perceived lack of good taste, when they are unable to cite the discourses that allow them recognition as having the right forms of taste and culture to participate on the course they have applied to. This is then projected on to the individual as the 'unworthy' candidate who is influenced by 'hip-hop' for example rather than those forms of fashion legitimated in higher education. However, the inability to afford regular visits to galleries and museums and to the 'right' kinds of shops, or to travel to those parts of the world deemed to represent 'high culture', operates as another form of injustice in the mis/recognition of the candidate (see Chapter Seven). The two forms of injustice operate together to deny the applicant parity of participation in the interview process, and ultimately in the higher education course. Fraser's approach to social justice would push WP strategies in the direction of interrogating the disciplinary and cultural values and practices of art and design higher education, which shape admissions tutors' judgments about potential, rather than seeking remedial approaches to regulate and 'correct' the (working-classed) candidate's taste in art and design.

Fraser argues that parity of participation requires the distribution of material resources, or the 'objective condition of participatory parity' (Fraser, 2003: 36).

This precludes 'forms and levels of economic dependence and inequality that impede parity of participation' as well as 'institutionalized norms that systematically depreciate some categories of people and the qualities associated with them', or the 'intersubjective condition of participatory parity' (Fraser, 2003: 36). Both forms of condition are central to participatory parity, encompassing both redistribution and recognition, without 'reducing either one to the other' (Fraser, 2003: 37). What is required is a dialogical approach to the parity of participation, in a 'democratic process of public deliberation' (Fraser, 2003: 43). However, as Fraser herself acknowledges, there is a dilemma of the circularity of this argument for, in order for the dialogical approach to work, the parity of participation in the dialogical approach is essential. Skeggs emphasizes the dilemma further:

> To make a recognition claim one must first have a recognizable identity, and this identity must be 'proper': that is, it must have recognizable public value. This immediately presents a problem for those who are not considered to have 'proper' identities and are continually misrecognized; it also presents a problem for those who are forced to inhabit an identity category not of their own making, as well as those who are forced to be visible in order to be seen to have a recognizable identity.
>
> (Skeggs, 2004: 178)

Fraser asserts that addressing such dilemmas and key questions, including for example: 'which people need which kind(s) of recognition in which contexts', requires the aid of critical social theory (Fraser, 2003: 47). In contemporary societies, people participate in a 'dynamic regime of ongoing struggles for recognition' although some will not have access to the resources needed, and some will not have access to the social esteem and status required, in order to participate fully and at the same level as other participants (Fraser, 2003: 57). Thus, critical theoretical perspectives concerned with dismantling contemporary social injustices help to account for the relation between maldistribution and misrecognition. Fraser proposes that 'perspectival dualism' as a framework helps to theorize the connections between both maldistribution and misrecognition, 'grasping at once their conceptual irreducibility, empirical divergence, and practical entwinement' (Fraser, 2003: 64). This theoretical approach is based on an understanding that claims for redistribution and recognition are inseparable, impinging on one another to give rise to unintended effects (Fraser, 2003: 64).

Debates about widening participation, which have focused mainly on redistributing resources through bursaries, outreach programmes and study skills support, have also given rise to derogatory discourses about students associated with WP threatening the standards and quality of higher education. This has been articulated, for example, in public statements referring to 'Mickey Mouse' courses, institutions and students. In this book I have argued that the redistribution of resources to students from poorer backgrounds must attend to cultural change within higher education, to deconstruct and redress the re/privileging of the values, subjectivities, knowledge and experiences of those from privileged groups and normalized identities. Privilege is not only about wealth and material resources, but also about the ways in which certain identities, subjectivities and dispositions are given more symbolic value in higher education contexts and through academic and cultural practices. Indeed, there is no redistribution without recognition (Fraser, 2003: 65). Similarly, a focus on the politics of recognition must necessarily have some distributive effects. This connects very strongly with the key point made in Chapter Nine that, as resources become scarcer, those funds allocated specifically for WP will create fiercer competition within institutions to secure those funds. It is imperative that the systems in place for the allocation of those funds are underpinned by the principles of perspectival dualism. Such systems must entrust those funds only to those who will ensure that (1) they will be redistributed to those social groups who have historically been under-represented in higher education; and/or (2) will develop strategies to disrupt the historical misrecognition of those social groups. Any reforms connected to recognition must also be concerned about struggles for redistribution of material and economic resources (Fraser, 2003: 66). Perspectival dualism 'aligns distribution and recognition with two other modes of social ordering – the economic and the cultural, which are conceived not as separate spheres but as differentiated and interpenetrating' (Fraser, 2003: 66).

Lois McNay highlights the significant strengths of Fraser's concept of recognition for understanding inequalities and exclusion both in terms of institutional subordination and as economic and material maldistribution (McNay, 2008: 147). Importantly, this theoretical perspective acknowledges that capitalism has become so complex that misrecognition does not necessarily accompany forms of economic injustice and vice versa (McNay, 2008: 148). The notion of misrecognition as a form of status subordination sheds light on the ways that institutionalized cultural value patterns have discriminatory effects on the differential positioning of subjects (McNay, 2008: 148). This is an important concept for understanding, for example, the ways that candidates from under-represented backgrounds in higher education might not be recognized as 'worthy' applicants due to the institutionalized cultural value patterns in different universities, disciplines, subjects and/or courses. By locating misrecognition at the level of the institution, rather than at the level of subjective construction, Fraser develops an 'objectivist' perspective of recognition, which enables concrete solutions or strategies aimed at dismantling status subordination (McNay, 2008: 149), again offering an important set of conceptual tools to develop transformative strategies for widening access to and participation in higher education, underpinned by aims of social justice.

Despite these significant strengths, McNay argues that Fraser's objectivist perspective of recognition tends to leave aside the important insights emerging from an understanding of the subjective dimensions of identity (McNay, 2008: 150). This leads to injustices of misrecognition being considered 'primarily as externally imposed injuries rather than as lived identities' (McNay, 2008: 150). McNay proposes Bourdieu's concept of habitus as a framework for understanding 'how economic imperatives are lived through cultural identities and that cultural norms can be lived as economic realities' (McNay, 2008: 156). Habitus foregrounds an idea of practice that conceptualizes agency as lived relation. A politicized understanding of agency must have 'some interpretive insight into the embodied context of action, which includes the intentions, motives and responses of the individuals involved' (McNay, 2008: 168). This helps to illuminate that people might occupy contradictory subject positions and the re/production of normative identities is a 'lived social relation that necessarily involves the negotiation of conflict and tension' (McNay, 2008: 169).

We need a theoretical framework of social inequalities and misrecognitions in higher education that enables an analysis of the ways that subjects' actions are shaped by their representations and understandings of the world, although 'the visible, that which is immediately given, hides the invisible which determines it' (Bourdieu, 1990: 126–127 in McNay, 2008: 181). An analytical framework for developing WP strategies and practices must enable the more subtle, invisible and insidious inequalities at play in higher education (which are always connected to wider social relations and contexts) to come to view, and to be linked to the level of subjectivity, emotion and the embodied context of action and practice.

In relation to these imperatives, I explore the importance of critical and feminist pedagogies for conceptualizing widening participation differently.

## Critical and feminist pedagogies

Throughout this book, I have argued that moving beyond hegemonic, neo-liberal, instrumentalist discourses of widening participation requires detailed and close attention to the complex workings of material inequality and cultural misrecognition. This kind of attention must include a drawing together of research, theory and practice, bringing together the different, competing and multiple perspectives to develop a transformative framework for widening participation. Such a framework must be sensitive to relations of difference and to formations of identity in the processes by which subjects become recognized and validated within higher education fields and everyday pedagogical practices.

Pedagogies remain a central area of lived, relational and embodied practice in higher education. Although hegemonic discourses at play in higher education policy construct largely instrumentalized notions of teaching and learning, the dynamics, relations and experiences of teaching and learning are intimately tied to the re/production of particular subjectivities and ways of being a university student or a teacher. Discourses of teaching and learning frame teacher and student experiences and identities largely in terms of 'styles', 'provision', 'needs' and 'delivery' and such language tends to be couched in a market-oriented perspective that often constructs teachers as service-providers and students as consumers in contemporary discourses of higher education. Such discourses tend to narrow and constrain our understanding of teaching and learning relations, experiences and identities in higher education. Although some attention might be paid to issues of power, this is often framed in terms of simplistic notions of student 'voice' and 'empowerment'. Concerns with 'diversity' are often tied to the perceived need for 'personalized', 'differentiated' and/or 'independent' learning. However, I have argued throughout this book that the insights of critical and feminist pedagogies might help to move towards transformative approaches to widening participation, making important connections with key concepts, including power, identity formation and processes of mis/recognition, redistribution and exclusion.

Critical and feminist pedagogies draw on theories of power to illuminate the complex relations between students and teachers in dynamic social spaces in which teaching and learning practices play out. In this framework, identities profoundly shape pedagogical experiences and perspectives and the different practices that get taken up by teachers and students. Power is not seen as monolithic within this conceptual framework; power is understood as shaping pedagogical relations and experiences in and across changing social, cultural, spatial and (micro)political contexts. Power is not an oppositional force that predictably benefits one group above the other but rather moves fluidly across and between differently positioned subjects. The teacher is not seen to 'have the power' to give to the students but rather power is generated, exercised and struggled over within lived social spaces such as classrooms and lecture theatres. Furthermore, power is not tied to one single source, but is interconnected to multiple dynamics, including, space, place, time, context, identity and subjectivity. Power shapes pedagogical practice in profound and unexpected ways and this is inextricably tied to questions of knowledge, authority and representation. As such, pedagogy, curriculum and assessment are not separate entities but overlapping and intersecting dimensions of educational practice in which power plays out in different ways, depending on context and subjectivities. Pedagogies are thus profoundly shaped by the different power relations at play, the changing contexts in which teaching and learning takes place, the resources available to teachers and students and the identities of teachers and students. Simultaneously, pedagogies are constitutive of identity formations through the discursive practices and regimes of truth at play in particular pedagogic spaces. Pedagogies both shape and are shaped by complex identity formations, epistemological frameworks and processes of recognition, as well as notions of 'right' to participate in higher education. Pedagogies do not simply reflect the classed, gendered and racialized subjectivities of teachers and students but pedagogies themselves are classed, gendered and racialized, intimately bound up with historical ways of being and doing within higher education spaces. Pedagogical practices are thus deeply implicated in the processes and politics of recognition and misrecognition.

# Developing participatory pedagogies

Drawing on the theoretical perspectives outlined above, in this final section of the chapter, I want to now explore the potential of what I name 'participatory pedagogies' for moving beyond current hegemonic discourses of 'widening participation', which are currently shaped predominately by neoliberal globalization. Participatory pedagogies are underpinned by explicit sets of social justice principles and ethical starting points. In practice, this might involve, for example, that teachers and students initiate their pedagogical relationship with an explicit plan of the ways they will work together ethically, critically and inclusively. This might also involve a commitment to creating interactive spaces for learning and teaching, where different forms of knowledge and experience might be drawn on and made available to help illuminate and make accessible the disciplinary or subject knowledge at the heart of the course. It might also involve an explicit discussion of the different perspectives, backgrounds and forms of knowledge of the participants whilst also subjecting these to critical reflection in collaborative processes of meaning-making. Participatory pedagogies understand concerns with curriculum and assessment as part of pedagogical practices and relations, not as separate entities. Thus, pedagogies are concerned not only with explicit practices of teaching and learning but also with the construction of knowledge, competing epistemological perspectives and the ways that learning and meaning might be assessed to support pedagogical and meaning-making processes.

The seminal work of Paulo Freire is a major influence on participatory pedagogies in its detailed critique of 'banking education' as a form of domination and its overall aim to recreate knowledge and meaning through critical, collaborative and educational dialogue with 'the oppressed': those social groups whose knowledge and experiences have been socially, culturally and historically undermined by 'the oppressor'. However, drawing on feminist post-structuralist critiques of Freirean perspectives, participatory pedagogies aim to grapple with the complexity of power as generative, fluid and struggled over. Although unpredictable, shifting and deeply regulatory, power is also tied to structural and intersecting social and cultural inequalities, such as class, gender and race, as well as generative possibilities of resistance, redistribution and reconstruction. This conceptualization of power destabilizes binary notions of the oppressor/oppressed, advantaged/disadvantaged, included/excluded, participant/non-participant, male/female, white/black and empowered/disempowered, which have shaped hegemonic assumptions of widening educational participation. Yet, feminist post-structuralism also pays attention to the ways that inequalities continue to be structured along axes and intersections of class, gender and race as well as tied to material injustices such as poverty. This perspective also reveals that binary notions tend to lock us into ways of thinking that are reproductive of, rather than challenging to, the status quo. Thus, participatory pedagogies aim to engage students and teachers in the deconstruction of hyper-rationalist discourses premised on binary distinctions. A key aim is to destabilize essentialist assumptions about class, ethnicity, gender, race and sexuality and open up spaces for critique and the collaborative re/construction of meanings, with an overarching aim of social justice in higher education. However, this framework also recognizes that individual teachers and students are not free to 'break loose' of hegemonic discourses and subjectivities, which are closely tied to wider social inequalities, structures and institutions. It is thus seen as imperative that teachers drawing on participatory pedagogies acknowledge the importance of helping all their students to gain access to the practices and epistemologies that have the greatest social and cultural legitimacy and power whilst simultaneously critiquing, problematizing, interrogating and unsettling those very practices and epistemologies. Simply dismissing hegemonic practices and epistemologies as irrelevant to those from backgrounds unfamiliar with such practices and knowledges might be another form of exclusion and marginalization (Mills and Gale, 2010: 82). Participatory pedagogies insist that teachers and students engage with hegemonic practices and knowledges, so that students from underrepresented backgrounds have the opportunity to access, participate in and critique them, as well as to deconstruct them to develop alternative ways of doing and knowing.

Importantly then, participatory pedagogies fully reject the notion that some groups of students are unable to engage with those practices and forms of knowledge granted the highest levels of social esteem. Such perspectives are based on flawed assumptions of deficit connected to the politics of misrecognition. Rather, the work of the pedagogue is to demystify these practices and forms of knowledge in order to make them accessible to those who have been historically excluded from the opportunity to engage with them. Potential and ability is seen as socially constructed and produced, and thus pedagogical interventions open up the opportunity for transformative subjectivities and practices. The quality of teaching and learning is assessed in relation to concerns with equality, including the redistribution of cultural, material and symbolic resources to those social groups who have been excluded and misrecognized in discursive and material educational fields.

One of the key aims of developing 'participatory pedagogies' is to value and recognize the richness and diversity of experiences and perspectives that all students bring to their learning and to pedagogical relationships. These experiences and perspectives are seen as key resources for processes of collaborative meaning-making, and part of their richness and depth is that they are embodied and contextualized forms of knowledge. Indeed, all forms of knowledge are understood to be shaped through complex social experiences, subjectivities and experiences – even knowledge claiming to be objective and value-free. As such, it is seen as imperative that pedagogy is designed in a way that creates the spaces for students to explore and develop their interests and experiences, to exchange ideas and dialogue, to make connections between the theoretical and the practical and to develop their understanding within the wider diverse community of learning to which they develop a strong sense of belonging. Social and cultural differences are drawn as a way of developing deeper levels of understanding rather than as a problem to be regulated and normalized or made to conform to a standard. This is particularly important for those students who feel 'different' or feel that they 'do not belong' in academic spaces, often due to narrow and limited pedagogical frameworks that only value certain forms of knowledge. It is of great importance that university teachers take seriously the development of 'safe learning spaces', where students are able to explore new and unfamiliar ideas with the constructive support of their peers and teachers, without fear of being mis-recognized or ridiculed. This involves creating challenging learning spaces – in which questioning and critical approaches are encouraged – but also enabling students to have access to, and work through, unfamiliar ideas without the fear of making 'mistakes'. This requires sophisticated levels of understanding on the part of the teacher of complex pedagogical relations and the operation of power in the classroom.

Emotional dynamics are as important as rational ones in developing a par-ticipatory pedagogic framework. Central to the development of participatory pedagogies are the passionate and compassionate orientations to teaching and learning relations and to the complex processes of meaning-making and identity-formation. This is not about charisma or individual personality; this is about carefully considered sets of values and ethics, which involve a sense of care and attention to the emotional as well as rational processes of teaching and learning in higher education. The passionate commitment of the teacher/researcher to her discipline or subject brings to life the competing sets of experiences and knowledge that create a dynamic and ongoing project of a field (or fields) of study. This also entails a passionate commitment to the potential contribution of transformation through learning and teaching pro-cesses and encounters. Compassion is central to participatory pedagogies; this involves serious dedication to the detailed and complex ethics of engaging in pedagogical relations and compassion for the perspectives, experiences and lives of others. Although I argue that teaching is always an interventionist project, as it is about dreaming and imagining other ways of being, knowing and doing, and challenging inequalities and misrecognitions, it is also about having compassion throughout the often difficult and challenging processes of teaching and learning, which might involve mixed feelings of distress, anx-iety, intimidation, frustration and anger, as well as pleasure, joy, elation and euphoria. This is not about naïve commitments to passion and compassion, in which problematic 'truths', judgements and assumptions are simply accepted, as they are re/presented in pedagogical spaces. This is a sophisticated form of compassion, which involves an ongoing commitment to the project of chal-lenging inequalities and mis/recognitions, despite the complex and unpredictable formations in which these emerge. Com/passionate pedagogies engage tea-chers and students in exploring the different formations of subjectivity, ontology and epistemology but also in subjecting these to critique and transformation in ways that are attentive, sensitive, and ethical to difference, contestation and the intricate workings of power.

## Final reflections

In this chapter, I have developed my consideration of the centrality of social justice for conceptualizing widening participation differently. Drawing on the work of Nancy Fraser, I have focused on her theory of social justice in relation to the complex issues raised by widening participation to consider in some detail the politics of redistribution and recognition. I have argued that Fraser's emphasis on both redistribution and recognition is key to the development of WP strategies, whilst also considering the importance of lived, embodied practice. I have focused on pedagogical practice as a central concern in relation to such considerations and the ways that universities might move away from utilitarian and neoliberal approaches to widening participation.

The project to widen participation in higher education demands that teachers and students engage critically with pedagogical practices and experiences, moving beyond rationalist and instrumentalist discourses. Notions of 'delivery' position teachers as service providers and students as passive recipients or demanding consumers, overlooking the relationship between pedagogy, subjectivity, power and knowledge. Universities committed to social justice must encourage critical reflexivity, so that the focus shifts from teachers and students constructed as lacking the right kinds of skills to attention to the ways that pedagogical practices might be implicated in the reproduction of exclusions and misrecognitions. This requires the development of com/passionate spaces for, and orientations to, critical dialogue, praxis and reflexivity, with teacher and student participants taking seriously the unpredictable, unstable and generative nature of power. In such pedagogical relations the possibility of developing inclusive, equitable and ethical practices in higher education, drawing together curriculum, pedagogy and assessment in an inclusive, participatory, redistributive and transformative framework for social justice in higher education, is developed and explored.

# 11 Beyond widening participation

In acknowledging the complex issues raised throughout this book, which emphasize the ways that power is exercised in intensely hierarchical institutions such as universities, the difficulties posed for a transformative approach to widening participation emerges. Indeed, in taking seriously the analysis presented in the book, how can those committed to a transformative project of widening participation help to shift practices away from the utilitarian approaches currently prioritized in policy and practice? If those who occupy positions of authority and power in relation to setting the framework and making key decisions re-privilege discourses of utilitarianism and deficit, then how can we expect to move away from such approaches? It is important of course to note the ways that higher education institutions, and the senior management teams within them, are regulated, subjected to surveillance, assessed and placed in global, national and local hierarchies in ways that profoundly constrain the possibilities for change and transformation. However, drawing on the critical tools of the body of theoretical work discussed in this book will move us towards praxis and will support the collaborative development of counter-hegemonic and subversive practices of resistance.

I have argued in this book that we must move beyond current hegemonic discourses and practices of higher education to reconceptualize widening participation as a project of transformation for social justice. Much of the current WP policy and practice emphasizes issues prior to access to higher education, most prominently 'raising aspirations' and raising levels of educational attainment. Although aspirations and attainment are certainly important, I have argued throughout the book that hegemonic utilitarian approaches to aspirations and attainment do not have the capacity to address deep-seated and long-standing historical injustices within education. Furthermore, although it is significant to address the complexities of under-representation in higher education prior to entry, I have argued strongly that it is equally important to attend to issues of inequality and misrecognition in terms of *participation in* higher education, beyond entry. Indeed, higher education practices that are connected to pedagogy, curriculum and assessment remain central areas of exclusion and it is therefore imperative to explore possibilities for developing structures, strategies and frameworks that support inclusive practices underpinned by a commitment to ethics and social justice.

One of the most challenging aspects of this is to involve those in the most privileged social positions, for example those in senior positions in prestigious universities, to participate in the questioning of practices and policies that reinforce inequalities, differences and misrecognitions across a range of higher educational contexts. This demands a critically reflexive framework for developing ethical, inclusive and participatory practices in higher education. Nancy Fraser's conceptualization of social justice (1997), which requires simultaneous attention to distribution *and* recognition, is particularly insightful and important in developing such a reflexive framework. This involves a deeply transformative reorientation to the project of widening participation, which engages those in the most privileged nations, institutions and social groups in subjecting themselves to change and transformation rather than the current context, which focuses on the 'disadvantaged' becoming more like the advantaged (Gewirtz, 2001; Archer and Leathwood, 2003). However, a revisioning of widening participation must also involve a broadening of the focus of participation: in higher education, but also beyond it, to consider other interconnected realms of social life, relations and learning, with particular detailed attention to the politics of redistribution and recognition and constructions of different forms of learning, students and education. This requires processes of re/memory in making connections between Fraser's framework for social justice and the silenced histories that have been key in re/shaping current unequal social relations, differences and inequalities across different social, cultural and global contexts (Livingston, 2009).

The transformative vision of widening participation that I have proposed in this book is a significant, long-term and radical one and is challenging in relation to discourses of difference and the neoliberal global frameworks currently regulating and producing educational policies and practices. However, the vision is worth keeping to the fore of our pedagogical and methodological imaginations. Indeed, it is possible that the global economic crisis offers us new ways of doing and understanding, and so we are presented with hope and an opportunity for 'a new imagination that is freed from the stifling neoliberal orthodoxy of the past decades' (Badat, 2010: 136). Developing reflexive practices and orientations, which place social justice, equality, ethics, redistribution and recognition as a central focus, is a helpful first step in the project of reconceptualizing widening participation. Further steps include resisting forms of neoliberal regulation, developing collaborative and counter-hegemonic practices and methodologies and rejecting the current modes of individualization. Reconceptualizing widening participation requires participants (e.g. educational leaders and managers, policy-makers, students and teachers) to problematize and reconstitute their practices in all dimensions of education, including approaches to pedagogy, assessment, quality, management and leadership, challenging discourses of difference and inequality (Burke and Jackson, 2007).

In contesting mainstream discourses of WP policy, it is paramount that the difference between *increasing* participation and *widening* participation is clarified (Archer *et al.*, 2003). Understandings, analyses and insights emerging from the body of critical theory and research drawn on in this book are crucial tools in the transformative project of developing counter-hegemonic practices that might begin to destabilize histories and relations of privilege and inequality in and across different higher education contexts. Such insights are invaluable in creating programmes, strategies and approaches to support all higher education participants, including, but not only, academics, in their work, giving them a language and a set of tools to expose subtle, insidious and almost invisible workings of power and privilege, which are tied to complex social, material, cultural and global inequalities and are connected to subjectivity and epistemological contestations. However, it is not just about developing the understanding and resources available to higher education participants. It is about transforming higher education institutional cultures and practices so that different forms of knowledge and different kinds of learners, subjects and knowers can be recognized and validated in and across pedagogical spaces. It is about redressing historical misrecognitions that have led to the privileging of particular epistemological frameworks in higher education (Gordon, 2007).

Chapter Nine has highlighted that widening participation can be experienced as a 'battleground' and this includes conflicts and struggles over scarce resources and funds, as well as for recognition and authority. In England, and in other national contexts, funds and resources will continue to be explicitly identified for widening participation, and there must be clear lines of responsibility and accountability attached to their use. One important way to draw on such funds includes investment in clear mechanisms to support the development of inclusive practices in higher education designed specifically to challenge and redress inequalities and misrecognitions. This might include investment in ethical admissions practices, in developing inclusive pedagogies, in re/considering the curriculum and in developing approaches to assessment that recognize rather than marginalize the 'voices' of students from traditionally under-represented backgrounds. In relation to this, it is important to interrogate taken-for-granted assumptions around 'quality' that are often in tension with issues of equality (Morley, 2003; Burke and Jackson, 2007), ensuring that accountability includes close attention to issues of ethics, inclusion, diversity and equality. This requires a very different approach to accountability than the neoliberal, new managerialist and largely bureaucratic mechanisms that are currently enforced. Accountability that supports the commitment to equality, social justice and ethical practice puts complex relations of power and politics of recognition at the centre of concern. Qualitative approaches to accountability are valued in such frameworks, which take notice of the experiences and accounts of those often silenced and marginalized in HE spaces, although quantitative data also help to make visible the operations of inequality at play.

Jill Gordon argues that, regardless of disciplinary or subject context, all those who teach in higher education must be held accountable to the subtle processes of exclusion at play across higher education curriculums:

> All of us, regardless of credentials, regardless of time since receiving advanced degrees or prominence in our respective fields, have an obligation to educate ourselves about the world around us, about developments in our fields, and most especially about people, events, and ideas about which our class, race and/or social position would normally insulate us from knowing. [ ... ] earning an advanced degree and entering a profession in the academy is still predominately the province of Whites who come from privileged backgrounds. [ ... ] Primarily, the obligation to educate ourselves means going out to meet the world, and not expecting it to come to us – or, perhaps more pointedly, not assuming that what has come to us constitutes 'the world'.
>
> (Gordon, 2007)

Gordon's words are important in understanding the complicated nature of power and responsibility in the transformative project of widening participation in higher education. If we are to embrace inclusive and reflexive practices within higher education institutions, WP must reach beyond those in posts with explicit WP responsibility. As Burke and Jackson argue (2007), we need to enrich and broaden our concepts of 'quality' and 'accountability' to hold those in positions of status, authority and power within universities accountable to issues of equality, ethics and inclusion. This demands careful attention to the subtle ways that the relations, practices and cultures within, between and across universities might serve to (unwittingly) perpetuate deep-seated, historical and trans/national inequalities, exclusions and misrecognitions. Furthermore, academics in elite higher education institutions must participate in helping students to recognize that 'the public good is not served well unless the less advantaged among the public are served well' (Brighouse, 2010: 308).

## Inclusive cultures and practices

In this book, I have argued that too much attention is paid to transforming the attitudes of individuals who have been socially excluded from higher educational participation and too little attention has been paid to the different higher education cultures and practices that generate exclusions. The right to higher education has been historically connected to flawed discourses of meritocracy, which assume that access to higher education has been dependent on potential, ability and hard work, rather than socio-economic, cultural and symbolic privilege and recognition. Furthermore, widening participation has become part of a wider political project of neoliberal globalization, with higher education strongly associated with economic imperatives, and teaching, learning and assessment often forming a part of disciplinary and regulatory technologies. Throughout the book, I have considered different critical theoretical perspectives and methodologies for reformulating higher education cultures and practices with the aim to unsettle and disrupt the privileging of certain forms of knowledge, practice and subjectivity and the misrecognition of 'Others'.

I have explored, for example, the ways that academic literacy practices require complex decoding of tacit understandings and conventions, which often remain mysterious to those who have not had access to academic capitals, networks and subjectivities. As a result, students who are unfamiliar with this practice are often misrecognized as intellectually inferior, 'weak' or lacking ability. The 'ability' to write in particular ways is misunderstood as a natural capacity rather than a social practice learned over time through access to certain resources, networks, epistemologies and educational provision. For example, the practice of 'being critical' is often a key criterion in the assessment of the academic essay and yet what it might mean to 'be critical' is rarely included as part of the taught curriculum. Being critical might have multiple meanings, including examining assumptions (own/others), making 'the familiar' 'strange', problematizing taken-for-granted perspectives, drawing on theories and concepts to develop questions and ideas, developing a line of argument, taking a position or stance and supporting this with literature from the field, weaving together different pieces of literature to support a claim, and moving away from simple description/summary. These ways of 'being critical' are not reflective of inherent ability but are learned social and disciplinary practices, which allow a subject to be recognized as a legitimate student of higher education and contribute to the production of particular forms of knowledge whilst excluding others. It is thus important to provide the opportunity for groups who have been excluded from this literacy practice to have access to the skills, understanding and knowledge required to produce writing that would be recognized as legitimate within specific disciplinary/ subject fields. However, there are two issues to consider in relation to this point. First, it is a mistake to reformulate this into a remedial understanding of the problem, so that additional help is provided to those students who are seen to 'lack' the 'right' skills. I have argued that writing in different academic contexts is not simply a skill, it is a practice embedded in a particular disciplinary context and it engages the writer in positioning themselves as an 'author/ity', so is inextricably tied to relations of power and struggles over meaning. The process of writing is not simply a set of rational techniques; it is both an intellectual and emotional process. Although academic writing practices are often tied to notions of objectivity, writing demands that the student locates the self in contested meanings and makes decisions and selections in the process of referencing literature in the field. Thus, it is a social practice; the author of the text is situated within a field of knowledge and practice. Simultaneously it is a discursive act; through the process of writing and producing a text, the student/author is constituted as (not) a student/ author, and (continuing) participation in higher education is often dependent on the process of the production of a particular form of text/self/authorship. Widening participation is thus intimately connected to sets of practices that are historically exclusive and that produce the discursive spaces of recognition as a university student.

I have also argued that academic literacy practices must not be separated from other higher education practices, including pedagogies, assessment and curriculum. For example, it is through learning and teaching practices that students might gain access to different literacy practices in which they might be recognized as an included subject. Pedagogies that seek to disrupt unequal gendered, classed and racialized power relations must include attention to the different literacy practices in which they engage, including ways of speaking and writing about knowledge and meaning. Assessment practices similarly must take into account the ways that different literacies are being privileged and the implications of this for inclusion, exclusion and participation. This does not necessarily mean discarding particular forms of assessment, which have historically been privileged in higher education (such as the essay), but thinking more carefully about the pedagogical and assessment practices that might support students in producing a particular piece of work for assessment. This might also mean considering other assessment practices that draw on different forms of knowledge, for example professional or personal forms of knowledge. These considerations all must be explicitly linked to the curriculum and how knowledge is being constructed; what forms of knowledge are being given legitimacy; and with what consequences for access, equality, inclusion, representation, voice, participation and social justice. Attention to subtle and implicit forms of misrecognition and symbolic violence must be a central concern in the development of inclusive, transformative and participatory practices.

## Transformative practices of widening participation: critical reflexive praxis

Unfortunately, there are no quick-fix, tick-box answers to the problem of moving beyond hegemonic utilitarian and neoliberal widening participation frameworks. The way forward demands a long-term, serious and complicated commitment to social justice and equity in higher education. It demands a broad and deep view of the operations of inequality both within and across different educational institutions and fields, as well as an understanding that these will always be inextricably connected to wider social relations and inequalities. Moving towards a transformative discourse of widening participation requires less attention to individual attitudes and much greater attention to the cultures, practices and histories that have greatly benefitted already highly privileged social groups and profoundly excluded others. This is not an easy process because it demands that those who have positions of privilege and authority subject their values, perspectives and judgements to critique and open up the opportunity to learn from and develop knowledge collaboratively with those groups who have historically been excluded from such endeavours. Furthermore, those who might be privileged in some social contexts might be marginalized in others. The workings of power in higher education and in relation to questions of the right to participate are fraught with contradictions, contestations and challenges.

However, let me be clear: I am not arguing that higher education institutions should simply discard the forms of knowledge and practice that have in many ways served universities and society so well for centuries past. Rather, it is to create the opportunities for these exclusive forms of knowledge and practice to become accessible, inclusive and participatory through processes of redistribution, as well as to subject these to critique and to the possibilities of change and transformation. In the processes of redistribution and critique, the forms of knowledge and practice will evolve, transform and change and, at the same time, those groups who have now become included will contribute to the development of alternative forms of knowledge and practice in higher education. This will open up the possibilities for other ways of doing, thinking, studying and knowing. However, it is important to strongly emphasize that this is not about lowering of standards or creating sub-standard courses and degrees. Indeed it is about strengthening standards and quality, as it requires all participants in higher education to develop deeper levels of criticality and reflexivity, bringing together theory and practice through a commitment to praxis. The impact of such approaches will not only be to widen participation in higher education, but to transform higher educational spaces in dedicated projects of creating dialectic spaces of ethical, inclusive and participatory meaning-making for the greater public good and social justice. This will no doubt have a positive impact on the economy, as different social groups are recognized, included and given the opportunity to be active and valued participants in the production of knowledge. However, this transformative framework will have an even more profound effect on social relations and identities, helping to challenge the divisions and hierarchies that are at the root of social exclusion, misrecognition, exclusion and marginalization. Higher education institutions must take centre stage in destabilizing those forms of knowledge and practice that work to create oppressive and exclusive conditions, which are toxic for everyone in society in the long term. Rather, the focus must be on developing higher education in ways that nurture, enrich and fully recognize the importance of diverse forms of knowledge, subjectivity and practice.

Paulo Freire talks about such processes in terms of the 'circle of knowledge' and the commitment of universities to rigour and standards, which depends on their engagement with what he calls the 'popular classes'. He argues that 'the university that fails to strive for greater rigour, more seriousness, in its research activities as in the area of instruction – which are never dichotomizable, true – cannot seriously approach the popular classes or make a commitment to them' (Freire, 2009: 169). This, he explains, is deeply connected to the circle of knowledge, which is the coming together of two moments of the same circle: the moments of understanding existing knowledge and producing new knowledge.

> There is no genuine instruction in whose process no research is performed by way of question, investigation, curiosity, creativity just as there is no research in the course of which researchers do not learn – after all, by coming to know, they learn, and after having learned something, they communicate, they teach. The role of the university ... is to immerse itself, utterly seriously, in the moment of this circle.
>
> (Freire, 2009: 169–70)

Freire's circle of knowledge represents the kind of praxis necessary for trans-formatory approaches to widening participation, which at its heart is a project of social justice. The circle that I argue for is one that allows resistance to the seductions of rationalist, linear, standardizing, homogenizing, normalizing, regulating, colonizing, exclusive and totalitarian regimes of knowing and being known. Instead the circle engages the cyclical, reflexive and partial spaces of knowing and being that participation in higher education should involve: the ongoing questioning of the assumptions and values that we bring to our learning, subjectivities and understanding. At the centre of the circle is a deep commitment to ethical practice in and beyond higher education, which demands that questions of equality, power and representation are at the fore of any pedagogical project.

As Patti Lather states in relation to the struggle for social justice in edu-cation: 'the conjunction in critical social theory of the various feminisms, neo-Marxisms and post-structuralisms feels fruitful ground for shifting us into ways of thinking that take us beyond ourselves' (Lather, 1991: 164). Those of us committed to the struggle for social justice in higher education have the fruits from such theoretical perspectives to draw on to move us beyond narrow individualism and towards transforming cultures and practices for widening participation in and beyond higher education. Reconsidering the right to higher education from a social justice perspective demands that the right is not determined within individualist, meritocratic frameworks that reduce the problem of widening participation to changing the attitudes of disadvantaged individuals deemed to have the potential to benefit from higher educational participation. The right to higher education is ultimately about deeply valu-ing and appreciating the significant contribution of higher education to social justice and the public good, to the complex processes of knowledge con-struction and to the ongoing development of different social groups and dif-ferent societies in the context of a long-term commitment to eradicating social inequalities. This requires multiple strategies, including the redis-tribution of privileged resources and opportunities, reflexive attention to the politics of recognition and subjective construction, and praxis that draws together the insights of critical, feminist and post-structural theories with embedded, transformative and participatory practices in higher education.

# Bibliography

Abbas, A. and McLean, M. (2010) 'Tackling Inequality Through Quality: A Comparative Case Study Using Bernsteinian Concepts' in E. Unterhalter and V. Carpentier (eds) *Global Inequalities and Higher Education: Whose Interests Are We Serving?* London: Palgrave Macmillan.

About Parliament (2010) 'Living Heritage: Going to School', http://www.parliament.uk/about/livingheritage/transformingsociety/school/overview/1870educationact.cfm. Accessed March 2010.

Adkins, L. (2004) 'Reflexivity and the Politics of Qualitative Research' in T. May (ed.) *Qualitative Research in Action*. London, Thousand Oaks, New Delhi: SAGE, 349–74.

Adnett, N. and Slack, K. (2003) 'Are There Economic Incentives for Non-Traditional Students to Enter HE? The Labour Market as a Barrier to Widening Participation', *Higher Education Quarterly* 61 (1): 23–36.

Alcoff, L. and Potter, E. (1993) *Feminist Epistemologies*. New York and London: Routledge.

Allen, W. R., Jayakumar, U. M., Griffin, K., Korn, W., and Hurtado, S. (2005) *Black Undergraduates from Bakke to Grutter: Freshmen Status, Trends and Prospects, 1971–2004*. Los Angeles, CA: Higher Education Research Institute, University of California.

Anderson, P. and Williams, J. (2001) *Identity and Difference in Higher Education: 'Outsiders Within'*. Aldershot, Burlington, VT, Singapore, Sydney: Ashgate.

Anthias, F. (1998) 'Evaluating "Diaspora": Beyond Ethnicity?', *Sociology* 32: 557–80.

Apple, M. (1986) *Teachers and Texts: A Political Economy of Class and Gender Relations in Education*. London: Routledge and Kegan Paul.

——(2006) *Educating the 'Right' Way: Markets, Standards, God, and Inequality*. London: Routledge.

Archer, L. (2003) *Race, Masculinity and Schooling: Muslim Boys and Education*. Berkshire: Open University Press.

Archer, L., Hutchings, M., Leathwood, C. and Ross, A. (2003) 'Widening Participation in Higher Education: Implications for Policy and Practice' in L. Archer, M. Hutchings and A. Ross (eds) *Higher Education and Social Class: Issues of Exclusion and Inclusion*. London: Routledge Falmer.

Archer, L. and Leathwood, C. (2003) 'Identities, Inequalities and Higher Education' in L. Archer, M. Hutchings and A. Ross (eds) *Higher Education and Social Class: Issues of Exclusion and Inclusion*. London: Routledge Falmer, 171–91.

Archer, L., Pratt, S.D. and Phillips, D. (2001) 'Working-class Men's Constructions of Masculinity and Negotiations of (Non) Participation in Higher Education', *Gender and Education* 13 (4): 431–49.

Atencio, M. and Wright, J. (2009) '"Ballet It's Too Whitey": Discursive Hierarchies of High School Dance Spaces and the Constitution of Embodied Feminine Subjectivities', *Gender and Education*, 21 (1): 31–46.

Atkinson, P. and Coffey, A. (2002) 'Revisiting the Relationship Between Participant Observation and Interviewing' in J. F. Gubrium and J. A. Holstein (eds) *Handbook of Interview Research*. Thousand Oaks, CA: SAGE.

Attwood, R. (2010) 'Review Finds "Clear Agreement" that Top-up Fees Have Not Deterred Students', *Times Higher Education*, 15 March.

Badat, S. (2010) 'Global Rankings of Universities: A Perverse and Present Burden' in E. Unterhalter and V. Carpentier (eds) *Global Inequalities and Higher Education: Whose Interests Are We Serving?* Hampshire: Palgrave.

Baker, S., Brown, B. J. and Fazey, J. A. (2006) 'Individualisation in the Widening Participation Debate', *London Review of Education* 4 (2): 169–82.

Ball, S. J., Bowe, R. and Gewirtz, S. (1995) 'Circuits of Schooling: A Sociological Exploration of Parental Choice of School in Social Class Contexts', *Sociological Review* 43: 52–78.

Banerjee, A., Bardhan, P., Basu, K., Chaudhuri, M. D., Ghatak, M., Guha, A. S., Majumdar, M., Mookherjee, D. and Ray, D. (2002) 'Strategy for Economic Reform in West Bengal', *Economic and Political Weekly*, 12 October.

Barefoot, B. O. (2004) 'Higher Education's Revolving Door: Confronting the Problem of Student Drop Out in US Colleges and Universities', *Open Learning* 19 (1): 9–18.

Barr, (2008) *The Stranger Within: On the Idea of an Educated Public*. Rotterdam: Sense Publishers.

Baxter, A., Tate, J. and Hatt, S. (2007) 'From Policy to Practice: Pupils' Responses to Widening Participation Initiatives', *Higher Education Quarterly* 61 (3): 266–83.

Bekhradnia, B. (2003) *Widening Participation and Fair Access: An Overview of the Evidence*. Higher Education Policy Institute Research Paper.

Bell, David (2003) 'Leading Change: African Conceptions of Leadership and Transformation in Higher Education in South Africa' in C. Prichard and P. Trowler (eds) *Realizing Qualitative Research into Higher Education*. Aldershot and Burlington, VT: Ashgate, 172–93.

Bell, J. M. and Hartmann, D. (2007) 'Diversity in Everyday Discourse: The Cultural Ambiguities and Consequences of "Happy Talk"', *American Sociological Review* 72 (6): 895–914.

Bennett, T., Savage, M., Silva, E., Warde, A., Gayo-Cal, M. and Wright, D. (2009) *Culture, Class, Distinction*. Oxford: Routledge.

Bernstein, B. (1975) *Class, Codes and Control, Vol. 3*. London: Routledge.

Bird, L. C., Cornforth, S., Davies, B., Milligan, A. and White, E. J. (2009) 'Inclusion and Mastery: Variations on the Theme of Subjection', *Gender and Education* 21: 47–62.

Blanden, J. and Machin, S. (2004) 'Educational Inequality and the Expansion of UK Higher Education', *Scottish Journal of Political Economy* 54: 230–49.

Bourdieu, P. (1984) *Distinction: A Social Critique of the Judgement of Taste*. London: Routledge.

——(1986) 'The Forms of Capital' in J. G. Richardson (ed.) *Handbook of Theory and Research for the Sociology of Education*. New York: Greenwood Press.

——(1991) *The Love of Art: European Art Museums and Their Public*. California: Stanford University Press.

——(1993) *The Field of Cultural Production: Essays on Art and Literature*. Cambridge: Polity Press.

Bourdieu, P. and Passeron, J.-C. (1977) *Reproduction in Education, Society and Culture*. London: SAGE.

Bourdieu, P. and Waquant, L. (1992) *An Invitation to Reflexive Sociology*. Chicago: University of Chicago Press.

Bowl, M. (2001) 'Experiencing the Barrier: Non-traditional Students Entering Higher Education', *Research Papers in Education* 16 (2): 141–60.

——(2003) *Non-Traditional Entrants to Higher Education: 'They Talk About People Like Me'*. Stoke-on-Trent, Trentham Books.

Brah, A. (1996) *Cartographies of Diaspora: Contesting Identities*. London and New York: Routledge.

Bridges, D. (2005) 'Widening Participation in Higher Education: "The Philosopher and the Bricklayer" Revisited'. Paper presented to Philosophy of Education Conference, Institute of Education, London, 1–3 April.

Brighouse, H. (2010) 'Globalization and the Professional Ethic of the Professoriat' in E. Unterhalter and V. Carpentier (eds) *Global Inequalities and Higher Education: Whose Interests Are We Serving?* Hampshire: Palgrave.

Brooks, R. (2005) *Friendship and Educational Choice: Peer Influence and Planning for the Future*, Basingstoke: Palgrave Macmillan.

Brown, G. (2007) Speech made by Prime Minister Gordon Brown at the University of Greenwich, 31 October 2007.

Brown, G. (2009) 'The Place of Aspirations'. Seminar paper, Dept of Geography, University of Leicester, 14 May 2009.

Brown, P. (2003) 'The Opportunity Trap: Education and Employment in a Global Economy', *European Educational Research Journal* 2 (1): 141–79.

Bryan, B., Dadzie, S. and Scafe, S. (1985) *Heart of the Race*. London: Virago.

Burke, P. J. (2002) *Accessing Education: Effectively Widening Participation*. Stoke-on-Trent: Trentham Books.

——(2004) 'Women Accessing Education: Subjectivity, Policy and Participation', *Journal of Access, Policy and Practice* 1 (2): 100–118.

——(2006) 'Men Accessing Education: Gendered Aspiration', *British Educational Research Journal* 32 (5): 719–34.

——(2008) 'The Implications of Widening Participation for Professionalism' in B. Cunningham (ed.) *Exploring Professionalism*. London: Institute of Education.

——(2009) 'Men Accessing Higher Education: Theorising Continuity and Change in Relation to Masculine Identities', *Higher Education Policy* 22 (1): 81–100.

——(2010) 'Masculinity, Subjectivity and Neoliberalism in Men's Accounts of Migration and Accessing Higher Education', *Gender and Education* 23 (2): 169–84.

Burke, P. J. and Hermerschmidt, M. (2005) 'Deconstructing Academic Practices Through Self-reflexive Pedagogies', in B. Street (ed.) *Literacies Across Educational Contexts: Mediating Learning and Teaching*. Philadelphia, PA: Caslon Press.

Burke, P. J. and Jackson, S. (2007) *Reconceptualising Lifelong Learning: Feminist Interventions*. London: Routledge.

Burke, P. J. and McManus, J. (2009) *Art for a Few: Exclusion and Misrecognition in Art and Design Higher Education Admissions*. London: National Arts Learning Network.

Burke, P. J. and Hayton, A. (2011) 'Is Widening Participation Still Ethical?' *Widening Participation and Lifelong Learning* 13 (1), April 2011.

Butler, J. (1993) *Bodies that Matter: On the Discursive Limits of 'Sex'*. London: Routledge.

Callender, C. (2003a) 'Student Financial Support in Higher Education: Access and Exclusion' in M. Tight (ed.) *Access and Exclusion: International Perspectives on Higher Education Research*. London: Elsevier Science.

——(2003b) 'The Contradictions of Higher Education Policy', ESRC Research Special, *The Edge*, (14) November 2003.

——(2009a) *Awareness and Knowledge of Institutional Bursaries and Scholarships Among Higher Education Advisors in Schools and Colleges*. Bristol: Office for Fair Access.

——(2009b) *Higher Education Institutions' Strategies to Increase the Awareness and Take-up of Institutional Bursaries and Scholarships*. Bristol: Office for Fair Access.

——(2010) 'Bursaries and Institutional Aid in Higher Education in England: Do They Safeguard Access and Promote Fair Access?', *Oxford Review of Education* 36: 1.

Carby, H. (1987) 'Black Feminism and the Boundaries of Sisterhood' in M. Arnot and G. Weiner (eds) *Gender and the Politics of Schooling*. London: Unwin Hyman.

Carpentier, V. (2010) 'Public-Private Substitution in Higher Education Funding and Kondratiev Cycles: The Impacts on Home and International Students' in Elaine Unterhalter and Vincent Carpentier (eds) *Global Inequalities and Higher Education: Whose Interests Are We Serving?* Hampshire: Palgrave.

Cassidy, S. (2003) 'Cambridge College Accused for Elitism After Rejecting Star Students', *The Independent*, 15 August.

Chowdry, H., Crawford, C., Dearden, L., Goodman, A. and Vignoles, A. (2009) *Widening Participation in Higher Education: Analysis Using Linked Administrative Data*. IFS Working Paper W10/04.

Claiborne, L. B., Cornforth, S., Davies, B., Milligan, A. and White, E. J. (2009) 'Inclusion and Mastery: Variations on the Theme of Subjection', *Gender and Education*, 21 (1): 47–61.

Clegg, S. (2005) *Academic Identities Under Threat?* Edinburgh: SRHE.

Coffey, A. and Atkinson, P. (1996) *Making Sense of Qualitative Data*. London, Thousand Oaks, New Delhi: SAGE.

Collins, P. H. (1990) *Black Feminist Thought: Knowledge, Consciousness, and the Politics of Empowerment*. Boston: Unwin Hyman.

Connell, R. W. (2000) *The Men and the Boys*. Cambridge, Oxford: Polity, Blackwell.

——(2005) *Masculinities*. Los Angeles, CA and Berkeley, CA: University of California Press.

Connolly, P. and Neill, J. (2001) 'Constructions of Locality and Gender and Their Impact on the Educational Aspirations of Working-class Children', *International Studies in Sociology of Education* 11 (2): 107–30.

Connor, H., Burton, R., Pearson, R., Pollard, E. and Regan, J. (1999) *Making the Right Choice: How Students Choose University and Colleges*. London: Institute for Employment Studies.

Copland, G. (2008) 'Introduction' in G. Copland, D. Sachdev and C. Flint (eds) *Unfinished Business in Widening Participation; The End of the Beginning*. London: Learning and Skills Council.

Creme, P. (2003) 'Why Can't We Allow Students to be More Creative?' *Teaching in Higher Education* 8 (2): 273–77.

Crenshaw, K. (1989) 'Demarginalizing the Intersection of Race and Sex: A Black Feminist Critique of Antidiscrimination Doctrine, Feminist Theory and Antiracist Politics', *University of Chicago Legal Forum* 4: 139–67.

Crozier, G. and Davies, J. (2007) 'Hard to Reach Parents or Hard to Reach Schools? A Discussion of Home-school Relations, with Particular Reference to Bangladeshi and Pakistani Parents', *British Educational Research Journal* 33 (3): 295–313.

Crozier, G. and D. Reay (2008) 'The Socio Cultural and Learning Experiences of Working Class Students in Higher Education', *Teaching and Learning Research Briefing* 44. London: Teaching and Learning Research Programme, ESRC.

Crozier, G., Reay, D., Clayton, J., Colliander, L. and Grinstead, J. (2008) 'Different Strokes for Different Folks: Diverse Students in Diverse Institutions – Experiences of Higher Education', *Research Papers in Education* 23(2): 167–77.

Currie, J., Thiele, B. and Harris, P. (2002) *Gendered Universities in Globalized Economies: Power, Careers and Sacrifices*. Lanham, MD, Boulder, CO, New York and Oxford: Lexington Books.

David, M., Coffey, A., Connolly, P., Nayak, A., and Reay, D. (2006) 'Troubling Identities: Reflections on Judith Butler's Philosophy for the Sociology of Education', *British Journal of Sociology of Education* 27(4): 421–24.

David, M., Parry, G., Vignoles, A., Hayward, G., Williams, J., Crozier, G., Hockings, C. and Fuller, A. (2009) *Widening Participation in Higher Education – A Commentary by the Teaching and Learning Research Programme*. London: Teaching and Learning Research Programme, ESRC.

Davies, B. (1997) 'The Subject of Post-structuralism: A reply to Alison Jones', *Gender and Education* 9 (3): 271–83.

——(2006) 'Subjectification: the relevance of Butler's Analysis for Education', *British Journal of Sociology of Education* 27 (4): 425–38.

Davis, K. (2008) 'Intersectionality as Buzzword: A Sociology of Science Perspective on What Makes a Feminist Theory Successful', *Feminist Theory* 9 (1): 67–85.

Dearing, R. (1997) *Higher Education in the Learning Society* (The Dearing Report). London: The National Committee of Inquiry into Higher Education.

Denham, J. (2008) Speech at HEFCE Conference 2008. London.

Department of Employment (1988) *Employment for the 1990s*. Great Britain: HMSO.

Desai, S. (2008) 'Caste in 21st Century India: Competing Narratives'. India Human Development Survey Working Paper No. 12.

Desai, S. and Kulkarni, V. (2008) 'Changing Educational Inequalities in India in the Context of Affirmative Action', *Demography* 45 (2): 254–70.

DfE (1991) *Higher Education: A New Framework*. London: HMSO.

DfEE (1998) *The Learning Age; A Renaissance for a New Britain*. London: HMSO.

——(1999) *Learning to Succeed – A New Framework for Post-16 Learning*. London: HMSO.

DfES (2001) *Schools Achieving Success*. London: DfES.

——(2003a) *The Future of Higher Education*. Norwich: HMSO.

——(2003b) *Widening Participation in Higher Education*. Norwich: HMSO.

——(2005) *Higher Standards, Better Schools for All*. London: DfES Publications.

——(2006a) *Aimhigher: Excellence Challenge: A Policy Evaluation Using the Labour Force Survey*. Research Report RR813. London: DfES Publications.

——(2006b) *Aimhigher Topic Paper*. London: DfES.

Diamond, J. (1999) 'Access: The Year 2000 and Beyond – What Next?', *Journal of Access and Credit Studies*, Summer 1999: 183–91.

Diawara, M. (1998) 'Homeboy Cosmopolitan: Manthia Diawara Interviewed by Silvia Kolbowski', *October*, 83 (Winter): 51–70.

Duggan, L. (2003) *The Twilight of Equality? Neoliberalism, Cultural Politics, and the Attack on Democracy*. Boston: Beacon Press.

Dyhouse, C. (2005) 'End of Award Report: Gaining Places: Stagnation and Growth in the Proportion of Women in Universities'. Swindon: ESRC. RES-000-22-0139-5K.

Dysthe, O. (2002) 'Professors as Mediators of Academic Text Cultures: An Interview Study with Advisors and Master's Degree Students in Three Disciplines in a Norwegian University', *Written Communication* 19 (4): 493–544.

ECU (2008) *Equality in Higher Education Statistical Report 2008*. London: Equality Challenge Unit.

Edwards, R. (2008) 'Actively Seeking Subjects?' in A. Fejes and K. Nicoll (eds) *Foucault and Lifelong Learning: Governing the Subject*. Oxford: Routledge.

Ellsworth, E. (1992) 'Why Doesn't This Feel Empowering? Working Through the Repressive Myths of Critical Pedagogy' in C. Luke and J. Gore (eds) *Feminisms and Critical Pedagogy*. London and New York: Routledge.

——(1997) *Teaching Positions*. New York and London: Teachers College Press.

Epstein, D., Elwood, J., Hey, V. and Maw, J. (1998) *Failing Boys? Issues in Gender and Achievement*. Buckinghamshire: Open University Press.

Evans, M. (2004) *Killing Thinking: the Death of the Universities*. London and New York: Continuum.

Fejes, A. (2008) 'Historicising the Lifelong Learner: Governmentality and Neoliberal Rule', in A. Fejes and K. Nicoll (eds) *Foucault and Lifelong Learning: Governing the Subject*. Oxford: Routledge.

Fitzgibbon, K. and Prior, J. (2006) 'Students' Early Experiences and University Interventions – A Timeline to Aid Undergraduate Student Retention' in *Widening Participation and Lifelong Learning*, 8 (3): 17–27.

Flax, J. (1995) 'Postmodernism and Gender Relations in Feminist Theory' in Blair and Holland with Sheldon (eds) *Identity and Diversity; Gender and the Experience of Education*. Avon: Open University.

Foskett, N. (2002) 'Marketing Imperative or Cultural Challenge? Embedding Widening Participation in the Further Education Sector', *Research in Post-Compulsory Education* 7 (1): 79–95.

Foucault, M. (1977) *Discipline and Punish: The Birth of the Prison*, trans. A. Sheridan. New York: Pantheon Books.

——(1980) 'Two Lectures', in C. Gordon (ed.) *Michel Foucault: Power/Knowledge*. London: Harvester Wheatsheaf.

——(1982) 'The Subject and Power', Afterword in H. Dreyfus and P. Rabinow (eds) *Michel Foucault: Beyond Structuralism and Hermeneutics* (2nd edn). Chicago, IL: University of Chicago.

——(1984) 'The Means of Correct Training' (from *Discipline and Punish*) in P. Rabinow (ed.) *The Foucault Reader*. London: Penguin Books.

——(1988) 'Practicing Criticism', an interview in D. L. Kritzman (ed.), *Michel Foucault: Politics, Philosophy, Culture*. London: Routledge, 152–56.

——(1991) *Discipline and Punish: The Birth of a Prison*. London: Penguin.

Fraser, N. (1997) *Justice Interruptus: Critical Reflections on the 'Postsocialist' Condition*. London and New York: Routledge.

——(2003) 'Social Justice in the Age of Identity Politics: Redistribution, Recognition and Participation' in N. Fraser and A. Honneth (2003) *Redistribution or Recognition? A Political-Philosophical Exchange*. London and New York: Verso.

Fraser, N. and Honneth, A. (2003) *Redistribution or Recognition? A Political-Philosophical Exchange*. London and New York: Verso.

Freire, P. (2009) *Pedagogy of Hope*. London: Continuum.

Frosh, S., Phoenix, A. and Pattman, R. (2002) *Young Masculinities: Understanding Boys in Contemporary Society*. Hampshire: Palgrave.

Gerson, K. and Horowitz, R. (2002) 'Observation and Interviewing: Options and Choices in Qualitative Research', in T. May (ed.) *Qualitative Research in Action*. London: SAGE, 199–224.

Gewirtz, S. (2001) 'Cloning the Blairs: New Labour's Programme for the Re-socialization of Working-class Parents', *Journal of Educational Policy* 16 (4): 365–78.

Gewirtz, S., Ball, S. J. and Bowe, R. (1995) *Markets, Choice and Equity in Education*. Buckingham: Open University Press.

Gillborn, D. (2008) *Racism and Education: Coincidence or Conspiracy?* London and New York: Routledge.

Gillborn, D. and Youdell, D. (2000) *Rationing Education: Policy, Practice, Reform and Equity*. Buckingham, Open University Press.

Gilroy, P. (2004) *Between Camps: Nations, Culture and the Allure of Race*. London: Routledge.

Goodwin, P. (2009) 'Building and Dwelling in the Zone' in Paul Goodwin and Monica de Miranda (eds) *Under-Construction*. Lisbon: DG Artes.

Gorard, S., Smith, E., May, H., Thomas, L., Adnett, N. and Slack, K. (2006) *Review of Widening Participation Research: Addressing the Barriers to Participation in Higher Education*. Bristol: HEFCE.

Gorard, S., with Adnett, N., May, H., Slack, K., Smith, E. and Thomas, L. (2007) *Overcoming the Barriers to Higher Education*. Stoke-on-Trent: Trentham Books.

Gordon, J. (2007) 'What Can White Faculty Do?', *Teaching in Higher Education* 12 (3): 337–48.

Government of India (1992) *Programme of Action on the National Education Policy*. New Delhi: Ministry of Human Resource Development.

——(1997) *Ninth Five-year Plan: 1997–2002*. New Delhi: Planning Commission.

——(2001) *Approach Paper to the Tenth Five-year Plan: 2002–2007*. New Delhi: Planning Commission.

——(2002) *Tenth Five-year Plan: 2002–2007*. New Delhi: Planning Commission.

Greenbank, P. (2006) 'The Evolution of Government Policy on Widening Participation', *Higher Education Quarterly* 60 (2): 141–66.

Guinier, L. and Sturm, S. (2001) *Who's Qualified?* Boston, MA: Beacon.

Gupta D. (2005) 'Caste and Politics: Identity Over System', *Annual Review of Anthropology* 21: 409–27.

Hall, S. (1992) 'Introduction: Identity in Question' in S. Hall, D. Held and T. McGrew (eds) *Modernity and Its Futures*. Cambridge: Polity Press.

——(1997) 'The Spectacle of the "Other"' in S. Hall (ed.) *Representation*. London: SAGE.

——(2000) 'Who Needs "Identity"?' in P. du Gay and P. Redman (eds) *Identity: A Reader*. London: SAGE.

Haney, L. (2004) 'Negotiating Power and Expertise in the Field' in T. May (ed.) *Qualitative Research in Action*. London, Thousand Oaks, New Delhi: SAGE, 349–74.

Haraway, D. (1988) 'Situated Knowledges: The Science Question in Feminism and the Privilege of Partial Perspective', *Feminist Studies* 14 (3): 575–99.

Harding, S. (1993) *The 'Racial' Economy of Science : Toward a Democratic Future*. Bloomington, IL and Indianapolis, IN: Indiana University Press.

Hayton, A. and Paczuska, A. (2002) 'Conclusion: Is Higher Education Gladdening Our Existence?' in A. Hayton and A. Paczuska (eds) *Access, Participation and Higher Education – Policy and Practice*. London: Kogan Page.

HEFCE (2003) *Funding for Widening Participation in Education: Responses to Consultation and Funding for 2003–2004 to 2005–2006*. http://www.hefce.ac.uk/pubs. Accessed 16 February 2010.

——(2005) *Young Participation in Higher Education*. http://www.hefce.ac.uk/pubs. Accessed 16 February 2010.

——(2006) *Widening Participation: A Review*. Accessed via http://www.hefce.ac.uk/widen/aim-high/review.asp. Accessed 16 February 2010.

——(2008) 'Widening Participation and Fair Access Research Strategy'. Higher Education Funding Council for England.

——(2009) 'Widening Participation'. http://www.hefce.ac.uk/widen. Accessed 24 May 2009.

Henkel, M. (2000) *Academic Identities and Policy Change in Higher Education*. London: Jessica Kingsley Publishers Ltd.

HEPI (2009) *Male and Female Participation and Progression in Higher Education*. Oxford: Higher Education Policy Institute.

Hey, V. and Evans, S. (2009) 'Destined for Success? Who is Made Intelligible in the Discursive Configuration of Class and Background' in symposium, Caught Between the Inertia of Archaism and the Frenzy of Hypermodernisation: Exploring a Cultural Sociology of Higher Education (Morley, Symposium Leader). Wales: SRHE annual conference, 2009.

Hills, J., Brewer, M., Jenkins, S., Lister, R., Lupton, R., Machin, S., Mills, C., Modod, T., Rees, T. and Riddell, S. (2010) *An Anatomy of Economic Inequality in the UK. A Report of the National Equality Panel*. London: Government Equalities Office.

Hockings, C., Cooke, S., Bowl, M., Yamashita, H. and McGinty, S. (2008) 'Learning and Teaching for Diversity and Difference in Higher Education: Towards More Inclusive Learning Environments', *Teaching and Learning Research Briefing* 41. London: Teaching and Learning Research Programme, ESRC.

Hooks, B. (1982) *Ain't I a Woman, Black Women and Feminism*. London: Pluto Press.

Howieson, C., Ozga, J. and Provan, F. (2003) *Student Retention in the University of Edinburgh, Final Report to the University of Edinburgh*. Edinburgh: Centre for Educational Sociology, Edinburgh University.

Ivanic, R. (1998) *Writing and Identity: The Discoursal Construction of Identity in Academic Writing*. Amsterdam and Philadelphia, PA: John Benjamins Publishing Company and John Benjamins North America.

Jackson, S. (2007) 'In Search of Lifelong Learning: Politics, Power and Pedagogic Challenges', Professorial Inaugural Lecture. London: Birkbeck, University of London.

Jones, A. (1993) 'Becoming a "Girl": Post-structuralist Suggestions for Educational Research', *Gender and Education* 5 (2): 157–65.

Jones, C. (2010) *HerStoria magazine*. Birkenhead: Jones5 Publishing Limited. http://www. herstoria.com/discover/HigherEducation.html. Accessed 2 June 2010.

Jones, R. and Thomas, L. (2005) 'The 2003 UK Government Higher Education White Paper: A Critical Assessment of its Implications for the Access and Widening Participation Agenda', *Journal of Education Policy* 20 (5): 615–30.

Kapur, D. and Mehta, P. B. (2007) *Indian Higher Education Reform: From Half-Baked Socialism to Half-Baked Capitalism*. Presented at the Brookings-NCAER India Policy Forum, New Delhi, 2 July.

Karabel, J. (2005) *The Chosen*. New York: Mariner Books.

Kenway, J. (1995) 'Feminist Theories of the State: To Be or Not To Be' in Blair and Holland with Sheldon (eds) *Identity and Diversity; Gender and the Experience of Education*. Avon: Open University.

Kettley, N. (2007) 'The Past, Present and Future of Widening Participation Research', *British Journal of Sociology of Education* 28 (3): 333–47.

Kogan, M. and Hanney, S. (2000) *Reforming Higher Education*. London and Philadelphia, PA: Jessica Kingsley Publishers.

Lamont, M. and Moraes da Silva, G. (2009) 'Complementary Rather than Contradictory: Diversity and Excellence in Peer Review and Admissions in American Higher Education', *21st Century Society* 4 (1): 1–15.

Lather, P. (1991) *Getting Smart: Feminist Research and Pedagogy With/in the Postmodern*. New York and London: Routledge.

Lave, J. and Wenger, E. (1991) *Situated Learning. Legitimate Peripheral Participation*. Cambridge: University of Cambridge Press.

Lawler, S. (2002) 'Narrative in Social Research' in T. May (ed.) *Qualitative Research in Action*. London, Thousand Oaks, New Delhi: SAGE.

——(2008) *Identity: Sociological Perspectives*. Cambridge: Polity Press.

Lea, M. R. and Street, B. (2000) 'Student Writing and Staff Feedback in Higher Education: An Academic Literacies Approach' in M. Lea and B. Stierer (eds) *Student Writing in Higher Education: New Contexts*. Buckingham: The Society for Research into Higher Education and Open University Press.

Leadbeater, C. (2004) 'Participation through Personalisation.' London: Demos. http://www. demos.co.uk/publications/personalisation. Accessed 14 March 2010.

——(2006) 'The Future of Public Services: Personalised Learning', *Schooling for Tomorrow. Personalised Education*. Paris: OECD Publications.

Leathwood, C. (2005) 'Assessment Policy and Practice in Higher Education: Purpose, Standards and Equity', *Assessment and Evaluation in Higher Education* 30 (3), June 2005: 307–24.

Leathwood, C. and Read, B. (2009) *Gender and the Changing Face of Higher Education: A Feminized Future?* Berkshire: Open University Press.

Leyva, Rodolfo (2009) 'No Child Left Behind: A Neoliberal Repackaging of Social Darwinism', *Journal for Critical Education Policy Studies* June 2009, 17 (1): 364–81.

Lillis, T. (2001) *Student Writing: Access, Regulation, Desire*. London: Routledge.

Lillis, T. M. and Ramsey, M. (1997) 'Student Status and the Question of Choice in Academic Writing', *Research and Practice in Adult Learning Bulletin* Spring (32): 15–22.

Livingston, G. (2009) 'Regulation, Resistance and Activism: Troubling Margin and Centre', Gender and Education Association Conference 2009. Institute of Education, University of London.

Lorde, A. (1984) *Sister Outsider*. Trumansburg: The Crossing Press.

Luke, C. and Gore, J. (eds) (1992) *Feminisms and Critical Pedagogy*. New York and London: Routledge.

Mac an Ghaill, M. (1994) *The Making of Men: Masculinities, Sexualities and Schooling*. Buckingham and Philadelphia: Open University Press.

Machin, S. and Vignoles, A. (2004) 'Educational Inequality: The Widening Socio-Economic Gap', *Fiscal Studies* 25: 107–28.

Maher, F. and Tetrault, M. (2006) *Privilege and Diversity in the Academy*. New York: Routledge.

Mahony, P. and Zmroczek, C. (eds) (1997) *Class Matters: 'Working-Class' Women's Perspectives on Social Class*. London: Taylor & Francis.

Martino, W. (1999) '"Cool Boys", "Party Animals", "Squids" and "Poofters": Interrogating the Dynamics and Politics of Adolescent Masculinities in School', *British Journal of Sociology of Education* 20 (2): 239–63.

Mauthner, M., Birch, M., Jessop, J. and Miller, T., (eds) (2002) *Ethics in Qualitative Research*. London, Thousand Oaks, CA, New York: SAGE.

Mauthner, N. S. and Doucet, A. (2003) 'Reflexive Accounts and Accounts of Reflexivity in Qualitative Data Analysis', *Sociology* 37 (3): 413–32.

McCall, L. (2005) 'The Complexity of Intersectionality', *Signs* 30 (3): 1771–1801.

McCausland, W. D., Mavromaras, K. and Theodossiou, I. (2005) 'Explaining Student Retention: The Case of the University of Aberdeen', *Widening Participation and Lifelong Learning* 7 (3): 24–26.

McGivney, V. (1999) *Excluded Men: Men Who Are Missing From Education and Training*. Leicester: National Institute of Adult Continuing Education.

McNay, L. (2008) *Against Recognition*. Cambridge: Polity.

McManus, J. (2006) 'Every Word Starts with "Dis": The Impact of Class on Choice, Application and Admissions to Prestigious Higher Education Art and Design Courses', *Reflecting Education* 2 (1): 73–84.

Milburn, A. (2009) *Unleashing Aspiration: The Final Report of the Panel on Fair Access to the Professions*. London: The Cabinet Office.

Miliband, D. (2006) 'Choice and Voice in Personalised Learning', *Schooling for Tomorrow. Personalised Education*. Paris: OECD.

Miller, J. (1995) 'Trick or Treat? The Autobiography of the Question', *English Quarterly* 27 (3).

——(1997) *Autobiography in Research*. Chicago: American Education Research Association.

Mills, C. and Gale, T. (2010) *Schooling in Disadvantaged Communities: Playing the Game From the Back of the Field*. Dordrecht: Springer.

Mirza, H. (2009) *Race, Gender and Educational Desire: Why Black Women Succeed and Fail*. Oxford: Routledge.

Morley, L. (1999) *Organising Feminisms: The Micropolitics of the Academy*. Hampshire: Macmillan Press.

——(2003) *Quality and Power in Higher Education*. Berkshire and Philadelphia, PA: Society for Research in Higher Education and Open University Press.

Morley, L. and Lugg, R. (2009) 'Mapping Meritocracy: Intersecting Gender, Poverty and Higher Educational Opportunity Structures', *Higher Education Policy* 22: 37–60.

Morris, M. and Golden, S. (2005) 'Evaluation of Aimhigher: Excellence Challenge Interim Report'. National Foundation for Educational Research, the Department for Education and Skills.

Mulholland, H. (2011) 'David Willetts Blames Feminism over Lack of Jobs for Working Men'. London: *Guardian*, 1 April.

Naidoo, R. (2003) 'Repositioning Higher Education as a Global Commodity: Opportunities and Challenges for Future Sociology of Education Work', *British Journal of Sociology of Education* 24 (2): 249–59.

——(2010) 'Global Learning in a Neoliberal Age: Implications for Development' in E. Unterhalter and V. Carpentier (eds) *Global Inequalities and Higher Education: Whose Interests Are We Serving?* Hampshire: Palgrave.

Nash, I. (2001) 'Leaders of the Learning Revolution', *The Times Educational Supplement* 23 March: 2.

Nicoll, K. and Fejes, A. (2008) 'Mobilizing Foucault in Studies of Lifelong Learning' in A. Fejes and K. Nicoll (eds) *Foucault and Lifelong Learning: Governing the Subject*. Oxford: Routledge.

Nixon, J., Marks, A., Rowland, S. and Walker, M. (2001) 'Towards a New Academic Professionalism: A Manifesto for Hope', *British Journal of Sociology of Education*, 22 (2): 227–44.

OECD (2005) *Education at a Glance*. Paris: OECD.

OFFA (2009) 'What Do We Mean by "Fair Access"?'. http://www.offa.org.uk/about/frequently-asked-questions/. Accessed 10 December 2009.

O'Leary, T. (2002) *Foucault and the Art of Ethics*, London and New York: Continuum.

Orr, S. (2007) 'Assessment Moderation: Constructing the Marks and Constructing the Students', *Assessment and Evaluation in Higher Education* 32 (6): 645–56.

Parr, J. (2000) *Identity and Education: The Links for Mature Women Students*. Aldershot: Ashgate.

Parra, Y. A. (2009) 'Power Relations, Forms of Female Subjectivity and Resistance' in N. Omelchenko (ed.) *The Human Being in Contemporary Philosophical Conceptions*. Newcastle Upon Tyne: Cambridge Scholars Publishing.

Paton, K. (2007) *Conceptualising 'Choice'; A Review of the Theoretical Literature*, Working Paper 5, Non-Participation in HE Project Series. London: Teaching and Learning Research Programme, ESRC.

Peelo, M. (2002) 'Who is Failing? Defining Student Failure', *Academy Exchange* 1: 17.

Piatt, W. (2009) 'Russell Group Response to Report on Fair Access to the Professions'. Russell Creating Opportunities Group. http://www.russellgroup.ac.uk/russell-group-latest-news/112–2009/3813-fair-access-to-the-professions. Accessed 17 August 2009.

Power, S., Edwards, T., Wigfall, V. and Whitty, G. (2003) *Education and the Middle Class*. Buckingham: Open University Press.

Prichard, C. and Trowler, P. (eds) (2003) *Realizing Qualitative Research into Higher Education*. Aldershot and Burlington: Ashgate.

Quinn, J. (2003) *Powerful Subjects*. Stoke on Trent: Trentham Books.

——(2005) 'Belonging in a Learning Community: The Re-imagined University and Imagined Social Capital', *Studies in the Education of Adults* 37 (1): 4–17.

Rabinow, P. (1984) (ed.) *The Foucault Reader: An Introduction to Foucault's Thought*. London: Penguin.

Randall, J. (2005) 'You Can't Brain Up by Dumbing Down Degrees', *The Daily Telegraph*, 25 November.

Raphael Reed, L. (1999) 'Troubling Boys and Disturbing Discourses on Masculinity and Schooling: A Feminist Exploration of Current Debates and Interventions Concerning Boys in School', *Gender and Education* 11 (1): 93–110.

Raphael Reed, L., Croudace, C., Harrison, N., Baxter, A. and Last, K. (2007) *Young Participation in Higher Education: A Sociocultural Study of Educational Engagement in Bristol South Parliamentary Constituency*. Research Summary; a HEFCE-funded Study. Bristol: The University of the West of England.

Reay, D. (1998) *Class Work: Mothers' Involvement in their Children's Primary Schooling.* London: UCL Press, Taylor & Francis Group.

——(2001) 'Finding or Losing Yourself? Working-class Relationships to Education', *Journal of Education Policy* 16 (4): 333–46.

——(2002) 'The Paradox of Contemporary Femininities in Education: Combining Fluidity with Fixity' in B. Francis and C. Skelton (eds) *Perspectives in Gender and Education.* Buckinghamshire: Open University Press.

——(2003) 'A Risky Business? Mature Working-class Women Students and Access to Higher Education', *Gender and Education* 15 (3): 301–17.

Reay, D. and Ball, S. J. (1997) '"Spoilt for Choice": The Working Classes and Educational Markets', *Oxford Review of Education* 23 (1): 89–101.

Reay, D., David, M. and Ball, S. J. (2005) *Degrees of Choice: Class, Race, Gender and Higher Education.* Stoke-on-Trent: Trentham Books.

Reay, D., Davies, J., David, M. and Ball, S. J. (2001) 'Choices of Degree or Degrees of Choice? Class, "Race" and the Higher Education Choice Process', *Sociology* 35 (4): 855–974.

Richardson, L. (2000) 'Writing: A Method of Inquiry' in N. K. Denzin and Y. S. Lincoln (eds), *Handbook of Qualitative Research.* London: SAGE.

Ricoeur, P. (1991) 'Narrative Identity' (trans. D. Wood), in D. Wood (ed.) *On Paul Ricoeur: Narrative and Interpretation.* London: Routledge.

Robbins, L. (1963) *Higher Education: A Report.* London: HMSO.

Rogoff, B., Turkanis, C. G. and Bartlett, L. (eds) (2001) *Learning Together: Children and Adults in a School Community.* New York: Oxford University Press.

Rose, N. (1992) *Powers of Freedom: Reframing Political Thought.* Cambridge: Cambridge University Press.

Ross, A. (2003) 'Higher Education and Social Access: to the Robbins Report' in L. Archer, M. Hutchings and A. Ross (eds) *Higher Education and Social Class: Issues of Exclusion and Inclusion.* London: RoutledgeFalmer, 21–44.

Ryan, A. (2005) 'New Labour and Higher Education' in *Oxford Review of Education* 31 (1): 87–100.

Said, E. (1977) *Orientalism.* London: Penguin Books.

Schwartz, S. (2004) *Fair Admissions to Higher Education: Recommendations for Good Practice.* London: Department for Education and Skills.

Shattock, M. (1994) *The UGC and the Management of British Universities.* Buckingham: Open University Press/SRHE.

Sheeran, Y., Brown, B. J. and Baker, S. (2007) 'Conflicting Philosophies of Inclusion: The Contestation of Knowledge in Widening Participation', *London Review of Education* 5 (3): 249–63.

Skeggs, B. (1997) *Formations of Class and Gender : Becoming Respectable.* London: SAGE.

Skeggs, B. (2002) 'Techniques for Telling the Reflexive Self', in T. May (ed.) *Qualitative Research in Action.* London, Thousand Oaks, CA, New Delhi: SAGE, 349–74.

——(2004) *Class, Self, Culture.* London and New York: Routledge.

Slack, K. (2003) 'Whose Aspirations Are They Anyway?', *International Journal of Inclusive Education* 7 (4): 325–35.

SPA, (2008) *Admissions Policies: Draft Guidance for Higher Education Providers.* Cheltenham: Supporting Professionalism in Admissions.

Spedding, T. and Gregson, M. (2000) 'Widening Participation in Colleges and Communities'. Paper presented to the British Education Research Association Conference, Cardiff.

Spivak, G. (1988) 'Can the Subaltern Speak?' in C. Nelson and L. Grossberg (eds) *Marxism and the Interpretation of Culture.* London: MacMillan.

Stanley, J. (1995) 'Pain(t) for Healing: The Academic Conference and the Classed/Embodied Self' in M. Morley (ed.) *Feminist Academics; Creative Agents for Change*. London: Taylor & Francis.

Stanley, L. (1992) *The Auto/Biographical I: Theory and Practice of Feminist Auto/Biography*. Manchester: Manchester University Press.

Stanley, L. and Wise, S. (1993) *Breaking Out Again*. London and New York: Routledge.

Strathern, M. (2000) 'The Tyranny of Transparency', *British Educational Research Journal* 26 (3), 309–21.

Sundaram, K. (2006) *On Backwardness and Fair Access to Higher Education in India: Some Results from NSS 55th Round Surveys 1999–2000*. Presented at the Round Table on 'De-Politicizing Backwardness – Alternative Approaches', Delhi University, 29–30 August.

Tamboukou, M. (1999) 'Spacing Herself: Women in Education', *Gender and Education* 11 (2): 125–39.

Thomas, L. (2005) *Widening Participation in Post-Compulsory Education*. London: Continuum.

Thompson, J. (2000) 'Introduction' in J. Thompson (ed.) *Stretching the Academy: The Politics and Practice of Widening Participation in Higher Education*. Leicester: NIACE.

Thornton, M. (2006) 'Widening Access, Widening Participation, Widening Success: An Indian Case Study', *Research in Post-Compulsory Education* 11 (1): 19–30.

Tight, M. (2003) *Researching Higher Education*. England: Society for Research in Higher Education and Open University Press.

Tomlinson, S. (2001) 'Some Success, Could Do Better: Education and Race 1976–2000' in R. Phillips and J. Furlong (eds) *Education, Reform and the State: Twenty-five Years of Politics, Policy and Practice*. London: Routledge, 192–206.

Torres, C. A. (1998) *Education, Power and Personal Biography: Dialogues with Critical Educators*. London and New York: Routledge.

——(2009) *Globalizations and Education: Collected Essays on Class, Race, Gender and the State*. New York: Teachers College, Columbia University.

——(2010) 'Globalization and Citizenship'. Keynote lecture given at the London Paulo Freire Institute, Roehampton University, 4 November 2010.

Torres, C. A. and Rhoads, R. A. (2006) 'Introduction: Globalization and Higher Education in the Americas' in R. A. Rhoads and C. A. Torres (eds) *The University, State and the Market: The Political Economy of Globalization in the Americas*. Stanford, CA: Stanford University Press, 3–38.

Trowler, P. (1998) *Education Policy*. East Sussex: The Gildredge Press.

UCU (2010) *Universities at Risk: The Impact of Cuts in Higher Education Spending on Local Economies*. London: University and College Union.

UGC (1993) *UGC Funding of Institutions of Higher Education, Report of Justice*. Dr. K. Punnayya Committee, 1992–92, University Grants Commission, New Delhi.

US Department of Education, National Center for Education Statistics (2002) *Findings from the Condition of Education 2002: Nontraditional Undergraduates*. Washington, DC: Government Printing Office.

US Department of Education (2003) *Digest of Education Statistics: 2002*. Washington, DC: Government Printing Office.

Usher, R. (1997) 'Telling a Story about Research and Research as Story-telling: Postmodern Approaches to Social Research' in G. McKenzie and D. Powell (eds) *Understanding Social Research: Perspectives on Methodology and Practice*. London: Falmer Press.

US Supreme Court (1978) *University of California Regents vs. Bakke*.

US Supreme Court (2003) *Grutter vs. Bollinger et al.*, Michigan Law School case.

UUK (2002) *Social Class and Participation: Good Practice in Widening Participation to Higher Education*. London: Universities United Kingdom.

Van Dyke, R., Little, B. and Callender, C. (2005) *Survey of Higher Education Students' Attitudes to Debt and Term-time Working and Their Impact on Attainment*. Bristol: HEFCE.

Vasagar, J. (2010) 'Go Directly to Work: High-flying Teens Leapfrog University', *Guardian*, 14 August.

Vasagar, J., and Williams, R. (2010) 'Universities Offer Lifeline to Top Students', *Guardian*, 19 August.

Vasagar, J. and Carrell, S. (2011) 'England's Newer Universities Face Biggest Cuts as Teaching Budgets Slashed', *Guardian*, 17 March.

Vignoles, A. (2008) 'Widening Participation in Higher Education: A Quantitative Analysis: Full Research Report', ESRC End of Award Report, RES-139-25-0234. Swindon: ESRC.

Walkerdine, V. (2003) 'Reclassifying Upward Mobility: Femininity and the Neo-liberal subject', *Gender and Education* 15 (3): 237–49.

Warmington, P. (2003) '"You Need a Qualification for Everything these Days." The Impact of Work, Welfare and Disaffection upon the Aspirations of Access to Higher Education Students', *British Journal of Sociology of Education* 24 (10): 95–108.

Webb, S. (1997) 'Alternative Students? Conceptualizations of Difference' in J. Williams (ed.) *Negotiating Access to Higher Education: The Discourse of Selectivity and Equity*. Buckingham: SHRHE and Open University Press.

Whitchurch, C. (2008a) 'Shifting Identities and Blurring Boundaries: The Emergence of Third Space Professionals in UK Higher Education', *Higher Education Quarterly* 62 (4) October: 377–96.

——(2008b) 'Beyond Administration and Management: Reconstructing the Identities of Professional Staff in UK Higher Education', *Journal of Higher Education Policy and Management* 30 (4) November: 375–86.

——(2009) 'Progressing Professional Careers in UK Higher Education', *Perspectives* 13 (1) January: 2–9.

Willets, D. (2010) Speech made at Universities UK Annual Conference, 9 September 2010, Cranfield University.

Williams, J. (1997) 'Institutional Rhetorics and Realities' in J. Williams (ed.) *Negotiating Access to Higher Education: The Discourse of Selectivity and Equity*. Buckingham: The Society for Research into Higher Education and Open University Press.

Williams, R. and Shepherd, J. (2010) 'GCSE Results: University Crisis to Hot School Students, Union Warns', *Guardian*, 24 August.

——(2010) 'Domino Effect Could See A-level Students Taking Opportunities from 16 Year Olds', *Guardian*, 24 August.

Winstead, T. (2009) 'The Transformative Possibilities of Higher Education: A Study of Working-class Women's Strategies of Hope and Resistance at a U.S. Community College'. Unpublished doctoral thesis, Institute of Education, University of London.

Women's Aid (2009) *Domestic Violence: Frequently Asked Questions. Factsheet 2009*. Bristol: Women's Aid Federation of England.

Woodrow, M. (2001) 'Politics Not Paper. Why Monitoring Matters for Widening Participation Projects', *Education Marketing* 23: 23–25.

Yorke, M. (2002) 'Academic Failure: A Retrospective View from Non-completing Students' in M. Peelo and T. Wareham (eds) *Failing Students in Higher Education*. Buckingham: Open University Press.

Youdell, D. (2006) *Impossible Bodies, Impossible Selves: Exclusions and Student Subjectivities*. Dordrecht: Springer.

Young, M. (1961) *The Rise of the Meritocracy 1870–2033: An Essay on Education and Equality*. London: Pelican Books.

# Index